Lineberger Memorial

Library

MACROBIUS

III

LCL 512

MACROBIUS

SATURNALIA

BOOKS 6–7

EDITED AND TRANSLATED BY

ROBERT A. KASTER

HARVARD UNIVERSITY PRESS
CAMBRIDGE, MASSACHUSETTS
LONDON, ENGLAND
2011

50 YBP ¹/₁₁   24.00

First published 2011

LOEB CLASSICAL LIBRARY® is a registered trademark
of the President and Fellows of Harvard College

Library of Congress Control Number 2010924777
CIP data available from the Library of Congress

ISBN 978-0-674-99672-4

*Composed in ZephGreek and ZephText by
Technologies 'N Typography, Merrimac, Massachusetts.
Printed on acid-free paper and bound by
The Maple-Vail Book Manufacturing Group*

CONTENTS

ABBREVIATIONS

CA	J. U. Powell, ed. *Collectanea Alexandrina*. Oxford, 1925
CAG	*Commentaria in Aristotelem Graeca*. 23 vols. Berlin, 1882–1909
CCAG	*Catalogus Codicum Astrologorum Graecorum*. 12 vols. Brussels, 1898–1924
CGF	G. Kaibel, ed. *Comicorum Graecorum Fragmenta*. Vol. 1, fasc. 1. Berlin, 1899
CIL	*Corpus Inscriptionum Latinarum*. 17 vols. Berlin, 1862–
CPG	F. G. Schneidewin and E. L. von Leutsch, ed. *Corpus paroemiographorum Graecorum*. Vol. 1. Göttingen, 1839
EGM	R. Fowler, ed. *Early Greek Mythography*. Vol. 1. Oxford, 2000
FCRR	H. Scullard. *Festivals and Ceremonies of the Roman Republic*. Ithaca, NY, 1981
FGrH	F. Jacoby, ed. *Die Fragmente der griechischen Historiker*. 4 parts. Leiden, 1957–
FHG	C. and T. Müller, ed. *Fragmenta Historicorum Graecorum*. 5 vols. Paris, 1878–1885
FLP²	E. Courtney, ed. *The Fragmentary Latin Poets*. 2nd ed. Oxford, 2003

ABBREVIATIONS

FPL[3]	J. Blänsdorf, ed. *Fragmenta Poetarum Latinorum*. 3rd ed. Stuttgart, 1995
GG	*Grammatici Graeci*. Leipzig, 1867–
GL	H. Keil, ed. *Grammatici Latini*. 7 vols. (with a supplement edited by H. Hagen). Leipzig, 1855–1880
GRF 1	H. Funaioli, ed. *Grammaticae Romanae Fragmenta*. Leipzig, 1907
GRF 2	A. Mazarino, ed. *Grammaticae Romanae Fragmenta Aetatis Caesareae*. Turin, 1955
HRR	H. Peter, ed. *Historicorum romanorum reliquiae*. 2nd ed. 2 vols. Leipzig, 1914
IAH	F. P. Bremer, ed. *Iurisprudentiae Antehadrianae*. 2 vols. Leipzig, 1898–1901
IAR[6]	P. E. Huschke, ed. *Iurisprudentiae Anteiustinianae Reliquiae*. 6th ed. E. Seckel and B. Kübler. 2 vols. Leipzig, 1908–1911
ICUR	J. B. de Rossi, ed. *Inscriptiones Christianae Urbis Romae*. 2 vols. Rome, 1861–1888
IG	*Inscriptiones Graecae*. 14 vols. Berlin, 1873–
IGBulg	G. Mikhailov, ed. *Inscriptiones Graecae in Bulgaria repertae*. Serdica, 1956–
ILS	H. Dessau, ed. *Inscriptiones Latinae Selectae*. 3 vols. Berlin, 1892–1916
Inscr. It.	*Inscriptiones Italiae*. 13 vols. Rome, 1931–
ISmyrna	*Die Inschriften von Smyrna*. 2 vols. Bonn, 1982–1900
LALE	R. Maltby. *Lexicon of Ancient Latin Etymologies*. Leeds, 1981
Lausberg	H. Lausberg. *Handbook of Literary Rhetoric*. Trans. M. T. Bliss, A. Jansen, D. E. Orton. Ed. D. E. Orton and R. D. Anderson. Leiden, 1998

LIMC	*Lexicon Iconographicum Mythologiae Classicae*. 8 vols. Zürich, 1981–
LSJ[9]	H. G. Liddell and R. Scott. *Greek-English Lexicon*, 9th ed. Rev. by H. S. Jones, with a revised supplement. Oxford, 1996
LTUR	E. M. Steinby, ed. *Lexicon Topographicum Urbis Romae*. 6 vols. Rome, 1993–2000
LTUR Sub.	A. La Regina, ed. *Lexicon Topographicum Urbis Romae: Suburbium*. 5 vols. Rome, 2001–
MRR	T. R. S. Broughton. *Magistrates of the Roman Republic*. Vols. 1–2: New York, 1951; Vol. 3 (supplement): Atlanta, 1986
OGIS	W. Dittenberger, ed. *Orientis Graeci Inscriptiones Selectae*. 2 vols. Leipzig, 1903–1905
ORF[2]	E. Malcovati, ed. *Oratorum Romanorum Fragmenta*. 2nd ed. Turin, 1955
Otto	A. Otto. *Die Sprichwörter und sprichwörtlichen Redensarten der Römer*. Leipzig, 1890
PCG	R. Kassel and C. Austin, ed. *Poetae Comici Graeci*. 8 vols. Berlin, 1983–
PEGr	A. Bernabé, ed. *Poetae Epici Graeci*. Stuttgart, 1996–
PLRE	A. H. M. Jones, J. R. Martindale, and J. Morris, ed. *Prosopography of the Later Roman Empire*. 3 vols. Cambridge, 1971–1992
PMGr	D. Page, ed. *Poetae Melici Graeci*. Oxford, 1962
RS	M. Crawford, ed. *Roman Statutes*. 2 vols. London, 1996
SRPF[3]	O. Ribbeck, ed. *Scaenicae Romanorum poesis fragmenta*. 3rd ed. 2 vols. Leipzig, 1897–1898

ABBREVIATIONS

SRRR	F. Speranza, ed. *Scriptorum Romanorum de re rustica reliquiae*. Messina, 1974–
SVF	J. von Arnim, ed. *Stoicorum veterum fragmenta*. 4 vols. Leipzig, 1903–1924
TLL	*Thesaurus Linguae Latinae*. Leipzig, 1900–
TrGF	B. Snell and R. Kannicht, ed. *Tragicorum Graecorum Fragmenta*. 5 vols. Göttingen, 1971–2004

SATURNALIA

‹LIBER SEXTVS›[1]

1 Hic Praetextatus, 'mirum,' inquit, 'in modum digessit Eustathius quae de Graeca antiquitate carmini suo Vergilius inseruit. sed meminimus viros inter omnes nostra aetate longe doctissimos, Rufium Caecinamque Albinos, promisisse se prodituros quid idem Maro de antiquis Romanis scriptoribus traxerit, quod nunc ut fiat tempus admonet.' 2. cumque omnibus idem placeret, tum Rufius Albinus: 'etsi vereor ne dum ostendere cupio quantum Vergilius noster ex antiquiorum lectione profecerit et quos ex omnibus flores vel quae in carminis sui decorem ex diversis ornamenta libaverit, occasionem reprehendendi vel imperitis vel malignis ministrem, exprobrantibus tanto viro alieni usurpationem nec considerantibus hunc esse fructum legendi, aemulari ea quae in aliis probes, et quae maxime inter aliorum dicta mireris in aliquem usum tuum opportuna derivatione convertere, quod et nostri tam inter se quam a Graecis et Graecorum excellentes inter se saepe fecerunt. 3. et ut de alienigenis taceam, possem pluribus edocere quantum se mutuo compilarint bibliothecae veteris auctores, quod tamen opportune alias si volentibus vobis erit

---

[1] *add. edd.*

---

[1] Cf. 1.24.19.   [2] Cf. Serv. on *A.* 8.517.

‹ BOOK SIX ›

Here Praetextatus said, 'Eustathius has done a marvelous 1
job of setting out the things Virgil borrowed from the ancient Greeks and inserted in his poetry. But I recall that
the men who are by far the most learned among all their
contemporaries—the two Albini, Rufius and Caecina—
undertook to put before us Virgil's borrowing from ancient
Roman authors,[1] and the hour suggests that now's the time
for their demonstration.' 2. Since this was agreeable all
around, Rufius Albinus began: 'I'm worried that as I eagerly show how much our Virgil profited from his reading
of earlier poets and how he plucked blossoms from all of
them, ornamental touches from a range of sources to increase his poetry's beauty, I'll provide the ignorant or malicious with an opportunity to criticize him and reproach the
great man for helping himself to others' goods, without
thinking that this is one of the benefits of reading, to imitate the things you approve in others and by a timely borrowing to turn to your own use the words of others that you
most admire[2]—a form of competition that our authors engaged in among themselves as much as with the Greek and
the best of the Greeks often engaged in with each other.
3. And to say nothing of non-Romans, I could tell you at
greater length how extensively the authors of our own ancient library borrowed from each other—but I will provide

probabo. unum nunc exemplum proferam quod ad probanda quae adsero paene sufficiet.

4. 'Afranius enim togatarum scriptor in ea togata quae Compitalia inscribitur, non inverecunde respondens arguentibus quod plura sumpsisset a Menandro, "fateor," inquit "sumpsi non ab illo modo sed ut quisquis[2] habuit quod conveniret[3] mihi quodque[4] me non posse melius facere credidi, etiam a Latino." 5. quod si haec societas et rerum communio poetis scriptoribusque omnibus inter se exercenda concessa est, quis fraudi Vergilio vertat, si ad excolendum se quaedam ab antiquioribus mutuatus sit? cui etiam gratia hoc nomine habenda est quod nonnulla ab illis in opus suum, quod aeterno mansurum est, transferendo fecit ne omnino memoria veterum deleretur, quos, sicut praesens sensus ostendit, non solum neglectui[5] verum etiam risui habere iam coepimus. 6. denique et iudicio transferendi et modo imitandi consecutus est ut quod apud illum legerimus alienum, aut illius esse malimus aut melius hic quam ubi natum est sonare miremur.

7. 'Dicam itaque primum quos ab aliis traxit vel ex dimidio sui versus vel paene solidos, post hoc locos integros

---

[2] quisque *ed. Colon. 1521* (*de hoc loco v. Kaster 2010, 77–78*)
[3] conveniret quod *Bentley*
[4] quod *Bothe*
[5] neglectui *ed. Colon. 1521*: non lectui ω

---

[3] The comedies of (e.g.) Plautus and Terence, set in Greece and based on Greek originals of the 4th–3rd cent. BCE, were called *fabulae palliatae*, "tales in Greek dress"; original comedies set in Rome on Roman themes were correspondingly called *fabulae togatae*, "tales in Roman dress."

that demonstration on another occasion, if you wish. Now I will give you a single example that will almost suffice to establish my claim.

4. 'When Afranius, the author of comedies in Roman dress,[3] was being accused of taking too much material over from Menander, he made the following very becoming reply in his comedy titled *Compitalia*: "I admit," he said, "I've borrowed not only from him but as any author had something that met my needs, and that I thought I couldn't improve upon, even when the other wrote in Latin."[4] 5. But if it's granted that writers of prose and poetry ought to engage in this sharing and exchange of material, who would blame Virgil if he borrowed some things from older writers to increase his refinement? We even owe him a debt of gratitude on this account, since by incorporating some of their material in his own work, which is destined to live forever, he saw to it that we not entirely forget those ancient authors whom—as current opinion shows—we have begun to consider not merely negligible but actually risible. 6. Thanks, furthermore, to the manner of his imitations and the good judgment he displayed in his borrowings, when we read another's material in his setting, we either prefer to think it actually his or marvel that it sounds better than it did in its original setting.

7. 'So here is the form my presentation will take: first, borrowings that range from half a line of Virgil to almost complete lines; then, whole passages borrowed with some

---

[4] Afranius of course wrote in verse (cf. 25–28 *SRPF*[3] 2:198), but M. appears to have quoted—or perhaps rather, closely paraphrased—what he wrote as prose (cf. Kaster 2010, 000).

cum parva quadam immutatione translatos sensusve ita
transcriptos ut unde essent eluceret, immutatos alios ut tamen origo eorum non ignoraretur, post haec quaedam de
his quae ab Homero sumpta sunt ostendam non ipsum ab[6]
Homero tulisse, sed prius alios inde sumpsisse, et hunc ab
illis, quos sine dubio legerat, transtulisse.

8. Vertitur interea caelum et ruit Oceano nox.

Ennius libro sexto:

vertitur interea caelum cum ingentibus signis.

9. axem umero torquet stellis ardentibus aptum.

Ennius in primo:

qui caelum versat stellis fulgentibus aptum,

et in tertio:

caelum prospexit stellis fulgentibus aptum,

⟨et⟩[7] in decimo:

hinc nox processit stellis ardentibus apta.

[6] ab CJ², *om.* ω
[7] et *om.* ω

---

[5] The three divisions correspond to the balance of 6.1, 6.2, and
6.3, respectively; on the sources see Introd. §4.
[6] At 5.5.5, *A.* 2.250–51 are said to be an imitation of Homer (*Il.*
8.485–86); but the point of similarity between Virgil and Ennius
("the heavens . . . revolve") does not appear in Homer.

small adjustment, or thoughts taken over in such a way that their place of origin is clear, or other passages that have in fact been changed, though their source is still recognizable; then I shall show that Virgil himself did not borrow some of the material taken from Homer, but rather that other earlier authors borrowed from Homer, and he in turn took it from those authors, whom he'd doubtless read.[5]

8. The heavens, meanwhile, revolve and night rushes on from Ocean. (A. 2.250)[6]

Ennius in Book 6[7] (205 Sk.):

The heavens, meanwhile, revolve with their vast constellations.

9. Upon his shoulder he makes the vault of heaven turn, studded with blazing stars. (A. 4.482)

Ennius in Book 1 (27 Sk.):

Who makes heaven wheel, studded with shining stars,

and Book 3 (145 Sk.):

He looked out at heaven, studded with shining stars,

and Book 10 (348 Sk.):

From this point night went on, studded with blazing stars.

---

[7] Citations of Ennius by book-number refer throughout to his *Annals*.

10. conciliumque vocat divum pater atque hominum rex.

Ennius in sexto:

tum cum corde suo divum pater atque hominum rex effatur.

11. est locus, Hesperiam Grai cognomine dicunt.

Ennius in primo:

est locus Hesperiam quam mortales perhibebant.

12. tuque, o Thybri tuo genitor cum flumine sancto
. . .

Ennius in primo:

teque, pater Tiberine, tuo cum flumine sancto . . .

13. accipe daque fidem: sunt nobis fortia bello pectora . . .

Ennius in primo:

accipe daque fidem foedusque feri bene firmum.

14. et lunam in nimbo nox intempesta tenebat.

Ennius in primo:

. . . cum superum lumen nox intempesta teneret.

---

8 Cf. also Enn. 591–92 Sk.

9 For the quasi-formulaic phrase "deepest night" (*nox intempesta*) cf. also *A.* 3.587 and 12.846 with 160 Sk.

10. And the father of gods and king of men summons his council. (*A*. 10.2)

Ennius in Book 6 (203–4 Sk.):

Then from his heart the father of gods and king of
   men
speaks out.[8]

11. There is a place, Hesperia the Greeks call it.
   (*A*. 1.530)

Ennius in Book 1 (20 Sk.):

There is a place that mortals speak of as Hesperia.

12. And you, father Thybris, with your holy
   stream. . . . (*A*. 8.72)

Ennius in Book 1 (26 Sk.):

And you, father Tiberinus, with your holy stream. . . .

13. Receive my solemn word and give me yours: we
   have hearts that are gallant
in war. . . . (*A*. 8.150–51)

Ennius in Book 1 (32 Sk.):

Receive my solemn word and give me yours, and
   strike a good, strong treaty.

14. And deepest night held the moon in a cloud. (*A*.
   3.587–88)

Ennius in Book 1 (33 Sk.):

. . . when deepest night held the light of heaven.[9]

15. Tu tamen interea calido mihi sanguine poenas
persolves . . .

Ennius in primo:

nec pol homo quisquam faciet impune animatus
hoc nec[8] tu, nam mi calido das[9] sanguine poenas.

16. Concurrunt undique telis
indomiti agricolae . . .

Ennius in tertio:

postquam defessi sunt, †stant et† spargere sese
hastis ansatis, concurrunt undique telis.

17. Summa nituntur opum vi.

Ennius in quarto:

Romani scalis summa nituntur opum vi,

et in sexto decimo:

reges per regnum statuasque sepulcraque quaerunt,
aedificant nomen, summa nituntur opum vi.

18. Et mecum ingentes oras evolvite belli.

8 nec *Baehrens*: nisi ω
9 das] dabis *DServ. ad A. 9. 420*

15. Still, you now will pay your debt to me with your
   hot
blood. . . . (*A.* 9.422†–23)

Ennius in Book 1 (94–95 Sk.):

No man alive, by god, will do this and go unpunished,
nor will you: you pay your debt to me with your hot
   blood.

16. From all sides the undaunted yeoman
come charging with their lances . . . . (*A.* 7.520–21)

Ennius Book 3 (143–44 Sk.):

After they become weary . . . of showering one
   another
with their thonged spears, they come charging from
   all sides with their lances.

17. They strive with all their might
and main. (*A.* 12.552*)

Ennius in Book 4 (151 Sk.):

On the ladders the Romans strive with all their might
   and main,

and Book 16 (404–5 Sk.):

By their rule kings seek statues, and memorials after
   death,
they build up their fame, they strive with all their
   might and main.

18. And unscroll with me the vast reaches of war.
   (*A.* 9.528†)

11

Ennius in sexto:

> quis potis ingentes oras evolvere belli?

19. Ne qua meis dictis esto[10] mora: Iuppiter hac stat.

Ennius in septimo:

> non semper vestra evertit: nunc Iuppiter hac stat.

20. Invadunt urbem somno vinoque sepultam.

Ennius in octavo:

> nunc hostes vino domiti somnoque sepulti.

21. tollitur in caelum clamor, cunctique Latini . . .

Ennius in septimo decimo:

> tollitur in caelum clamor exortus utrisque.[11]

22. quadrupedante putrem sonitu quatit ungula
   campum.

Ennius in sexto:

> explorant Numidae:[12] totam quatit ungula terram,

idem in octavo:

---

10 dictis esto] esto dictis *Verg*.   11 utrisque] utrimque
Merula   12 Numidae *ed. Ven. 1472*: (h)umidae ω

---

10 Cf. also *A*. 12.462 and Enn. 545 Sk.

11 There being no event in *Annals* 6 with which Numidian cavalry can plausibly be linked, editors generally assume that the number M. gives is incorrect and assign the fragment to Book 7, where the second Punic War was treated.

Ennius in Book 6 (164 Sk.):

Who can unscroll the vast reaches of war?

19. Let no delay attend my words: now Jupiter stands
on our side. (A. 12.565)

Ennius in Book 7 (232 Sk.):

He does not always overturn your [interests]: now
Jupiter stands on our side.

20. They attack a city buried in sleep and drink.
(A. 2.265)

Ennius in Book 8 (288 Sk.):

Now the enemy were overcome by wine and buried
in sleep.

21. A cry is raised to heaven, and all the Latins . . .
(A. 11.745)

Ennius in Book 17 (428 Sk.):

On both sides a cry begins and is raised to heaven.[10]

22. The hoof shakes the crumbling plain with its four-
footed beat. (A. 8.596)

Ennius in Book 6 (242 Sk.):[11]

The Numidians go scouting: the hoof shakes the
earth all round,

again in Book 8 (263 Sk.):

consequitur, summo sonitu quatit ungula terram,

idem in septimo decimo:

it eques et plausu cava concutit ungula terram.

23. unus qui nobis cunctando restituit[13] rem.

Ennius in duodecimo:

unus homo nobis cunctando restituit rem.

24. corruit in vulnus: sonitum super arma dederunt.

Ennius in sexto decimo:

concidit et sonitum simul insuper arma dederunt.

25. et iam prima novo spargebat lumine terras.

Lucretius in secundo:

. . . cum primum aurora respergit[14] lumine terras.

26. . . . flammarum longos a tergo involvere[15] tractus.

Lucretius in secundo:

nonne vides longos flammarum ducere tractus?

---

13 restituit (*ex sequent., lapsu Macrob.*)] -is *Verg.*
14 cum primum aurora respergit] primum aurora novo cum spargit *Lucr.*   15 involvere] albescere *Verg.*

---

12 Cf. Serv. on *A.* 6.845.
13 Serv. on this verse rightly cites *Il.* 4.504.
14 Cf. DServ. on *A.* 9.459.
15 *A.* 4.584–85 (cf. §31 below) are treated as a direct imitation of Homer at 5.6.15 (cf. also 5.9.11).

[The cavalry] follows, and the hoof shakes the earth
   with a din,

again in Book 17 (431 Sk.):

The cavalry passes, the hollow hoof shakes the earth
   with its beat.

23. The one man who restored our state by his delay.
   (A. 6.846)[12]

Ennius in Book 12 (363 Sk.):

One man restored our state by his delay.

24. He fell forward onto his wound, his arms
   clattered atop him. (A. 10.488)[13]

Ennius in Book 16 (411 Sk.):

He collapsed and at once his arms clattered atop him.

25. And [Aurora] was starting to dapple the lands
   with a new day's light. (A. 4.584)[14]

Lucretius in Book 2 (144):

. . . when first the dawn dapples the earth with light.[15]

26. . . . coiling long trailers of flame from behind. (G.
   1.367)

Lucretius in Book 2 (207):

Don't you see [them] drawing long trailers of flame?

27. . . . ingeminant abruptis nubibus ignes.

Lucretius in secundo:

nunc hinc, nunc illinc abruptis[16] nubibus ignes . . .

28. . . . belli simulacra ciebat.

Lucretius in secundo:

. . . componunt,[17] complent: belli simulacra cientur.[18]

29. simulacraque luce carentum.

Lucretius in quarto:

. . . cum saepe figuras
contuimur miras simulacraque luce carentum.

30. asper, acerba tuens, retro redit . . .

Lucretius in quinto:

asper, acerba tuens, immani corpore serpens . . .

31. Tithoni croceum linquens Aurora cubile.

Furius in primo annali:

interea Oceani linquens Aurora cubile.

---

[16] abruptis] -ti *Lucr.*
[17] componunt] camporum *Lucr.*
[18] cientur] cientes *Lucr.*

27. . . . the clouds explode, the fires redouble.
(A. 3.199)

Lucretius in Book 2 (214):

Now on this side, now on that the clouds explode, the
fires . . .

28. . . . was summoning up
images of war. (A. 5.674)

Lucretius in Book 2 (324):

. . . arrange and fill: images of war are summoned up.

29. and images of those who've
lost the light of life. (G. 4.472)

Lucretius in Book 4 (38–39):

. . . when often we spy uncanny
shapes and likenesses of those who've lost the light of
life.

30. Fierce, with bitter glances, he retreats. . . .
(A. 9.794)

Lucretius in Book 5(33):

Fierce, with bitter glances, the snake of monstrous
bulk . . .

31. Aurora was leaving Tithonus' saffron-hued bed.
(A. 4.585)

Furius in Book 1 of his *Annals* (fr. 7 *FPL*[3]):

Meanwhile Aurora was leaving Ocean's bed.

32. quod genus hoc hominum quaeve hunc tam
    barbara morem . . . ?

Furius in sexto:

quod genus hoc hominum, Saturno sancte create?

33. . . . rumoresque serit varios ac talia fatur . . .

Furius in decimo:

rumoresque serunt varios et multa requirunt.

34. . . . nomine quemque vocans reficitque ad[19]
    proelia pulsos.

Furius in undecimo:

. . . nomine quemque ciet, dictorum tempus adesse
commemorat,

deinde infra :

confirmat dictis simul atque exsuscitat acris
ad bellandum animos reficitque ad proelia mentes.

35. Dicite, Pierides: non omnia possumus omnes.

Lucilius in quinto:

maior erat natu: non omnia possuma omnes.

[19] ad] in *Verg*.

---

[16] The tag "we cannot all do all things" seems to be treated as a
Virgilian original at 5.16.7.

32. What race of men is this, what barbarous [land permits] such behavior . . . ? (*A.* 1.539)

Furius in Book 6 (fr. 11 *FPL*³):

What race of men is this, holy offspring of Saturn?

33. . . . and sows the seeds of varied rumor and speaks as follows . . . (*A.* 12.228)

Furius in Book 11 (fr. 12 *FPL*³):

They sow the seeds of varied rumors and ask many questions.

34. . . . calling on each by name, and refreshes them for battle after their repulse. (*A.* 11.731)

Furius in Book 11 (fr. 13 *FPL*³):

He calls on each by name, tells them the time for what was said
is at hand,

then further on (fr. 14 *FPL*³):

He bucks them up with his words, at the same time rousing their
keen spirits for war and readying their thoughts again for battle.

35. Speak, maidens of Pieria: we cannot all do all things (*E.* 8.63)

Lucilius in Book 5 (224):

He was the elder: we cannot all do all things.[16]

36. Diversi circumspiciunt, hoc acrior idem . . .

Pacuvius in Medea:[20]

diversi circumspicimus, horror percipit.

37. Ergo iter inceptum peragunt[21] rumore secundo.

Sueius in libro quinto:

. . . redeunt, repetita ferunt[22] rumore secundo.

38. Numquam hodie effugies: veniam, quocumque vocaris.

Naevius in Equo Troiano:

numquam hodie effugies, quin mea manu moriare.[23]

39. Vendidit hic auro patriam dominumque potentem imposuit: fixit leges pretio atque refixit.

Varius de morte:

vendidit hic Latium populis agrosque Quiritum eripuit, fixit leges pretio atque refixit.

40. . . . ut gemma bibat et Sarrano dormiat ostro.

Varius de morte:

. . . incubet ut Tyriis atque ex solido bibat auro.

[20] Medea (cf. DServ. ad A. 11.543)] Medo Schrijver et al.
[21] peragunt (codd. Ra Verg., Non. 385.7, ex A. 6.384)] celerant codd. cett. Verg.
[22] repetita ferunt Courtney: referunt petita ω
[23] mea moriaris manu Ribbeck

36. Scattered, they look all around, more fiercely now
he again . . . (A. 9.416)

Pacuvius in his *Medea* (224 *SRPF*³ 1:119):

Scattered, we look all around, dread seizes [us].

37. With a murmur of approval, then, they resume
the journey begun. (A. 8.90)

Sueius in Book 5 (fr. 7 *FPL*³):

. . . with a murmur of approval they return, carrying
what they'd recovered.

38. You'll never escape today: to wherever you
challenge me, I'll come. (E. 3.49)

Naevius in his *Trojan Horse* (14 *SRPF*³ 1:9):

You'll never escape today dying by my hand.

39. This one sold his homeland for gold and installed
a mighty
despot: for a price he posted and rescinded laws.
(A. 6.621–22)

Varius in his *On Death* (fr. 1 *FPL*³):

This one sold Latium to the nations and from native
Romans took
their fields, for a price he posted and rescinded laws.

40. . . . that he might drink from a gem-encrusted
cup and sleep on Tyrian purple. (G. 2.506)

Varius in his *On Death* (fr. 2 *FPL*³):

. . . that he might lie on Tyrian cloth and drink from
solid gold.

41. "talia saecla," suis dixerunt, "currite," fusis.

Catullus:[24]

currite, ducenti subtemine,[25] currite fusi.

42. . . . felix, heu nimium felix, si litora tantum
numquam Dardaniae tetigissent nostra carinae.

Catullus:

Iuppiter omnipotens, utinam non[26] tempore primo
Cnosia Cecropiae tetigissent litora puppes.

                43. . . . magna ossa lacertosque
extulit[27] . . .

Lucilius[28] in septimo decimo:

                . . . magna ossa lacertique
apparent homini . . .

            44. . . . placidam per membra quietem
irrigat.

Furius in primo:

. . . mitemque rigat per pectora somnum.

et Lucretius in quarto:

. . . nunc quibus ille modis somnus per membra
    quietem
inrigat[29] . . .

---

[24] Catullus S: -tulus ω (*sic et in §42*)
[25] ducenti subtemine] ducentes subtegmina *Catull.*
[26] non] ne *Catull.*   [27] extulit] exuit *Verg.*

41. "Hasten on, age of gold," they sang to their
shuttles. (*E.* 4.46)

Catullus (64.327):

Hasten, shuttles, hasten on, as the weft leads the way.

42. . . . happy, alas, all too happy, if only Trojan
ships had never touched our shores. (*A.* 4.657–58)

Catullus (64.171–72):

Almighty Jupiter, would that Athenian ships
had never touched Cretan shores in the first place.

43. . . . he raised high his big-boned
arms . . . (*A.* 5.422–23)

Lucilius in Book 17 (548–49):

. . . the fellow's big-boned
arms are evident . . . .

44. . . . causes peaceful rest to seep
through his limbs. (*A.* 1.691–92)

Furius in Book 1 (fr. 9 *FPL*[3]):

. . . makes gentle sleep seep through his breast.

and Lucretius in Book 4 (907–8):

. . . Now in the way that sleep makes rest seep
through
the limbs. . . .

---

[28] Lucilius *ed. Basil. 1535 in marg.*: Lucius *a*, Lucretius β_2
[29] inrigat] -get *Lucr.*

45. . . . camposque liquentes.

Lucretius in sexto [simile de mari]:[30]

. . . et liquidam molem camposque natantes . . .

46. . . . et[31] geminos, duo fulmina belli,
Scipiadas . . .

Lucretius in tertio:

. . . Scipiades,[32] belli fulmen, Carthaginis horror.

47. . . . et ora
tristia temptantum sensu torquebit amaro.

Lucretius in secundo:

. . . foedo pertorquent ora sapore.

48. . . . morte obita quales fama est volitare figuras.

Lucretius in primo:

. . . cernere uti videamur eos[33] audireque coram,
morte obita quorum tellus amplectitur ossa.

hinc est et illud Vergilii:

. . . et patris Anchisae gremio complectitur ossa.

[30] secl. Jan
[31] et] aut Verg.
[32] Scipiades] -das Lucr.
[33] eos ed. Lugd. Bat. 1670 ex Lucr.: eas ω

---

[17] At G. 2.246 Servius cites Lucr. 4.224, which has a slightly
different text.

45. . . . and the liquid plains.
(A. 6.724)

Lucretius in Book 6 (405):

. . . and the liquid mass and floating plains . . .

46. . . . and the pair of Scipios, two thunderbolts of war . . . (A. 6.842–43).

Lucretius in Book 3 (1034):

. . . Scipios, the thunderbolt of war, the terror of Carthage.

47. . . . And will pucker the lips of those who try it with its bitter taste. (G. 2.246–47)[17]

Lucretius in Book 2 (401):

. . . pucker the lips with the disgusting taste.

48. . . . like the shapes that flit about, they say, after death. (A. 10.641)

Lucretius in Book 1 (134–35):

. . . so that we seem to see and hear before us those whose bones the earth enfolds after death.

From the latter comes this Virgilian line (A. 5.31):

. . . and enfolds the bones of father Anchises in its bosom.

49. . . . ora modis attollens pallida miris.

Lucretius in primo:

. . . sed quaedam simulacra modis pallentia miris . . .

50. tum gelidus toto manabat corpore sudor.

Ennius in sexto decimo:

tunc timido manat ex omni corpore sudor.

51. labitur uncta vadis abies . . .

Ennius in quarto decimo:

labitur uncta carina, volat super impetus undas.

          52. . . . ac ferreus ingruit imber.

Ennius in octavo:

hastati spargunt hastas, fit ferreus imber.

        53. apicem tamen incita summum
hasta tulit.

Ennius in sexto [decimo]:[34]

. . . tamen induvolans secum abstulit hasta
insigne.

[34] decimo *seclusi* (*ut ex §50 irrepens*), †decimo† *initio Enniani coniungit Skutsch post Strzlecki*

---

[18] Cf. also 396 Sk., in the passage (391–98 Sk.) quoted at 6.3.3.
[19] Cf. also *A.* 4.398 and 505 Sk.

49. . . . his face looming, uncanny pale. (*A.* 1.354)

Lucretius in Book 1 (123):

. . . but certain images, uncanny pale . . .

50. Then a clammy sweat trickles over his entire body. (*A.* 3.175)

Ennius in Book 16 (417 Sk.):

Then in his fear sweat trickles from his entire body. [18]

51. The greased keel glides over the shallows . . . (*A.* 8.91)

Ennius in Book 14 (376 Sk.):

The greased keel glides, its onrush flies over the waves.[19]

52. . . . and an iron rain comes rushing down. (*A.* 12.284)

Ennius in Book 8 (266 Sk.):

The spearmen send their spears broadcast, an iron rain arises.

53. Still, the speeding spear carried off the topmost peak of his helmet. (*A.* 12.492–93)

Ennius in Book 6 (173–74 Sk.):

. . . Still, the spear as it fled carried off the emblem.

54. pulverulentus eques furit: omnes arma requirunt.

Ennius in sexto:

. . . balantum pecudes quatit: omnes arma requirunt.

55. nec visu facilis nec dictu affabilis ulli.

Accius in Philoctete:

. . . quem neque tueri contra neque adfari[35] queas.

56. aut spoliis ego iam raptis laudabor opimis
aut leto insigni.

Accius in armorum iudicio:

　　　　　　　nam tropaeum ferre me a forti viro
pulchrum est; si autem vincar, vinci a tali nullum[36] est
　　probrum.

57. Nec si miserum fortuna Sinonem
finxit, vanum etiam mendacemque improba finget.

Accius in Telepho:

nam si a me regnum fortuna atque opes
eripere quivit, at virtutem nequit.[37]

58. Disce, puer, virtutem ex me verumque laborem,
fortunam ex aliis.

[35] adfari] fari *Ribbeck*
[36] *post* nullum *add.* mi *G. Hermann*, nullum est a tali *Bothe*
[37] nequit (*contra metrum*)] necquit *Ribbeck in app.*

---

[20] The subject is perhaps "terror" or "the wolf" (Skutsch).

54. The dusty cavalryman is in a rage, all look for
their arms. (*A.* 7.625)

Ennius in Book 6 (169 Sk.):

. . . makes[20] the bleating flocks quiver, all look for
their arms.

55. For no man an easy sight to see nor agreeable to
address. (*A.* 3.621)

Accius in *Philoctetes* (538 *SRPF*[3] 1:237):

. . . whom you could neither look upon nor address.

56. I shall win glory, whether by snatching the richest
spoils
or by a distinguished death. (*A.* 10.449–50)

Accius in *The Judgment of Arms* (148–49 *SRPF*[3] 1:179):

For it is a fine thing for me to take a trophy
from a hero; but if I should lose, losing to such a man
is no shame.

57. No, even if a wicked fortune has molded Sinon in
the shape
of a wretch, it shall not also make him an empty liar.
(*A.* 2.79–80)

Accius in *Telephus* (619–20 *SRPF*[3] 1:250):

For if fortune could take from me my kingdom
and my wealth, she was not able to steal my honor.

58. Learn of courage from me, my child, and real
labor,
but learn of luck from others. (*A.* 12.435–36)

Accius in armorum iudicio:

> virtuti sis[38] par, dispar fortunis patris.

> 59. iam iam nec maxima Iuno
> nec Saturnius haec oculis pater aspicit aequis.

Accius in Antigona:

> iam iam neque di regunt,
> neque profecto deum summus rex omnibus curat.[39]

> 60. num capti potuere capi? num incensa cremavit
> Troia viros?

Ennius in decimo, cum de Pergamis loqueretur:

> . . . quae neque Dardaniis campis potuere perire
> nec cum capta capi nec cum combusta cremari.

> 61. . . . multi praeterea, quos fama obscura recondit.

Ennius in Alexandro:

> multi alii adventant, paupertas quorum obscurat
> nomina.

> 62. audentes fortuna iuvat.

Ennius in septimo:

> fortibus est fortuna viris data.

[38] virtuti sis G: -tis is Pβ_2 (-tis his N), -ti is C
[39] rex omnibus curat] res curat hominibus *Buecheler*

---

[21] Soph. *Ajax* 550–51 is the common model of both.

Accius in *The Judgment of Arms* (156 SRPF³ 1:180):

> Be like your father in courage, unlike him in luck.[21]

> 59. Now, now neither greatest Juno
> nor the father, Saturn's son, looks impartially upon
> these deeds. (*A.* 4.371–72)

Accius in *Antigone* (142–43 SRPF³ 1:178):

> Now, now neither the gods are in charge
> nor, surely, does the gods' supreme ruler care for all.

> 60. Couldn't they stay captive once captured?
> Couldn't Troy in flames
> have consumed her heroes? (*A.* 7.295–96)

Ennius in Book 10, when he's speaking about Pergamum (344–45 Sk.):

> . . . which could neither perish on the Dardanian
> plains
> nor stay captive when captured nor burn when set
> afire.

> 61. . . . many men besides, whose fame is clouded
> and obscure. (*A.* 5.302)

Ennius in *Alexander* (36 SRPF³ 1:23 = 68 Jocelyn):

> Many others come, whose renown poverty makes
> obscure.

> 62. Fortune favors the bold. (*A.* 10.254)

Ennius in Book 7 (233 Sk.):

> Good fortune has been granted to heroes.

63. Recoquunt patrios fornacibus enses

et

curvae rigidum falces conflantur in ensem.

Lucretius in quinto:

inde minutatim processit ferreus ensis
versaque in obscenum[40] species est falcis aënae.

64. pocula sunt fontes liquidi atque exercita cursu
flumina.

Lucretius in quinto:

at[41] sedare sitim fluvii fontesque vocabant.

65. Quos rami fructus, quos ipsa volentia rura
sponte tulere sua, carpit.

Lucretius in quinto:

quod sol atque imbres dederant, quod terra crearat
sponte sua, satis id placabat pectora donum.

2   'Post versus ab aliis vel ex integro vel ex parte translatos,
vel quaedam immutando verba tamquam fuco alio tinctos,
nunc locos locis componere sedet animo, ut unde formati
sint quasi de speculo cognoscas.

---

[40] obscenum (*cf. A. 4. 455*)] opprobrium *Lucr.*
[41] at *Lucr.*: ad ω

63. In their furnaces they forge anew their fathers'
    swords (*A.* 7.636)

and

curved scythes are recast to make a sturdy sword.
    (*G.* 1.508)

Lucretius in Book 5 (1293–94):

From that source, little by little, there came the iron
    sword
and the bronze scythe's shape was turned to
    something foul.

64. To drink they have clear springs and rivers
    running
wild. (*G.* 3.529–30)

Lucretius in Book 5 (945):

But streams and springs invited them to soothe their
    thirst.

65. The fruit that the branches, the field themselves
    with a will
offered all on their own, he plucks. (*G.* 2.500–1)

Lucretius in Book 5 (937–38):

What the sun and rain had given, what the earth had
    borne
all on its own soothed their hearts, a sufficient gift.

'So much for lines borrowed wholly or in part from 2
other authors, or lines that are, as it were, tinged a different hue by the change of certain words: now it's my aim to
compare parallel passages, so that you might recognize the
model after which its mirror image was formed.

2. Nec sum animi dubius, verbis ea vincere magnum
quam sit et angustis hunc addere rebus honorem.
sed me Parnassi deserta per ardua dulcis
raptat amor: iuvat ire iugis, qua nulla priorum
Castaliam molli devertitur orbita clivo.

3. Lucretius in primo:

nec me animi fallit quam sint obscura, sed acri
percussit thyrso laudis spes magna meum cor
et simul incussit suavem mi[42] in pectus amorem
Musarum, quo nunc instinctus mente vigenti
avia Pieridum peragro loca nullius ante
trita solo.

4. 'Accipite et alterum locum Maronis illi unde traxerat
comparandum, ut eundem colorem ac paene similem so-
num loci utriusque reperias.
Vergilius:

si non ingentem foribus domus alta superbis

[42] mi *ed. Ven. 1500, Lucr.*: mihi ω

2. I have not a doubt in my mind how great a task it is to master
this topic with my words and add this luster to a paltry theme.
But a passion for sweet Parnassus carries me along over
places deserted and steep: it is a delight to traverse the ridges where
no forerunner's path turns down the gentle slope toward Castalia. (G. 3.289–93*)

3. Lucretius in Book 1 (922–27):

Nor am I deceived how obscure my subject is, but a great
hope of glory has struck my heart with a fierce inspiration
and at the same time instilled in my chest an alluring love
of the Muses: aroused now by that love, my thoughts quickening,
I make my way over the Muses' trackless places that have til now
been trod by no man's foot.

4. 'Now here's another passage of Maro that you should compare with his source, to see how both passages have the same coloring and almost sound alike.

Virgil (G. 2.461–43):

If a lofty household with arrogant doors does not spew

35

mane salutantum totis vomit aedibus undam,
nec varios inhiant pulchra testudine postes . . .

et mox :

at secura quies et nescia fallere vitam,[43]
dives opum variarum, at laetis[44] otia fundis,
speluncae vivique lacus, at frigida tempe
mugitusque boum mollesque sub arbore somni
non absunt, illic saltus ac lustra ferarum
et patiens operum exiguoque adsueta iuventus.

5. Lucretius in libro secundo:

. . . si non aurea sunt iuvenum simulacra per aedes
lampadas igniferas[45] manibus retinentia dextris,
lumina nocturnis epulis ut suppeditentur,
nec domus argento fulgens auroque renidens[46]
nec citharam[47] reboant laqueata aurataque templa,[48]
cum tamen inter se prostrati in gramine molli
propter aquae rivum sub ramis arboris altae

---

[43] vitam (*codd.* PRachrsv *Verg.*)] vita R, *codd. cett. Verg., Serv. et alii gramm.*

[44] laetis (*agnosc. Schol. Bern. ad loc.*)] latis *Verg.*

[45] igniferas PG: igne feras Nβ_2

[46] fulgens . . . renidens] fulget . . . renidet *Lucr.* (fulgenti *Lachmann*)

[47] citharam] -rae *Lucr.*

[48] templa *ed. Ven. 1513 e Lucr.*: tempe ω (*cf. 6.4.21* tecta)

a huge wave of morning visitors from every nook and
    cranny,
if they do not goggle at doorposts made intricate with
    fine tortoise-shell . . . ,

followed soon by (*G.* 2.467–72),

Still, there's tranquility, secure and unschooled in the
    ways
that lead life astray, rich in a range of goods; still,
    there's the rest
that comes to fertile fields, the grottoes and natural
    pools;
still, there are cool valleys, lowing cattle, the soft
    times
of sleep beneath a tree; the mountain passes and
    haunts of beast
are there, and young men inured to toil and
    accustomed to little.

5. Lucretius in Book 2 (24–33):

. . . if dwellings there do not have gilded statues of
    youths
throughout, holding fiery torches in their right hands
to give light to banquets that last through the night,
if the household there does not shine with silver and
    gleam with gold,
if precincts there do not echo, coffered and gilded,
    with the lyre,
when—nonetheless—they loll in casual clusters on
    the soft grass
by a watery stream under a tall tree's limbs

non magnis opibus iucunde corpora curant,
praesertim cum tempestas arridet et anni
tempora conspergunt viridantes floribus herbas.

6. Non umbrae altorum nemorum, non mollia
    possunt
prata movere animum, non qui per saxa volutus
purior electro campum petit amnis..

Lucretius in secundo:

nec tenerae salices atque herbae rore virentes[49]
fluminaque ulla[50] queunt summis labentia ripis
oblectare animum subitamque avertere curam.

7. ipsius vero pestilentiae, quae est in tertio Georgicorum,
color totus et liniamenta paene omnia tracta sunt de de-
scriptione pestilentiae quae est in sexto Lucretii. nam Vergiliana incipit:

hic quondam morbo caeli miseranda coorta est
tempestas, totoque autumni incanduit aestu
et genus omne neci pecudum dedit, omne ferarum.

Lucretii vero sic incipit:

haec ratio quondam morborum et mortifer aestus

[49] virentes] vigentes *Lucr.*
[50] ulla (*cod.* O² *Lucr.*)] illa *Lucr.*

and see to their bodies' needs pleasantly and at no
    great cost,
especially when the weather smiles and
the season sprinkles the green grass with flowers.

6. The shadows of tall groves, the gently rippling
meadows cannot lift the spirit, nor the stream, more
    lucid
than amber, that tumbles over rocks and seeks the
    plain. (G. 3.520–22)

Lucretius in Book 2 (361–63):

Neither tender willows and grasses green and dewy
nor rivers gliding past the tops of their banks can
beguile the mind and turn aside a sudden anxious
    thought.

7. The whole coloring and almost all the brush-strokes of
the depiction of the plague in Book 3 of the *Georgics*
(478*–566) are drawn from the description in Book 6 of
Lucretius (1138–1286). The Virgilian description begins
(478–80),

Here, once upon a time, from a heaven-borne illness
    a dreadful
season arose and burned the whole seething length of
    autumn,
giving over to death all beasts of the farm, all beasts
    of the wild.

Lucretius' description begins this way (1138–40):

Once upon a time, this guiding principle of disease
    and a deadly

finibus in Cecropis funestos reddidit agros
vastavitque vias, exhausit civibus urbem.

8. sed quatenus totum locum utriusque ponere satis longum est, excerpam aliqua ex quibus similitudo geminae
descriptionis appareat. Vergilius ait:

tum vero ardentes oculi atque attractus ab alto
spiritus, interdum gemitu gravis, imaque longo
ilia singultu tendunt, it naribus ater
sanguis et oppressas[51] fauces premit aspera lingua.

9. Lucretius ait:

principio caput incensum fervore gerebant,
et duplices oculos suffusa luce rubentes.
sudabant etiam fauces intrinsecus artae[52]
sanguine, et ulceribus vocis via saepta coibat,
atque animi interpres manabat lingua cruore,
debilitata malis, motu gravis, aspera tactu.

10. Vergilius ait:

haec ante exitium primis dant signa diebus,

---

[51] oppressas] obsessas *Verg.*
[52] artae] atrae *Lucr.*

sweltering made the field a morgue in the land of
    Cecrops,
laying waste the byways, draining the city of its
    citizens.

8. But insofar as quoting all of both passages is quite a long
task, I'll present some excerpts that will make the similarity of the two descriptions apparent. Virgil says (505–8):

Then indeed the eyes are bright and bloodshot, a sigh
    is drawn
from deep in the chest, now and again weighed down
    with a groan,
long, gasping breaths strain the gut, black blood
    pours
from the nostrils, the tongue becomes rough and
    blocks the throat.

9. Lucretius says (1145–50):

At first, they walked about with heads on fire with
    fever,
their two eyes bloodshot and gleaming.
Their throats, too, were constricted, they oozed
blood, the pathway of the voice was blocked and
    closed with sores,
and the tongue, the mind's interpreter, dripped with
    gore,
weakened by the illness, clumsy in its movement,
    rough to the touch.

10. Virgil says (503),

These were the signs they gave in the first days
    before they died,

et quae darent signa supra retulit, id est:[53]

> demissae aures, incertus ibidem
> sudor et ille quidem morituris frigidus, aret
> pellis et attactu[54] tractanti dura resistit.

11. Lucretius ait:

> multaque praeterea mortis tunc signa dabantur:
> perturbati[55] animi, mens in maerore metuque,
> triste supercilium, furiosus vultus et acer,
> sollicitae porro plenaeque sonoribus aures,
> creber spiritus aut ingens raroque coortus,
> sudorisque madens per collum splendidus umor,
> tenuia sputa, minuta, croci contacta colore
> salsaque, per fauces raucas vix edita tussis.[56]

12. Vergilius ait:[57]

> profuit inserto latices infundere cornu
> Lenaeos: ea visa salus morientibus una.
> mox erat hoc ipsum exitio.

Lucretius ait:

> nec ratio remedi communis certa dabatur:
> nam quod alis[58] dederat vitalis aëris auras
> volvere in ore licere[59] et caeli templa tueri,
> hoc aliis erat exitio letumque parabat.

---

[53] id est αε: idem PRF
[54] attactu (*cod.* n *Verg.*)] ad tactum *Verg.*
[55] perturbati] -ta *Lucr.*
[56] raucas . . . tussis] rauca . . . tussi *Lucr.*
[57] ait PG, *om.* Nβ₂   [58] alis] ali *Lucr.*
[59] licere *ed. Ven. 1513, Lucr.*: liceret ω

42

and he recounted the signs immediately preceding, namely (500–2),

> Their ears drooped and at the same time a fitful
> sweat arose, the clammy sort typical of the dying;
> their hide was hot and did not yield when palpated.

11. Lucretius says (1182–89):

> Then they gave many signs of death besides:
> mind disturbed, thoughts sunk in grief and fear,
> brow distraught, looks wild and fierce,
> ears beset by constant roaring to boot,
> breathing rapid or an occasional great sigh,
> neck clammy with a glistening slick of sweat,
> spittle thin and sparse, bright yellow and salty,
> coughing that scarcely escaped their rasping throats.

12. Virgil says (509–11):

> It did some good to pour liquid Bacchus in through a
> funnel: that seemed the only help for the dying.
> Soon this proved deadly itself.

Lucretius says (1226–29):

> Nor was there at hand any generally reliable cure: the
>   thing
> that had allowed some to feel on their faces the sky's
> life-giving breeze and to see the precincts of heaven
> proved deadly for others and sealed their doom.

13. Vergilius ait:

praeterea nec mutari iam[60] pabula refert
quaesitaeque nocent artes, cessere magistri.

Lucretius ait:

nec requies erat ulla mali: defessa iacebant
corpora, mussabat tacito medicina timore.

14. Vergilius ait:

ipsis est aër avibus non aequus et illae
praecipites alta vitam sub nube relinquunt.

Lucretius ait:

nec tamen omnino temere illis sedibus[61] ulla
comparebat avis nec tristia saecla ferarum
exsuperant[62] silvis, languebant pleraque morbo
et moriebantur.

nonne vobis videntur membra huius descriptionis ex uno
fonte manasse? 15. sed rursus locos alios comparemus:

gaudent perfusi sanguine fratrum,
exilioque domos et dulcia limina mutant.

Lucretius in tertio:

---

[60] nec mutari iam] iam nec mutari *codd. plerique Verg.*, nec
iam mutari *codd. cett. Verg.*
[61] sedibus] solibus *Lucr.*
[62] exsuperant] exibant *Lucr.*

13. Virgil says (548–49):

> Besides, it makes no difference now to change their feed,
> healing arts do harm when applied, their masters withdraw in defeat.

Lucretius says (1178–79):

> Nor did the evil known any respite: their bodies lay exhausted, physicians reduced to muttering in silent fear.

14. Virgil says (546–47):

> The air was cruel to the very birds, who fell headlong and left their life beneath a lofty cloud.

Lucretius says (1219–22):

> And still it was not altogether easy to find a single bird
> in their former dwellings, nor did the grim generations
> of beasts survive in the woods, but most were dying,
> enfeebled by the disease.

Don't the components of this description appear to have flowed from a single source? 15. But now let's compare some other passages:

> They delight in being soaked in their brothers' blood
> and trade their homes' sweet thresholds for exile.
> (G. 2.510–11)

Lucretius in Book 3 (70–72):

sanguine civili rem conflant divitiasque
conduplicant avidi, caedem caede accumulantes;
crudeles gaudent in tristi funere fratris.

16. multa dies variusque[63] labor mutabilis aevi
rettulit in melius: multos alterna revisens
lusit et in solido rursus fortuna locavit.

Ennius in octavo:

> multa dies in bello conficit unus . . .
et rursus multae fortunae forte recumbunt.
haud quaquam quemquam[64] semper fortuna secuta
> est.

17. o praestans animi iuvenis, quantum ipse feroci
virtute exsuperas, tanto me impensius aequum est
consulere atque omnes metuentem expendere
causas . . .

Accius in Antigona:

quanto magis te istius modi esse intellego,
tanto, Antigona, magis me par est tibi consulere et
parcere.

---

[63] variusque (*codd. nonnull. Verg., Non. 380.40*)] variique *codd.
cett. Verg., edd.*
[64] quaquam quemquam *ed. Ven. 1513*: quaquam αδ, quemquam F

They scrape together an estate from the blood of
    citizens and greedily
double their wealth, heaping up slaughter with
    slaughter;
they cruelly delight in a brother's baleful burial.

16. Time and the varied toils that the changeable
    seasons bring
have made many things better: fortune, returning
    now in this guise, now
in that has mocked many, then given them back their
    footing. (A. 11.425–27)

Ennius in Book 8 (258–60 Sk.):

        One day accomplishes much in war . . .
and many fortunes chance to sink back again.[22]
Fortune has attended almost no one at every
    moment.

17. O young man of surpassing spirit, the more you
    exult
in your fierce valor, the more earnestly should I
take counsel and fearfully weigh all factors . . .
    (A. 12.19–21)

Accius in *Antigone* (136–37 SRPF[3] 1:177):

The more I know that your nature is such, Antigone,
the more proper it is that I take thought for you and
    spare you.

---

[22] Mention of fortunes "sink[ing] back again" suggests that a
line has been lost in which fortunes were said to rise.

18. o lux Dardaniae, spes o fidissima Teucrum

et reliqua. Ennius in Alexandro:

> o lux Troiae, germane Hector,
> quid ita cum tuo[65] lacerato corpore miser?
> aut qui te sic respectantibus tractavere nobis?[66]

19. frena Pelethronii Lapithae gyrosque dedere
imposti dorso atque equitem docuere sub armis
insultare solo et gressus glomerare superbos.

Varius de morte:

> quem non ille sinit lentae moderator habenae
> qua velit ire, sed angusto prius ore[67] coercens
> insultare docet campis fingitque morando.

20. talis amor Daphnin, qualis cum fessa iuvencum
per nemora atque altos quaerendo bucula lucos
propter aquae rivum viridi procumbit in ulva
perdita nec serae meminit decedere nocti.

---

[65] quid ita cum tuo (*lacunam post* ita *stat. Ribbeck*)] quid te ita
cum tuo *Eyssenhardt*, quid te ita contuo *Voss* (*prob. Timpanaro*),
alii alia (*de metro incerto v. Jocelyn 1967, 231–32*)

[66] respectantibus tractavere nobis] tractavere nobis respectantibus *Ribbeck*, miser <es> (<ades> *Mariotti*) *ad initium versus
transtul. et finem post* respectantibus *stat. Vahlen*

[67] ore] orbe *Torrentius* (*ad Hor. c. 1.10.6* [1608])

18. O light of Troy, most trusted hope of the
    Teucrians. (*A.* 2.281)

and so on. Ennius in *Alexander* (57–59 *SRPF*³ 1:25 = 69–71
Jocelyn):

O light of Troy, true brother Hector, why do I,
unhappy man, [see] you with your body thus
    mutilated?
Who treated you in that way, as we looked on?

19. Bridles and the training course the Pelethronian
    Lapiths gave us,
mounted on horseback, and they taught the
    horseman under arms
to bound upon the earth and gallop with proud
    strides. (*G.* 3.115–17)

Varius *On Death* (fr. 3 *FPL*³):

The one who guides the supple rein does not allow
    him
to go where he pleases but uses the bit to keep him in
    check,
teaching him to bound upon the plains, training him
    by holding him back.

20. Such a love [grips] Daphnis as when a heifer,
    wearied
by searching for her calf through the glades and lofty
    groves,
collapses in the green sedge next to a watery stream,
in despair, and does not think to yield to the late
    night. (*E.* 8.85–88)

49

Varius de morte:

> ceu canis umbrosam lustrans Gortynia vallem,
> si veteris potuit cervae comprendere[68] lustra,
> saevit in absentem et circum vestigia lustrans[69]
> aethera per nitidum tenues sectatur odores.
> non amnes illam medii, non ardua tardant
> †perdita†[70] nec serae meminit decedere nocti.

> 21. . . . nec te, tua funera mater
> produxi pressive oculos aut vulnera lavi.

Ennius in Cresphonte:[71]

> neque terram inicere neque cruenta convestire
>   corpora
> mihi[72] licuit neque miserae lavere lacrimae[73] salsum
>   sanguinem.

> 22. namque canebat uti magnum per inane coacta
> semina terrarumque animaeque marisque fuissent,
> et liquidi simul ignis, ut his exordia primis
> omnia et ipse tener mundi concreverit orbis,
> tum durare solum et discludere Nerea ponto

---

[68] comprendere] deprendere *Baehrens*
[69] lustrans] latrans *Vliet* (*ad Gratt. 212* [*1645*])
[70] 'culmina *vel tale aliquid libenter reponam' Willis*
[71] Cresphonte *Schrijver, Bothe*: cres(s)i- ω
[72] corpora/mihi *Bothe*: mihi corpora ω
[73] mihi licuit neque miserae lavere lacrimae] [mihi] licuit neque m. l. l. <latice> *O. Skutsch*

---

23 M.'s text of this line is that attested by all ancient and medieval witnesses; it is judged corrupt by all modern editors, since it

Varius *On Death* (fr. 4 *FPL*[3]):

> Like a hound of Gortyn scouring a shady valley,
> if it has been able to find an old hind's haunts,
> it is furious to get at her, though she's gone, tracing
>   out the tracks
> this way and that, trying to catch the faint scent in
>   the bright air.
> The rivers that stand in the way, the steep . . . do not
> slow it down nor does it think to yield to the late
>   night.

> 21. . . . . Nor did I, your mourning[23] mother,
> lead your procession or close your eyes or bathe your
>   wounds. (*A.* 9.486–87)

Ennius in *Cresphon* (126–7 *SRPF*[3] 1:34 = 138–39 Jocelyn):

> I was not allowed to place some earth upon you or
>   dress your bloodied
> body, my unhappy tears were not allowed to wash
>   away the salty blood.

> 22. For he sang of how through the great void the
>   seeds
> of lands and air and sea had been combined,
> and of molten fire too, how from these first bodies
> all things got their start and the world's still-plastic
>   sphere coalesced,
> how the earth then began to harden and confine
>   Nereus

can be construed only if *funera*, a noun ("deaths/funerals"), is
treated (as Servius says) as an adjective = *funerea* ("mourning").

coeperit[74] et rerum paulatim sumere formas,
iamque novum terrae stupeant lucescere solem.

23. Lucretius in quinto, ubi de confusione orbis ante
hunc statum loquitur:

hic[75] neque tum solis rota cerni lumine claro[76]
altivolans poterat, neque magni sidera mundi,
nec mare nec caelum, nec denique terra nec aër
nec similis nostris rebus res ulla videri,
sed nova tempestas quaedam molesque coorta.
diffugere inde loci partes coepere paresque
cum paribus iungi res et discludere mundum
membraque dividere et magnas[77] disponere partes.

24. et infra:

. . . hoc est, a terris magnum[78] secernere caelum
et seorsum mare, uti secreto umore pateret,
seorsus item puri secretique aetheris ignes.

et infra:

. . . omnia enim magis haec ex levibus atque rotundis
‹ seminibus ›.[79]

25. . . . cum fatalis equus saltu super ardua venit

---

[74] coeperit *ed. Ven. 1472 e Verg. (cf. 6.4.11)*: -erat ω
[75] hic *Lucr.*: his ω
[76] claro (*cf. Catull. 64.408*)] largo *Lucr.*
[77] magnas] magna *codd.* OQ *Lucr.*
[78] magnum] altum *Lucr.*
[79] seminibus *addidi, om.* ω

in the sea, and gradually take on familiar shapes,
and how the lands look amazed on the new light of
    the sun. (*E*. 6.31–37)

23. Lucretius in Book 5, where he talks about the cha-
otic condition of the world before its present state (432–
39):

At that time neither the wheel of the sun could be
    seen, flying high,
its light blazing, nor the stars of the great firmament
nor the sea nor the sky, neither the earth nor the air,
nor did a single thing appear as it does to us now,
but a new season, a novel shape of things had begun.
From that point segments of space began to separate
and like things began to be joined with like, shutting
    off the firmament,
defining the component parts, and arranging the
    massive segments.

24. and further on (446–48):

. . . that is, to set great heaven apart from the earth,
and the sea on its own, so that it lies open, its waters
    set apart
and on their own, too, the unmixed and well defined
    fires of the ether.

and further on (455–56):

. . . for all these consist of lighter and rounder
    seeds.

25. . . . when destiny's horse came with a bound over
    lofty

Pergama et armatum peditem gravis attulit alvo.

Ennius in Alexandro:

> nam maximo
> saltu superabit[80] gravidus[81] armatis equus
> qui suo partu ardua perdat Pergama.

26. tum pater omnipotens, rerum cui summa[82]
    potestas,
infit: eo dicente deum domus alta silescit
et tremefacta solo tellus, silet arduus aether,
tum venti[83] posuere, premit placida aequora pontus.

Ennius in Scipione:

> mundus caeli vastus constitit silentio
> et Neptunus saevus undis asperis pausam dedit.
> Sol equis iter repressit ungulis volantibus,
> constitere[84] amnes perennes, arbores vento vacant.

27. itur in antiquam silvam, stabula alta ferarum.
procumbunt piceae, sonat icta securibus ilex

80 superabit *Bothe post Voss*: -vit ω
81 gravidus *ed. Ven. 1528*: gravibus ω
82 summa (*codd. plerique Verg.*)] prima *codd. cett. Verg., Tib., edd.*
83 venti] Zephyri *Verg.* (*cf. 5.13.38*)
84 constitere *ed. Ven. 1528* (constatere C): consistere ω

Pergamum and bore the armed soldiery, pregnant, in its womb. (*A.* 6.515–16)

Ennius in *Alexander* (59–61 *SRPF*[3] 1:25 = 72–73 Jocelyn):

> For with a very great
> bound a horse pregnant with armed men cleared the way
> to destroy lofty Pergamum with its offspring.

26. Then the father almighty, whose power is supreme in all things,
speaks: and as he speaks the gods' lofty house falls quiet,
the earth is shaken to it foundation, high heaven is silent,
then the west winds fall, the sea holds it calm surface in check. (*A.* 10.100–3)[24]

Ennius in *Scipio* (fr. 31 *FLP*[2] p. 27)

> The vast vault of heaven stood still and silent,
> and fierce Neptune gave the rough waves a respite.
> The Sun checked his horses' course even as their hooves flew,
> the ceaseless rivers stood still, the trees lacked for wind.

27. They go into the ancient wood, the deep resting place of beasts,
the pitch-pines fall, the holm oak resounds with the axes' blows,

---

[24] The passage is treated as a direct imitation of Homer at 5.13.37–38.

fraxineaeque trabes, cuneis et fissile robur
scinditur, advolvunt ingentes montibus ornos.

Ennius in sexto:

incedunt arbusta per alta, securibus caedunt,
percellunt magnas quercus, exciditur ilex,
fraxinus frangitur atque abies consternitur alta,
pinus proceras[85] pervortunt, omne sonabat
arbustum fremitu silvai frondosai.

28. diversi magno[86] ceu quondam turbine venti
confligunt Zephyrusque Notusque et laetus Eois
Eurus equis.

Ennius in septimo decimo:

concurrunt veluti venti, cum spiritus Austri
imbricitor Aquiloque suo cum flamine contra
indu[87] mari magno fluctus extollere certant.

29. Nec tamen, haec cum sint hominumque
    boumque labores
versando terram experti, nihil improbus anser
‹Strymoniaeque grues et amaris intiba fibris
officiunt aut umbra nocet›.[88]

---

[85] proceras *ed. Ven. 1472*: -res ω (-ros P)
[86] diversi magno] adversi rupto *Verg.* (*cf. 5.13.14*)
[87] indu *ed. Paris. 1585*: inde ω
[88] Strymoniaeque . . . nocet *addidi* (*v. Kaster 2010, 80*)

---

25 The passage is treated as a failed combination of two Homeric passages at 5.13.14–15.

the ash beams too, wedges split the cleft oak,
they roll huge flowering ashes down the mountains.
   (A. 6.179–82)[25]

Ennius in Book 6 (175–79 Sk.):

They stride into the lofty copses, they hack with their
      axes,
the send great oaks flying, the holm oak is cut down
the ash smashed, the towering fir laid low,
they overturn tall pines, the whole copse
re-echoes with the leafy wood's rumbling.

28. Just as in a great cyclone winds from different
      quarters clash,
the west wind, the south, and the east wind that
      delights
in the horses of Dawn (A. 2.416–18)

Ennius in Book 17 (432–34 Sk.):

They clash like the winds, when the south wind's
      gust,
bringing the rain, and the north with its own
      opposing blast
compete to raise swells on the great sea.

29. Still, when the toil of men and oxen have made
      these
attempts in tilling the soil, the wicked goose and
      cranes
from the Strymon and chicory's bitter leaves work
their mischief, or else the shade does harm.
   (G. 1.118–21)

Lucretius in quinto:

> sed[89] tamen interdum magno quaesita labore,
> cum iam per terras frondent atque omnia florent,
> aut nimiis torrens[90] fervoribus aetherius sol
> aut subiti perimunt imbres gelidaeque pruinae,
> flabraque ventorum violento turbine vexant.

30. 'Sunt alii loci plurimorum versuum quos Maro in opus suum cum paucorum immutatione verborum a veteribus transtulit. et quia longum est numerosos versus ex utroque transcribere, libros veteres notabo, ut qui volet illic legendo aequalitatem locorum conferendo miretur. 31. in primo Aeneidos tempestas describitur, et Venus apud Iovem queritur de periculis filii, et Iuppiter eam de futurorum prosperitate solatur. hic locus totus sumptus a Naevio est ex primo libro belli Punici. illic enim aeque Venus, Troianis tempestate laborantibus, cum Iove queritur, et sequuntur verba Iovis filiam consolantis spe futurorum. 32. item de Pandaro et Bitia aperientibus portas locus acceptus est ex libro quinto decimo Ennii, qui induxit Histros duos in obsidione erupisse porta et stragem de obsidente hoste fecisse.

33. 'Nec Tullio compilando, dummodo undique ornamenta sibi conferret, abstinuit:

> O fama ingens, ingentior armis,
> vir Troiane . . .

---

[89] sed] et *Lucr.*   [90] torrens] torret *Lucr.*

---

26 The passage is treated as a direct imitation of Homer at 5.11.26–29.

Lucretius in Book 5 (213–17):

> But still sometimes, when all the gains that great toil
> seeks are in leaf and flower throughout the land,
> either the heavenly sun, blazing with extreme heat,
> destroys them, or sudden rains and chill frosts,
> and gusts of wind in a wild cyclone assail them.

30. 'There are other long passages that Maro transferred from the ancients into his own work with the change of a few words. Since copying out numerous verses from both sources would be a lengthy process, I will just note his models, so that a person so inclined might read and compare the passages and marvel at their similarity. 31. In Book 1 of the *Aeneid* a storm is described (81–123), and Venus complains to Jupiter about the dangers her son faces (227–53), and Jupiter comforts her by telling her that her posterity will flourish (254–96). All of this is taken from Book 1 of Naevius' *Punic War* (fr. 14 *FPL*[3]): there too Venus complains to Jupiter while the Trojans are beset by a storm, and after her complaint Jupiter comforts her by speaking of her posterity's great expectations. 32. Similarly, the passage about Pandarus and Bitias' opening the gates of the camp (*A.* 9.672–818) was taken over from Book 15 of Ennius (fr. iv),[26] where he presented two Histrian soldiers breaking out of the gate of the camp under siege and wreaking havoc on the besieging enemy.

33. 'Nor did he avoid borrowing from Cicero, provided he could augment his work's adornment from whatever source (*A.* 11.124–45):

> O great in fame, in arms greater,
> man of Troy . . . ,

nempe hoc ait Aeneam famam suam factis fortibus super-
gressum, cum plerumque fama sit maior rebus. sensus hic
in Catone Ciceronis est his verbis: "contingebat in eo quod
plerisque contra solet, ut maiora omnia re quam fama
viderentur: id quod non saepe evenit, ut expectatio cogni-
tione, aures ab oculis vincerentur." 34. Item:

>   proximus huic, longo sed proximus intervallo.

Cicero in Bruto: "duobus igitur summis Crasso et Antonio
L. Philippus proximus accedebat, sed longo intervallo tamen proximus."

3   'Sunt quaedam apud Vergilium quae ab Homero credi-
tur transtulisse, sed ea docebo a nostris auctoribus sumpta
qui priores haec ab Homero in carmina sua traxerant. quod
quidem summus Homericae laudis cumulus est quod, cum
ita a plurimis adversus eum vigilatum sit coactaeque omnium vires manum contra fecerint, "ille velut pelagi rupes
immota resistit."

2. 'Homerus de Aiacis forti pugna ait:

> Αἴας δ' οὐκέτ' ἔμιμνε· βιάζετο γὰρ βελέεσσι·
> δάμνα μιν Ζηνός τε νόος καὶ Τρῶες ἀγαυοὶ
> βάλλοντες· δεινὴν δὲ περὶ κροτάφοισι φαεινὴ

the point being, of course, that Aeneas' heroic deeds were still greater than his renown, though in most cases it is the other way around. This is Cicero's meaning when he says, in his *Cato* (fr. 14), "In his case it turned out that he was in every respect greater in fact than he was said to be, which is the opposite of what is usually the case: it has rarely happened that acquaintance outstrips expectation, that what one sees surpasses what one has heard." 34. Similarly (*A.* 5.320):

> closest after him, but closest by a wide margin.

Cicero in *Brutus* (173): "To the two greatest [orators], Crassus and Antonius, Lucius Philippus came closest, but still, closest by a wide margin."

'There are some things in Virgil that he is believed to 3 have borrowed from Homer, but I will show that these were taken over from our own authors who had previously taken them from Homer and incorporated them in their poetry. And in fact I think this is the crowning touch to Homer's glory: though so many authors have watched in wait against him and all have gathered their forces to assail him, "he stands against them unmoved, like a crag in the sea" (*A.* 7.586).

2. 'About Ajax's heroic fighting Homer says (*Il.* 16.102–11):

> Aias no longer held firm, overpowered by the
>   missiles:
> the resolve of Zeus was breaking him, and the lordly
>   Trojans
> with their spear-casts. About his temples the shining
>   helmet

πήληξ βαλλομένη καναχὴν ἔχε, βάλλετο δ' αἰεὶ
κὰπ φάλαρ' εὐποίηθ'· ὁ δ' ἀριστερὸν ὦμον
  ἔκαμνεν
ἔμπεδον αἰὲν ἔχων σάκος αἰόλον· οὐδ' ἐδύναντο
ἀμφ' αὐτῷ πελεμίξαι ἐρείδοντες βελέεσσιν.
αἰεὶ δ'[91] ἀργαλέῳ ἔχετ' ἄσθματι, κὰδ δέ οἱ ἱδρὼς
πάντοθεν ἐκ μελέων ῥέεν ἄσπετος,[92] οὐδέ πη
  εἶχεν
ἀμπνεῦσαι· πάντη δὲ κακὸν κακῷ ἐστήρικτο.

3. hunc locum Ennius in quinto decimo[93] ad pugnam C. Aelii[94] tribuni his versibus transfert:

undique conveniunt velut imber tela tribuno:
configunt parmam, tinnit hastilibus umbo,
. . .[95]
aerato sonitu galeae, sed nec pote quisquam
undique nitendo corpus discerpere ferro.
semper abundantes hastas frangitque quatitque.
totum sudor habet corpus multumque laborat,
nec respirandi fit copia. praepete ferro
Histri tela manu iacientes sollicitabant.

91 δ' ed. Basil. 1535, om. a
92 ῥέεν ἄσπετος (cf. Il. 18.403)] πολὺς ἔρρεεν Hom.
93 XV β₂ (quod recip. Skutsch): XII a (duodecimo ed. Ven. 1472)
94 C. Aelii Merula (cf. Livy 41.1.7, 4.3): caelii ω
95 unum versum excedisse statuit Vahlen, dubitavit Skutsch

clattered terribly as it was struck, the helmet's well-
made
bosses bore constant blows, his left shoulder wearied
of holding the gleaming shield ever in place. Nor
could they
shake him, though they pressed about him with their
shafts.
A hard panting seized him, the sweat poured down
from his limbs all about, without cease, and he had
no point
at which to catch his breath: woe was piled upon woe,
entirely.

3. In Book 15 Ennius applies this passage to the fighting of
the tribune Gaius Aelius, with these lines (391–98 Sk.):

From every side the missiles converge on the tribune
like a shower:
they pierce his small shield, its boss rings as it's struck
by the shafts,
. . .
with the helmet's bronze re-echoing, but neither can
anyone
tear at his body with a blade, though they press from
every side.
All the while he breaks and brandishes the shafts that
come full spate.
Sweat seizes his entire body, the strain is great,
nor has he any chance to catch his breath. With
winged steel
the Histrians harry him as they hurl their spears.

4. hinc Vergilius eundem locum de incluso Turno gratia elegantiore composuit:

> ergo nec clipeo iuvenis subsistere tantum
> nec dextra valet, obiectis sic undique telis
> obruitur. strepit adsiduo cava tempora circum
> tinnitu galea et saxis solida aera fatiscunt
> discussaeque iubae capiti nec sufficit umbo
> ictibus: ingeminant hastis et Troes et ipse
> fulmineus Mnestheus. tum toto corpore sudor
> liquitur et piceum—nec respirare potestas—
> flumen agit, fessos quatit aeger anhelitus artus.

5. Homerus ait:

> ἀσπὶς ἄρ᾿ ἀσπίδ᾿ ἔρειδε, κόρυς κόρυν,[96] ἀνέρα δ᾿
> ἀνήρ.

Furius in quarto annali:

> pressatur pede pes, mucro mucrone, viro vir.

hinc Vergilius ait:

> haeret pede pes densusque viro vir.

[96] κόρυν ed. Colon. 1521: PTN a

---

[27] DServ. on A. 9.808 takes the "whole passage" to be based on Homer.

[28] The passage is treated as a direct (and failed) imitation of Homer at 5.13.27; cf. also Ennius 584 Sk..

4. Drawing on that passage Virgil treated the same subject—in this case, Turnus shut up in the Trojan camp—with greater finesse and charm (*A.* 9.806–14):[27]

> The young warrior, then, has not the strength to
>   stand his ground
> with shield or weapon-hand, so overwhelmed is he by
>   the spears
> hurled from every side. Around his hollow temples
>   his helmet
> rings without stop, rocks open cracks in the solid
>   bronze,
> the crests are knocked from his head and the shield's
>   boss
> cannot withstand the blows: they redouble their casts,
>   the Trojans
> and Mnestheus himself, a thunderbolt. Then over all
>   his body
> sweat pours and—no chance for breath—forms
> a pitchy cascade, a sickly panting shakes his wearied
>   limbs.

5. Homer says (*Il.* 13.131 = 16.215):

> Shield pressed against shield, helmet against helmet,
>   man against man.

Furius Book 4 of his *Annals* (fr. 10 *FPL*[3]):

> Foot thrusts against foot, sword-tip to sword-tip, man
>   to man.

Hence[28] Virgil says (*A.* 10.361*):

> Foot treads on foot, one man pressed to another.

6. Homeri est:

> οὐδ᾽ εἴ μοι δέκα μὲν γλῶσσαι, δέκα δὲ στόματ᾽
> εἶεν . . .

hunc secutus Hostius poeta in libro secundo belli Histrici
ait:

> non si mihi linguae
> centum atque ora sient totidem vocesque
> liquatae . . .

hinc Vergilius ait:

> non mihi si linguae centum sint oraque centum . . .

7. Homerica descriptio est equi fugientis in haec verba:

> ὡς δ᾽ ὅτε τις στατὸς ἵππος, ἀκοστήσας ἐπὶ
> φάτνῃ,
> δεσμὸν ἀπορρήξας θείῃ πεδίοιο κροαίνων,
> εἰωθὼς λούεσθαι ἐϋρρεῖος ποταμοῖο,
> κυδιόων· ὑψοῦ δὲ κάρη ἔχει, ἀμφὶ δὲ χαῖται
> ὤμοις ἀΐσσονται· ὁ δ᾽ ἀγλαΐηφι πεποιθὼς
> ῥίμφά ἑ γοῦνα φέρει μετά τ᾽[97] ἤθεα καὶ νομὸν
> ἵππων

8. Ennius hinc traxit:

> et tum, sicut equus qui de praesepibus fartus

[97] τ᾽ ed. Paris. 1585, Hom., om. a

6. Homer's line is (*Il.* 2.489):

Not if I had ten tongues, ten mouths. . . .

The poet Hostius followed Homer in Book 2 of his *Histrian War* (fr. 3 *FPL*³):

Not if I had one hundred
tongues and as many mouths and a clear-sounding
voice. . . .

Hence²⁹ Virgil says (*A.* 6.625):

Not if I should have one hundred tongues, one
hundred mouths . . .

7. Homer describes a fleeing horse in these terms (*Il.* 6.506–11):

As when a stabled horse, well-fed at his fodder,
snaps his tether and gallops over the plain,
accustomed to bathe in the fine-flowing river,
exulting: he holds his head high, and about his
shoulders his mane flutters. He is confident in his
glory
as his legs carry him swiftly to the haunts and
pastures of horses.

8. Ennius drew upon those lines (535–39 Sk.):

And then, just like a horse that has eaten his fill in the
stable

---

²⁹ The passage is treated as a direct imitation of Homer at 5.7.16. Serv. on *A.* 6.625 points to Lucretius (fr. 1.2); cf. also Enn. 469–70 Sk.

vincla suis magnis animis abrupit et inde
fert sese campi per caerula laetaque prata
celso pectore: saepe iubam quassat simul altam,
spiritus ex anima calida spumas agit albas.

Vergilius:

qualis ubi abruptis fugit praesepia vinclis . . .

et cetera. 9. nemo ex hoc viles putet veteres poetas, quod
versus eorum scabri nobis videntur. ille enim stilus Enniani saeculi auribus solus placebat, et diu laboravit aetas secuta ut magis huic molliori filo adquiesceretur. sed ulterius
non moror Caecinam quin et ipse prodat quae meminit
Maronem ex antiquitate transtulisse.'

4   Tum Caecina: 'in versibus vel in locis quantum sibi
Maro ex antiquitate quaesiverit, Rufius ut memor et veteris et novae auctorum copiae disseruit. ego conabor ostendere hunc studiosissimum vatem et de singulis verbis veterum aptissime iudicasse et inseruisse electa operi suo
verba, quae nobis nova videri facit incuria vetustatis. 2. ut
ecce "addita" pro "inimica" et "infesta" quis non aestimet
poetam arbitrio suo novum verbum sibi voluisse fabricari?
sed non ita est. nam quod ait:

              . . . nec Teucris addita Iuno
       usquam aberit,

---

30 A "word for word" adaptation of Homer, acc. to Serv. on
A. 11.492.

31 Cf. 1.4.17–27, on ancient usage misunderstood as "novel"
from ignorance of antiquity.

and, spirits high, snapped his tether, thereafter
passing through the green, luxuriant meadows on the
    plain,
chest high and proud: he gives his lofty mane a
    frequent shake
as his breath sends sprays of white foam from his hot
    soul.

Virgil (A. 11.492):

As when, his tether snapped he flees the stable . . .

and the rest.[30] 9. Let no one form a low opinion of the ancient poets because their verses strike us as rough. That's
the only style that pleased Ennius' contemporaries, and
succeeding generations labored long to acclimatize themselves to the more finely spun style we know. But I don't
want to keep Caecina waiting any longer to present his own
recollections of Maro's borrowings from antiquity.'

Then Caecina said, 'Rufius has shown, with the knowl-   4
edge of the full range of ancient and more recent texts,
how much Maro profited from antiquity both in writing
specific lines and in treating whole topics. I will try to show
that this most scholarly bard formed very apt judgments
about individual words the ancient authors used and inserted in his work some choice elements of diction that our
own disregard for antiquity causes us to think his own devising.[31] 2. For example, who would not suppose that in using "inflicted" [addita] in the sense of "inimical" and "hostile" the poet wanted to craft a new usage? But that's not
the case: his saying (A. 6.90*–91),

            . . . nor will Juno at anywhere cease
    to be inflicted on the Trojans—

id est adfixa et per hoc infesta, hoc iam dixerat Lucilius in libro quarto decimo his versibus:

> si mihi non praetor siet additus atque agitet me,
> non male sit: ille, ut dico, me exenterat[98] unus.

3. . . . mane salutantum totis vomit aedibus undam.

pulchre "vomit undam"—et antique, nam Ennius ait,

> et Tiberis flumen[99] vomit in mare salsum,

unde et nunc vomitoria in spectaculis dicimus, unde homines glomeratim ingredientes in sedilia se fundunt. 4. agmen pro actu et ductu quodam ponere non inelegans est ut:

> leni fluit agmine Thybris—

immo et antiquum est, Ennius enim in[100] quinto ait,

> quod per amoenam urbem leni fluit agmine flumen.

5. quod ait

> crepitantibus urere flammis,

non novum usurpavit verbum, sed prior Lucretius in sexto posuit:

[98] exenterat *Eyss.*: exten- ω
[99] flavom *post* et *inser. Ilberg, post* flumen *Skutsch*
[100] in *add. ed. Ven. 1472, om.* ω

meaning "fastened" to them and so "hostile" to them—
has a precedent in Book 14 of Lucilius, where he writes
(474–75):

> If that praetor were not inflicted on me and giving
>   me a hard time,
> I'd be fine: but I tell you, he's the one person who's
>   gutting me.

> 3. . . . . spews a huge wave of morning callers from
>   every nook and cranny (G. 2.462).

"Spews [*vomit*] a wave" is a nice touch—and ancient, for
Ennius says (453 Sk.),

> and the Tiber spews its stream into the salty sea.

That's the source of the so-called *vomitoria* we have in
venues for shows, which allow people entering in a mass to
disperse into their seats. 4. Using "column" [*agmen*] to
mean "movement" and a kind of "directed motion" is not
an indelicate touch (A. 2.782),

> the Thybris flows with its gentle column—

no indeed, but it's also ancient: so Ennius' phrasing in
Book 5 (163 Sk.),

> the river that flows with its gentle column through
>   the charming city.

5. In saying (G. 1.85)

> burn with crackling [*crepitantes*] flames,

he did not help himself to a new word, but Lucretius used
it previously in Book 6 (154–55):

71

nec res ulla magis quam Phoebi Delphica laurus
terribili sonitu flamma crepitante crematur.

> 6. Tum . . . ferreus hastis
horret ager.

"horret" mire se habet, sed et Ennius in quarto decimo:

horrescit telis exercitus asper utrimque,

et in Erectheo:

arma arrigunt,[101] horrescunt tela,

et in Scipione:

sparsis hastis longis campus splendet et horret.

sed et ante omnes Homerus:

ἔφριξεν δὲ μάχη φθισίμβροτος[102] ἐγχείῃσιν.

7. splendet tremulo sub lumine pontus.

"tremulum lumen" de imagine rei ipsius expressum est.
sed prior Ennius in Melanippe,

lumine sic tremulo terra et cava caerula candent,

et Lucretius in sexto:

praeterea solis radiis iactatur aquai
umor et in lucem tremulo rarescit ab aestu.

---

[101] arrigunt (*obel. notat Jocelyn*)] arriguntur *Jan dubitanter*,
rigent *ed. Colon. 1521*

[102] φθισίμβροτος *ed. Colon. 1521, codd. plerique Hom.*:
ΦΕΙϹΙΜ- *a*

nor does anything burn with a more dreadful sound
of crackling flame than Phoebus' Delphic laurel.

> 6. Then . . . the iron field
> bristles with lances. (*A.* 11.601*–2)

"Bristles" [*horret*] is a remarkable usage, but Ennius has it,
too, in Book 14 (384 Sk.):

> On both sides the fierce host bristles with lances,

and in *Erectheus* (131 *SRPF*[3] 1:35 = 143 Jocelyn):

> Their arms are raised, their missiles bristle,

and in *Scipio* (fr. 33 *FLP*[2] p. 33):

> When the long lances have been broadcast, the plain
> gleams and bristles.

But Homer has it, too, before all others (*Il.* 13.339):

> The man-destroying battle bristled with lances.

> 7. The sea gleams beneath [the moon's] quavering
> light. (*A.* 7.9)

"Quavering [*tremulum*] light" is coined to suggest just
what the phenomenon looks like. But Ennius used it earlier in *Melanippe* (251 *SRPF*[3] 1:58 = 250 Jocelyn),

> Thus the earth and the hollow vault of heaven glow
> with a quavering light,

as does Lucretius in Book 6 (874–75):

> Besides, the water's moisture is set in motion by the
> sun's
> rays and evaporates in the light because of the
> quavering heat.

8. hic candida populus antro
imminet et lentae texunt umbracula vites.

sunt qui aestiment hoc verbum "umbracula" Vergilio auctore compositum, cum Varro rerum divinarum libro decimo dixerit: "non nullis magistratibus in oppido id genus
umbraculi concessum"; et Cicero in quinto de legibus:
"visne igitur—quoniam sol paululum a meridie iam de-
vexus videtur, neque dum satis ab his novellis arboribus
omnis hic locus opacatur—descendatur ad Lirim eaque
quae restant in illis alnorum umbraculis persequamur?" similiter in Bruto: "sed ut e[103] Theophrasti doctissimi hominis umbraculis . . . ."

9. Transmittunt cursu campos atque agmina cervi
pulverulenta fuga glomerant.

quod ait speciose "transmittunt" pro "transeunt," sic et Lucretius in secundo:

et circumvolitant equites mediosque repente
transmittunt valido quatientes impete campos.

sed et "Paestanum et Vibonensem," Cicero ait,[104] "pedibus
aequis[105] transmisimus," quod est "transivimus."

103 ut e N, *Cic.*: ut et PGRA, et ut C, et F
104 Paestanum et Vibonenem, Cicero ait *ed. Lugd. Bat. 1597*:
pestanus vibonensis sic ait ω
105 aequis *Salmasius*: -quos ω

---

32 The sheets (*pedes*, lit. "feet") were ropes that adjusted the
angle of the sail relative to the ship's prow-to-stern axis: when the
sheets were let out the same length on both port and starboard, it
meant that the wind was dead astern.

8. Here a dazzling poplar looms
over the cave and pliant vines weave shadings
[*umbracula*]. (*E.* 9.41–42†)

There are those who suppose that Virgil coined the word "shadings" on his own authority, though in Book 10 of *Divine Antiquities* Varro said (fr. 82), "Some magistrates in the town were granted that sort of shading," and in Book 5 of his *Laws* Cicero said (fr. 2 Powell), "Would you like, then—since the sun seems a bit lower in the sky than noon and this whole space doesn't receive sufficient cover from these saplings—to go down to the Liris and pursue the rest of the discussion in the alders' shading?," and similarly in *Brutus* (37), "But as from out of the shading of that very learned fellow Theophrastus . . . ."

9. The stags pass over the plain at a gallop and gather their dusty column in flight. (*A.* 4.154–55)

The attractive use of "pass over" [*transmittunt*] for "cross over" [*transeunt*] is found in Lucretius, too, in Book 2 (329–30),

And the horsemen fly about and suddenly pass over
the middle of the plain, making it shake with their
mighty charge.

But Cicero, too, says "We passed over [the bays] of Paestum and Vibo with sheets dead even"[32] (cf. *Att.* 16.6.1), that is, "we crossed over."

10. Quam tota cohors imitata relictis
ad terram defluxit equis.

sic Furius in primo:

ille gravi subito devinctus[106] vulnere habenas
misit equi lapsusque in humum[107] defluxit et armis
reddidit aeratis sonitum.

11. Tum durare solum et discludere Nerea ponto
coeperit.

ferit aures nostras hoc verbum "discludere" ut novum, sed
prior Lucretius in quinto:

diffugere inde loci partes coepere paresque
cum paribus iungi res et discludere mundum.

12. pastorem, Tityre, pingues
pascere oportet oves, deductum dicere carmen.

"deductum" pro "tenui et subtili" eleganter positum est:
sic autem et Afranius in Virgine:

verbis pauculis
respondit tristis voce deducta <mihi>[108]
malleque se non quiesse dixit.

---

[106] devinctus] devictus P1 (*quod recip. Blänsdorf, Courtney*)
[107] humum *ed. Ven. 1472*: unum ω
[108] mihi *add. Bothe, om.* ω (*utrum librarii an Macrob. lapsu
haud scio*)

---

[33] Furius probably wrote *devictus* = "subdued," found in one
MS; but *devinctus* = "subjugated" appears to be the reading M.
knew.

10. Following her lead her companions left
their mounts and flowed down [*defluxit*] to the
ground. (*A.* 11.500–1)

Thus Furius in Book 1 (fr. 8 *FPL*[3]):

That one there, suddenly subjugated[33] by a weighty
wound,
let go the horse's reins and, tottering, flowed down to
the ground,
and raised a crash with his brazen arms.

11. The earth then began to harden and confine
Nereus
in the sea. (*E.* 6.35–36)

This word "confine" [*discludere*] strikes our ears as a
new coinage, but Lucretius used it previously in Book 5
(437–38):

From that point segments of space began to separate
and like things began to be joined with like, confining
the firmament.

12. A shepherd, Tityrus, should feed
his flock 'til they're fat but keep his song fine-spun.
(*E.* 6.4–5)

"Fine-spun" [*deductum*] for "thin and delicate" is a nice
usage—but Afranius uses it too, in his *Maiden* (339–41
SRPF[3] 2:249):

With a few little words
she answered me sadly, her tone fine-spun,
and said she wished she had not fallen asleep;

item apud Cornificium:

　　deducta mihi voce garrienti.

13. sed haec ab illo fluxerunt quod Pomponius in Atellania quae Kalendae Martiae inscribitur ait:

　　　　vocem deducas oportet, ut mulieris videantur
　　verba.—iube modo adferatur munus,[109] ego vocem
　　　　reddam
　　tenuem et tinnulam,

et infra:

　　etiam nunc vocem deducam.

　　　　　　　14. . . . proiectaque saxa Pachyni
　　radimus . . .

"proiecta," si secundum consuetudinem dicatur, intelligi-tur "abiecta," si secundum veteres, "porrecta"[110] "porro iacta," ut alibi ait,

　　　　proiecto dum pede laevo
　　aptat se pugnae.

15. sed et Sisenna in secundo dixit: "et Marsi propius suc-cedunt atque ita scutis proiectis tecti saxa certatim lenta manibus coniciunt in hostes." et in eodem: "vetus atque in-

---

　　[109] munus *ed. Paris. 1585*: unus ω
　　[110] porrecta *scripsi* (*cf. DServ. ad A. 3.599*): proiecta ω

and similarly in Cornificius (fr. 1 *FPL*[3]),

> . . . as I was going on in fine-spun tones.

13. But these usages are derived from what Pomponius wrote in his Atellan farce[34] titled *The First of March* (57–60 *SRPF*[3] 2:280–81):

> You should make your tone fine-spun, so they seem a woman's
> words.—Just order that my gift[35] be brought, and I'll make my tone
> slight and tinkling,

and further on,

> Even now shall I make my tone fine-spun.

> 14. . . . and we scrape by the jutting [*proiecta*] rocks
> of Pachynus. (*A.* 3.699†–700)

proiecta means "downcast" according to current usage, but "extended" [*porrecta*]—"cast straight ahead" [*porro iacta*]—according to the ancients' usage, as he says elsewhere (*A.* 10.587*–88),

> while with left foot extended [*proiecto*]
> he readies himself for battle.

15. But Sisenna too, in Book 2, said (fr. 8), "The Marsi also approach and, thus protected by their extended [*proiectis*] shields, hurl heavy rocks at the enemy," and in the same

---

[34] Cf. 1.4.21n.   [35] The speaker is a man pretending to be a woman on the Matronalia (1 March), a holiday when men brought married women gifts.

gens erat arbor ilex, quae circum proiectis ramis maiorem
partem loci summi tegebat." et Lucretius in tertio:

quamlibet immani proiectu corporis exstet . . .

16. . . . et[111] tempestivam silvis evertere pinum.

hoc verbum de pino "tempestiva" a Catone sumpsit, qui ait
(*Agr.* 31.2), "pineam nuc‹eam hanc atque aliam materiem
o⟩nn⟩em[112] cum effodies, luna decrescente eximito post
meridiem, sine vento austro; tum vero[113] erit tempestiva
cum semen suum maturum erit."

17. 'Inseruit operi suo et Graeca verba, sed non primus
hoc ausus; auctorum enim veterum audaciam secutus est.

18. dependent lychni laquearibus aureis,

sicut Ennius in nono:

. . . lychnorum lumina bis sex,

et Lucretius in quinto:

quin etiam nocturna tibi, terrestria quae sunt,
lumina, pendentes lychni.

Lucilius in primo:

[111] et] aut *Verg.*
[112] hanc atque aliam materiem omnem *suppl. Marinone*[2] *ex
Catone* (nuceam *iam Jan*): nucem ω
[113] tum vero] tum *codd. Catonis, Plin. NH 16.193*

book (fr. 9), "Ancient and massive was the holm oak, which covered the greater part of the summit with branches that extended [*proiectis*] all around." Lucretius, too, in Book 3 (987),

> however monstrous the extent [*proiectu*] of his
> body. . . .

> 16. . . . and to overturn the seasonable pine in the
> woods. (*G.* 1.256)

He took this application of the word "seasonable" [*tempestiva*] to the pine from Cato, who says (*Agr.* 31.2), "When you uproot pine, walnut, and any other wood, do it after noon at the time of a waning moon, when there is no south wind; then, indeed, it will be seasonable [*tempestiva*], when its seed will be ripe."

17. 'He inserted Greek words, too, in his work, but he was not the first to dare this: he had the boldness of ancient authors as his model.

> 18. *lychni* [lamps] hang from the golden coffered
> ceiling (*A.* 1.726*),

just like Ennius in Book 9 (311 Sk.),

> . . . twice six lights of *lychni*,

and Lucretius in Book 5 (294–95),

> Indeed, consider the terrestrial sources of light
> at night, hanging *lychni*,

Lucilius in Book 1 (16–17):

porro "clinopodas" "lychnosque" ut diximus
   σεμνῶς[114]
ante "pedes lecti" atque "lucernas."

19. et quod dixit,

         . . . nec lucidus aethra
siderea polus . . .

Ennius prior dixerat in sexto decimo:

                interea fax
occidit Oceanumque rubra tractim obruit aethra.

et Iulius[115] in Teuthrante:

flammeam per aethram late[116] fervidam ferri facem.

20. Daedala Circe,

quia Lucretius dixerat:

daedala tellus.

21. Reboant silvaeque et longus Olympus,

quia est apud Lucretium:

nec cithara[117] reboant laqueata aurataque tecta.[118]

22. sed hac licentia largius usi sunt veteres, parcius Maro:
quippe illi dixerunt et "pausam" et "machaeram" et "aso-

---

114 σεμνῶς] cemnoc ω
115 Iulius *Bothe*: ilius ω
116 late *Schrijver*: alte ω
117 cithara] citharae *Lucr.*
118 tecta] templa *Lucr.*

Furthermore, as we previously called a bed's feet and lamps

clinopodes and *lychni*, to strike a certain tone . . .

19. There's also this turn of phrase (*A.* 3.585–86),

. . . nor the vault of heaven alight
with the *aethra* [brilliance] of stars . . . ,

which Ennius previously used in Book 16 (415–16 Sk.),

Meanwhile the torch of heaven
set and a reddening *aethra* slowly covered the surface
of Ocean,

and Julius in *Teuthras* (3 *SRPF*³ 1:263):

Through the fiery *aethra* the blazing torch is borne
abroad.

20. *daedala* [skillful] Circe (*A.* 7.282),

after Lucretius' phrase (1.7, 228):

daedala earth.

21. And the woods and distant Olympus *reboant* [re-echo] (*G.* 3.223),

after Lucretius' phrae (2.28),

nor do the golden coffered ceilings *reboant* with the
lyre.

22. But the ancients used this license more extensively, Maro more sparingly, seeing that *they* used the words *pausa* [pause], and *machaera* [short sword] and *asôtia*

tiam" et "malachen" et alia similia. 23. nec non et Punicis Oscisque verbis usi sunt veteres, quorum imitatione Vergilius peregrina verba non respuit, ut in illo

silvestres uri adsidue . . . :

"uri" enim Gallica vox est, qua feri boves significantur.

et camuris hirtae sub cornibus aures

"camuris" peregrinum verbum est, id est in se redeuntibus. et forte nos quoque camaram hac ratione figuravimus.

5 'Multa quoque epitheta apud Vergilium sunt quae ab ipso ficta creduntur, sed et haec a veteribus tracta monstrabo. sunt autem ex his alia simplicia, ut Gradivus, Mulciber, alia composita ut Arquitenens, Vitisator. sed prius de simplicibus dicam.

2. et discinctos Mulciber Afros:

Mulciber est Vulcanus, quod ignis sit et omnia mulceat ac domet. Accius in Philoctete:

<blockquote>heu Mulciber!
arma ignavo invicta es[119] fabricatus manu,</blockquote>

et Egnatius de rerum natura libro primo:

[119] invicta es] es invicta *Bothe*, invicta fabricatus es *Jan*

---

[36] *pausa* and *machaera* are both used from the time of Plautus and Ennius; the first attested use of *malachê* is in Pliny the elder (but cf. Varro *Latin Language* 5.103), of *asotia*, in Gellius.

[37] Contrast Serv. on *G*. 2.374, who derives the word from Greek ὄρος ("mountain").   [38] Cf. Paul. Fest. p. 38.14, Non. p. 43, DServ. on *G*. 3.55.   [39] Lat. *camara* is certainly derived from Gk. καμάρα, and *camura* might be also.

[profligacy] and *malachê* [mallow] and others like them.[36]
23. In fact the ancients also used Punic and Oscan words,
and following their example Virgil did not reject foreign
words, for instance (G. 2.374)

> without cease the woodland *uri* . . . :

uri is a Gallic word used to denote wild oxen.[37]

> And shaggy ears beneath *camura* horns (G. 3.55*):

camura is a foreign word that means "curving back on
themselves";[38] and perhaps we Romans came up with the
word *camara* [arched window or ceiling] along the same
lines.[39]

'Virgil uses many epithets that he is believed to have
made up, but I shall show that these too were drawn from
the ancients. Some of these are simple forms, like *Gradivus* or *Mulciber*, others are compounds, like *Arquitenens*
or *Vitisator*.[40] But I'll talk about the simple forms first.

2. And Mulciber [had fashioned] the Africans with
their flowing robes (A. 8.724*†):

Mulciber is Vulcan, because as fire he softens [*mulcere*]
and masters all things.[41] Accius in *Philoctetes* (558–59
*SRPF*³ 1:240):

> alas Mulciber!
> you have crafted invincible arms with a futile hand,

and Egnatius in Book 1 of *On Nature* (fr. 1 *FPL*³):

---

[40] Respectively, Mars, Vulcan (cf. §2), Apollo ("the Bow-
holder," cf. §8), and Dionysus ("the Vine-planter," but cf. §11).
[41] Cf. Paul. Fest. p. 129.5–7.

denique Mulciber ipse ferens[120] altissima caeli
†contingunt . . . [121]

        3. . . . haedique petulci floribus insultent.

Lucretius in secundo:

praeterea teneri tremulis cum[122] vocibus haedi
corniferas norunt matres agnique petulci.

4. illud audaciae maximae videri possit, quod ait in Bucolicis:

et liquidi simul ignis,

pro "puro" vel "lucido" seu pro "effuso et abundanti," nisi
prior hoc epitheto Lucretius usus fuisset in sexto:

hac etiam fit uti de causa mobilis ille
devolet in terram liquidi calor[123] aureus ignis.

5. "tristis" pro "amaro" translatio decens est ut

. . . tristisque lupini,

et ita Ennius in libro Saturarum[124] quarto:

neque triste quaeritat sinapi,
neque cepe maestum.

---

[120] ferens] furens *Bergk,* petens *Baehrens*
[121] contingunt (*obel. notant Jan, Willis*): contingit *Bergk,* dein
quae Mulciber ipse ferit altissima caeli/contingunt *Marinone²*
[122] cum *e Lucr.*: in ω
[123] calor (*codd. Lucr.*)] color *Serv. ad E. 6.33, edd.*
[124] Saturarum *Colonna ap. ed. Lugd. Bat. 1597:* Sabinarum ω

And then Mulciber himself, bearing (?) . . . the
    highest point in heaven. . . .

        3. . . . and *petulci* [= butting][42] goats
gambol on the blossoms. (*G.* 4.10*–11)

Lucretius in Book 2 (367–68):

Besides, the tender young goats with their quavering
    voices
and the *petulci* lambs recognize their horned
    mothers.

4. What he says in the *Bucolics* might seem extremely bold
(*E.* 6.33*†),

and at the same time of *liquidus* fire—

whether *liquidus* denotes "pure" or "shining" or denotes
"wild and excessive"—save that Lucretius previously used
this epithet in Book 6 (204–5):

For this reason it happens that the swift, golden
warmth of *liquidus* fire swoops down upon the earth.

5. Using *tristis* ["sad"] to mean "bitter-tasting" is an attractive extension, as in

. . . and of *tristis* lupine (*G.* 1.75*†),

and Ennius uses it that way in Book 4 of his *Satires* (fr. 14
*FLP*²),

he looks neither for *tristis* mustard
nor for mournful onion.

[42] Cf. Fest. p. 226.4–12. (citing Afranius in addition to Virgil
and Lucretius).

6. "auritos" lepores non Maro primus usurpat, sed Afranium sequitur, qui in prologo ex persona Priapi ait:

> nam quod vulgo praedicant
> aurito me parente natum, non ita est.

7. et ut composita subiungam, quod ait Vergilius,

> vidit, turicremis cum dona imponeret aris. . . ,

iam Lucretius in secundo dixerat:

> nam saepe ante deum vitulus delubra decora
> turicremas propter mactatus concidit aras.

8. . . . . quam pius Arquitenens . . .

hoc epitheto usus est Naevius belli Punici libro secundo:

> deinde pollens sagittis   inclitus arquitenens
> sanctusque Delphis[125] prognatus   Pythius Apollo.

idem alibi:

> cum tu arquitenens, sagittis pollens dea . . .

sed et Hostius libro secundo belli Histrici:

---

[125] Delphis] Iove *Buecheler, alii alia*

---

[43] Cf. Paul. Fest. p. 8.7–8.

[44] Naevius cannot have thought that Delphi, rather than Delos, was Apollo's birthplace: if the archetype's *Delphis* is what M. wrote (not *Deli*), it is an error comparable to his referring to Palinurus when he meant Misenus (5.7.9).

[45] Here the epithet refers to Apollo's sister, Diana.

6. Maro was not the first to speak of hares as *auriti* ["eared"] (*G.* 1.308),[43] but he follows Afranius, who said in one of his prologues, speaking in the character of Priapus (402–3 *SRPF*[3] 2:258),

> As for the widely circulated claim
> that I was born from an *auritus* father, it's not true.

7. And to add an account of compound epithets, the word that Virgil uses (*A.* 4.453),

> When she placed the offering on the *turicremae*
>   ["incense-burning"] altars, she saw . . . ,

Lucretius had already used in Book 2 (352–53):

> For often before the gods' handsome shrines the calf
> falls, slaughtered hard by the *turicremae* altars.

8. . . . [the island] which the devoted *Arquitenens* . . .
    (*A.* 3.75)

Naevius used this epithet in Book 2 of the *Punic War* (fr. 24 *FPL*[3]),

> Then the master of arrows,   the famed *Arquitenens*,
> the holy one born at Delphi[44]   Pythian Apollo,

as he does elsewhere (fr. 62 *FPL*[3]),

> When you, *Arquitenens*,   mistress of arrows,
>   goddess. . . .[45]

But Hostius does so too, in Book 2 of his *Histrian War* (fr. 4 *FPL*[3]),

SATURNALIA

dia Minerva ⟨simul⟩,[126] simul autem invictus Apollo
arquitenens Latonius.

9. silvicolae Fauni[127] . . . ,

Naevius belli Punici libro primo:

silvicolae homines   bellique inertes

Accius in Bacchis:

et nunc silvicolae ignota invisentes loca.

10. . . . despiciens mare velivolum,

Laevius[128] in Helena:

tu qui
permensus ponti maria alta
velivola. . .

Ennius in quarto decimo:

. . . cum procul aspiciunt hostes accedere ventis
navibus velivolis.

idem in Andromache:[129]

. . . rapit ex alto naves velivolas.

11. vitisator curvam servans sub imagine falcem,

126 simul *add. Bergk, om.* ω
127 Fauni] -no *Verg.*   128 Laevius *Ribbeck*: Livius ω
129 Andromache A: dromache ω

---

46 With Courtney (*FLP*[2] p. 127) I take the meter to be dactylic
tetrameter.   47 Virgil uses the epithet here not of Dionysus
but of the native Italian figure "father Sabinus"; I follow Fordyce

Divine Minerva together, together too invincible
    Apollo,
Arquitenens, son of Leto.

9. *silvicolae* ["forest-dwelling"] Fauns . . . (*A.* 10.551):

Naevius in Book 1 of the *Punic War* (fr. 10 *FPL*³),

silvicolae people   and worthless in war,

Accius in *Bacchae* (237 *SRPF*³ 1:192):

and now the *silvicolae* going to see places unknown.

10. . . . looking down upon the *velivolum* ["swift-
    sailing"] sea (*A.* 1.224*):

Laevius in *Helen* (fr. 11 *FPL*³),[46]

            You who
have traversed the sea's deep
velivola expanses . . . ,

Ennius in Book 14 (379–80 Sk.),

    . . . when from afar they see the enemy advance with
        the winds
on their *velivolae* ships.

and again in *Andromache* (74 *SRPF*³ 1:27 = 111 Jocelyn),

    . . . hurries the *velivolae* ships from the deep.

11. a *vitisator* ["vine-planter"] holding his curved
    pruning-hook in the representation (*A.* 7.179):[47]

and Horsfall in taking the difficult phrase *sub imagine* as = "in the
representation" (a statue is being described), but with no great
confidence that it is correct.

91

Accius in Bacchis:

> o Dionyse,
> pater optime vitisator, Semela
> genitus,[130] Euhie[131] . . .

12. . . . almaque curru
noctivago Phoebe

Egnatius de rerum natura libro primo:

> roscida noctivagis astris labentibus Phoebe
> pulsa loco cessit concedens lucibus altis.

13. Tu nubigenas, invicte, bimembris . . . ,

Cornificius in Glauco:

> . . . centauros foedare bimembres.

14. caprigenumque pecus nullo custode per herbas,

Pacuvius in Paulo:

> . . . quamvis caprigeno pecori grandior gressio est;[132]

---

[130] genitus] genite *pensitavit Jan*   [131] Euhie *vel* Euie
Scaliger (Euie *et Jan dubitanter*): euhia ω
[132] quamvis . . . gressio est] qua via caprigeno generi gradibilis
Prisc. GL 2.196.5 (*unde* qua vix c. g. gradilis *G. Hermann*)

---

[48] *bimembres* = "having limbs of two sorts," i.e., centaurs; they
are called "born from a cloud" because when Ixion tried to rape
Hera, Zeus substituted a cloud in her image, from which Cen-
taurus ("Prick-breeze"), ancestor of the centaurs, was born after
Ixion's attack.

92

Accius in *Bacchae* (240–42 *SRPF*[3] 1:193),

> o Dionysus,
> best father, *vitisator*, Semela's
> child, Euhie. . . .

> 12. . . . and kindly Phoebe
> in her *noctivagus* ["night-wandering"] chariot
> (*A*. 10.215):

Egnatius in Book 1 of his *On Nature* (fr. 2 *FPL*[3]),

> As the *noctivaga* stars glided on, dewy Phoebe
>   withdrew,
> driven from her place, yielding to the lights high in
>   heaven.

> 13. You, invincible one, [slay] the *bimembres* born
>   from a cloud . . . (*A*. 8.293):[48]

Cornificius in *Glaucus* (fr. 2 *FPL*[3]),

> . . . to mangle the *bimembres* centaurs.

> 14. and no guardian over the *caprigenum* ["goat-
>   born"] flock through the pasture (*A*. 3.221):

Pacuvius in *Paulus* (5 *SRPF*[3] 1:325),

> . . . though the *caprigenum* flock have a longer
>   stride,[49]

---

[49] The transmitted text, translated here, can hardly be correct, though it is not clear whether the fault lies with M., his source, or his scribes: the version of the line quoted by the grammarian Priscian—"where the path is passable for the goat-born race"—is surely closer to what Pacuvius wrote.

Accius in Philoctete:

> . . . caprigenum trita ungulis;

idem in Minotauro:

> . . . taurigeno semine ortum fuisse an humano?

15. decenter et his epithetis Vergilius usus est: pro sagitta "volatile ferrum," et pro Romanis "gentemque togatam," quorum altero Sueius, altero Laberius usus erat. nam Sueius in libro quinto ait,

> . . . volucrumque volatile telum.

ac Laberius in Ephebo:

> licentiam ac libidinem ut tollam petis
> togatae stirpis.

idem infra:

> id circo ope nostra dilatatum est dominium
> togatae gentis.

6   'Figuras vero quas traxit de vetustate, si volentibus vobis erit, cum repentina memoria suggesserit, enumerabo. sed nunc dicat volo Servius quae in Vergilio notaverit ab ipso figurata, non a veteribus accepta, vel ausu poetico nove quidem sed decenter usurpata. cotidie enim Romanae indoli enarrando eundem vatem, necesse est ha-

---

50 If *volucrumque*—"and of winged things/birds" (gen. plur.) —is what Sueius wrote, it depends grammatically on words that M. did not quote, or that were lost in transmission, and cannot be intelligibly translated.

Accius in *Philoctetes* (544 *SRPF*[3] 1:238),

> . . . [a path] worn by the hooves of the *caprigeni*,

who also says, in *Minotaur* (463 *SRPF*[3] 1:226),

> . . . that he was sprung from *taurigenum* ["bull-born"]
> seed or human seed.

15. Virgil made handsome use of the following epithets too: for an arrow, "flying iron" (*A.* 4.71), and for the Romans, "the toga-clad race" (*A.* 1.282), the first of which Sueius used, the other, Laberius. For in Book 5 Sueius says (fr. 8 *FPL*[3]),

> . . . the flying missile,[50]

and Laberius in *The Ephebe* (58–59),

> You ask that I remove the licentious lustfulness
> of the toga-clad stock,

and also farther along (56–57),

> For that reason, with my aid, the dominion of the
>   toga-clad race
> has been extended.

'If you like, I will list the figures that he borrowed from 6 the ancient writers, when I've gathered them up, spur-of-the-moment, from my memory. But right now I'd like Servius to speak about the figurative usages that he's noticed in Virgil that were *not* taken over from earlier writers but were rather shaped by the poet himself or adopted, with a poet's daring, in a novel yet becoming way. For since he spends each day explaining the same bard to our talented youth, he must inevitably have quite a ready supply

beat huius adnotationis scientiam promptiorem.' placuit universis electio in reliqua suffecti, et adhortati sunt Servium ut quae in se refusa sunt adnotaret.

2. Ille sic incipit: 'vates iste venerabilis varie modo verba, modo sensus figurando multum Latinitati leporis adiecit. qualia sunt haec:

supposita de matre nothos furata creavit,

ut ipsa creaverit quos creari fecit; ⟨et⟩[133]

3. tepidaque recentem
caede locum,

cum locus recens caede nove dictus sit; et

haec ait, et socii cesserunt aequore iusso,

pro eo quod iussi cesserunt; et

. . . caeso sparsurus sanguine flammas,

qui ex caesis videlicet profunditur; ⟨et⟩[134]

4. vota deum primo victor solvebat Eoo,

[133] et *addidi, om.* ω
[134] et *addidi, om.* ω

of such observations.' All agreed to the choice of Servius as a substitute to continue the balance of the topic, and they urged him to remark on the matters that Caecina referred to him.

2. He began this way: 'That venerable bard increased the charm of the Latin language in diverse ways, now with figures of speech, now with figures of thought. Here are some examples:

> She stealthily created bastards from a mare she
>   substituted (A. 7.283),

as though she herself created those that she caused to be created; and (A. 9.455–56*)

>   3. a place fresh
>   with warm slaughter,

since "a place fresh with slaughter" is an unprecedented expression; and (A. 10.444*)

> So he spoke, and his allies withdrew from the bidden
>   field ,

instead of saying that they withdrew at his bidding; and (A. 11.82*)

> . . . . intending to spatter the flames with slaughtered
>   blood,

where of course the blood is spilled by those who have been slaughtered; and (A. 11.4)

4. as victor he was paying the gods' vows at first dawn,

pro "quae dis vota sunt"; et

   . . . me consortem nati concede sepulcro,

alius dixisset, "et me consortem nato concede sepulcri." et

   illa viam celerans per mille coloribus arcum,

id est "per arcum mille colorum." 5. et

   hic alii spolia occisis direpta Latinis
   coniciunt igni,

pro "in ignem." et

   corpore tela modo atque oculis vigilantibus exit,

"tela exit" pro "vitat." et

   . . . senior leto canentia lumina solvit,

pro "vetustate senilia." 6. ⟨et⟩[135]

   . . . exesaeque arboris antro

pro "caverna." et

   . . . frontem obscenam rugis arat,

[135] et *addidi, om.* ω

---

51 The difference, between using a phrase with an ablative of quality and one with a genitive of quality, is a matter of tone in the Latin (the former being an archaism in Virgil's day) and difficult to reflect in English.

52 The effect at issue is not the slight difference in English between "escape" and "avoid" but the relatively rare use of the verb

instead of "vows made to the gods"; and (A. 10.906)

> . . . grant that I be my son's partner in his tomb,

where another would have said, "And grant that I share a tomb with my son"; and (A. 5.609*)

> She hurried her way over a bow with a thousand
> > colors,

that is, "over a bow of a thousand colors";[51] 5. and (A. 11.193)

> Here others hurl for the fire [igni] spoils stripped
> > from slain Latins,

for "onto the fire [in ignem]"; and (A. 5.438*)

> With his body and watchful eyes he just escapes the
> > missiles,

"escapes the missiles" for "avoids";[52] and (A. 10.418*)

> . . . the old man relaxed his hoary [canentia] eyes in
> > death,

for "eyes made old by long time's passage"; 6. and (G. 4.4)

> . . . in the cave of a tree that had been eaten away,

for "in the hollow"; and (A. 7.417)

> . . . plows wrinkles into her foul forehead,

exire ("to go out") as a transitive verb with a direct object. Equally striking, but unremarked, is Virgil's use of tela ("missiles") to denote the punches thrown in a boxing match.

"arat" non nimie sed pulchre dictum. ⟨et⟩[136]

ter secum . . .
. . . aerato circumfert tegmine silvam,

pro "iaculis"; et "vir gregis" pro "capro." 7. et illa quam pulchra sunt: "aquae mons," "telorum seges," "ferreus imber," ut apud Homerum:

λάϊνον ἕσσο χιτῶνα κακῶν ἕνεχ᾽, ὅσσα ἔοργας

et

dona laboratae Cereris,

et

oculisque[137] aut pectore noctem
accipit,

et

vocisque offensa resultat imago,

et

pacemque per aras
exquirunt,

et

paulatim abolere Sychaeum
incipit.

[136] et *addidi, om.* ω
[137] oculisque ω (*codd. aliquot Verg.*)] oculisve *codd. cett. Verg.*

where "plows" is not overdone but nicely chosen; and (*A.* 10.887–88)

> thrice he turns and with him . . .
> . . . bears a forest on his shield's brazen covering,

where "forest" stands for "spears"; and "man of the flock" (*E.* 7.7*) for "he-goat"; 7. and these phrases, so beautiful: "a mountain of water" (*A.* 1.105), "a crop of missiles" (*A.* 3.46*), "iron rain" (*A.* 12.284*)—as we find in Homer (*Il.* 3.57),

> you would long since have worn a stone tunic[53] for all the woes you've caused—

and "gifts of worked Ceres" (*A.* 8.181*), and (*A.* 4.530–31)

> and welcomes night with eyes or
> heart,

and (*G.* 4.50*)

> and a likeness of the voice strikes [the rocks] and rebounds,

and (*A.* 4.56–57*)

> and they seek peace
> among the altars,

and (*A.* 1.720–21)

> she begins, little by little, to banish
> Sychaeus.

---

[53] I.e., would have been stoned to death (spoken to Paris).

8. 'Saepe etiam verba pro verbis pulchre ponit:

oraque corticibus sumunt horrenda cavatis,

"ora" pro "personis," et

discolor unde auri per ramos aura refulsit.

quid est enim "aura" auri, aut quemadmodum aura "reful-
get"? sed tamen pulchre usurpavit. et

simili frondescit virga metallo,

quam bene usus est "frondescit metallo"! 9. et

nigri cum lacte veneni

. . . [138] nigro imponere nomen lactis? et

haud aliter iustae quibus est Mezentius irae,

"odio esse" aliquem usitatum, "irae esse" inventum Maronis est.

10. 'Item de duobus incipit dicere et in unum desinit:

interea reges, ingenti mole Latinus
quadriiugo vehitur curru,

ut est apud Homerum:

[138] *lacunam post* veneni *statuit Jan (bene 'quo modo potuit
veneno' vel sim. exempli gratia obtulit)*

---

[54] A brief lacuna was identified here by Jan, whose plausible
stop-gap ("quo modo potuit veneno") is reflected by the words in
square brackets.

8. 'Often, too, he uses one word in another's place, to good effect:

And they take on fearsome faces of hollowed-out
     bark (*G.* 2.387),

where "faces" stands for "masks," and (*A.* 6.204*)

     whence the contrasting breeze of gold gleamed
          through the branches—

for what is gold's "breeze," or how does a breeze "gleam"?
Yet it's a handsome turn—and (*A.* 6.144*),

     the branch is in leaf with a like metal—

what a nice touch, "is in leaf with metal"!—9. and
(*A.* 4.514*),

     with the milk of black poison—

[how did he come to] apply the name of "milk" to black
[poison]?[54]—and (*A.* 10.714)

     Just so, those for whom Mezentius is an object of
          righteous anger—

that someone "is an object of hatred" is a familiar expression, but "is an object of anger" is Maro's own coinage.
10. 'Similarly, there are places where he begins by
speaking of two people and ends by speaking only of one
(*A.* 12.161–62*),

     Meanwhile the kings, Latinus with his massive form
     is carried in a chariot with a team of four,

as we find in Homer (*Od.* 12.73–74),

οἱ δὲ δύω σκόπελοι ὁ μὲν οὐρανὸν εὐρὺν ἱκάνει
ὀξείῃ κορυφῇ, νεφέλη δέ μιν ἀμφιβέβηκεν.

et

protinus Orsilochum et Buten, duo maxima Teucrum
corpora, sed Buten aversum cuspide fixit

et cetera.

11. Iuturnam misero, fateor, succurrere fratri
suasi,

cum solitum sit dici "Iuturnae suasi," et

urbem quam statuo, vestra est,

⟨pro "urbs quam statuo vestra est"⟩;[139] et

tu modo, quos in spem statues submittere gentis,
praecipuum iam inde a teneris impende laborem,

pro "in eos impende."

12. ʿFacit pulcherrimas repetitiones:

nam neque Parnassi vobis iuga, nam neque Pindi
ulla moram fecere.

---

[139] pro "urbs quam statuo vestra est" *addidi e Serv. ad A.*
1.573, om. ω

---

[55] The comparison of the Virgilian passages with the Homeric
is misleading: Homer never does return to describe the second
of the two crags, whereas Virgil goes on to treat the second
king (Turnus) in the first passage (*A.* 12.164–65) and the second
brother in the other (*A.* 11.694–98).

[56] Cf. DServ. on *A.* 10.10.

The two crags, one reaches to broad heaven
with its jagged crest, and cloud surrounds it;

and (A. 11.690–91),

Straightway, Orsilochus and Butes, the two most
massive
of the Trojans, but Butes' back he pierced with his
spear-point,

and so on.[55]

11. I persuaded that Juturna—I admit it—come to
the aid of her poor
brother (A. 12.813–14),

though the customary idiom is "I persuaded Juturna";[56]
and (A. 1.573*)

Which city I am founding is yours,

for "the city which I am founding is yours"; and (G. 3.73–
74†)

Just see to it that, those you plan to breed as the
herd's future hope,
invest your chief effort right from the time they are
young,

for "invest in those."

12. 'He uses repetitions to very good effect:

For neither Parnassus' ridges, for neither Pindus'
caused
you any delay. (E. 10.11–12)

quae vobis, quae digna, viri, pro talibus ausis?[140]

vidisti quo Turnus equo, quibus ibat in armis?

13. 'Nec interpositiones eius otiosae sunt:

"si te nulla movet tantarum gloria rerum,[141]
at ramum hunc"—aperit ramum qui forte[142] latebat—
"agnoscis,"[143]

"Vt sceptrum hoc"—dextra sceptrum nam forte
    gerebat—
"numquam fronde levi. . . ,"

14. 'Et illa mutatio elegantissima est ut de quo loqueba-
tur subito ad ipsum verba converteret:

. . . ut bello egregias idem disiecerit urbes,
Troiamque Oechaliamque et[144] duros mille labores
rege sub Eurystheo fatis Iunonis iniquae
pertulerit: "tu nubigenas invicte bimembris . . . "

et reliqua. 15. illa vero intermissio

quos ego—sed motos praestat componere fluctus,

tracta est a Demosthene: ἀλλ᾽ ἐμοὶ μὲν—οὐ βούλομαι

---

[140] talibus ausis (*codd. aliquot Verg., cf. A. 2.535, 12.351*)]
laudibus istis *codd. cett. Verg., Serv., Tib., edd.*

[141] tantarum gloria rerum (*cf. A. 4.232, 272*)] tantae pietatis
imago *Verg.*

[142] forte] veste *Verg.*

[143] agnoscis] adgnoscas *Verg.*

[144] et (*codd.* Rbr *Verg.*)] ut *codd. cett. Verg., Tib.*

What am to give you, what worthy things, men, to
match your bold undertaking? (*A.* 9.252)

Did you see the horse, see the arms Turnus wore as
he rode? (*A.* 9.269)

13. 'His parenthetical interventions are effective too:

If the glorious reputation of such deeds does not
move you,
still, this bough (he shows the bough he chanced to
have hidden)
is not unfamiliar (*A.* 6.405–7),

As this scepter (for he chanced to hold the scepter in
his right hand)
will never with delicate foliage . . . (*A.* 12.206–7*),

14. 'A very subtle effect is achieved, too, by the change
of course whereby he begins by speaking about a person
and then turns to address him directly (*A.* 8.290–93):

. . . how the same hero scattered noble cities in war,
Troy and Oechalia, and bore to the end a thousand
hard labors under king Eurystheus because of the
destiny imposed
by cruel Juno: "You, invincible one, the hybrids born
from a cloud . . . "[57]

and so on. 15. But the way he breaks off here (*A.* 1.135)

whom I'll—but better now to settle the troubled seas

is drawn from Demosthenes (18.3): "But as far as I'm con-

[57] Cf. 6.5.13n.

δυσχερὲς οὐδὲν εἰπεῖν[145] ἀρχόμενος τοῦ λόγου, οὗτος δὲ ἐκ[146] περιουσίας ἐμοῦ[147] κατηγορεῖ. 16. haec vero quam poetica indignatio:

> "pro Iuppiter! ibit

hic. . . ?," ait,

haec miseratio:

> o patria, o[148] rapti nequiquam ex hoste Penates!

et illa trepidatio:

> ferte citi ferrum, date tela et scandite[149] muros:
> hostis adest!,

et conquestio:

> mene igitur socium tantis[150] adiungere rebus,
> Nise, fugis?

17. 'Quid et illa excogitatio novorum intellectuum ut

> mentitaque tela,

et

> ferrumque armare veneno,

et

[145] εἰπεῖν οὐδὲν *Dem.*
[146] ἐκ *om. a*
[147] ἐμοῦ] μου *Dem.*
[148] o] et *Verg.*
[149] et scandite (*codd. plerique Verg., Tib.*)] ascendite *codd. cett. Verg., edd.*
[150] tantis] summis *Verg.*

cerned—no, I do not wish to speak harshly at the start of my speech, though *he* has the advantage in denouncing me." 16. How poetic this expression of outrage is (*A.* 4.590*–91),[58]

> "By god!," she said,
> will he just leave . . . ?,"

and this expression of pity (*A.* 5.632),

> O my homeland, o Penates rescued—in vain—from the enemy!

and this expression of agitation (*A.* 9.37*†),

> Quick, bring a sword, hand out the lances, mount the walls:
> the enemy is upon us!,

and lament (*A.* 9.199–200),

> Is it me, then, Nisus, you're trying to avoid enlisting as an ally in such an exploit?

17. 'Consider, too, the way he comes up with wholly new ways of expressing certain thoughts, like (*A.* 2.422*)

> and counterfeit weapons,

and (*A.* 9.773*)

> and arm the spear-point with poison,

and (*G.* 2.36)

---

[58] For the treatment of *pathos*, see 4.2–3; the first example here is cited at 4.2.2.

cultusque[151] feros mollire[152] colendo,

‹et›[153]

exuerint silvestrem animum,

et

virgineumque alte bibit acta cruorem,

ut apud Homerum de hasta

λιλαιομένη χροὸς ἆσαι

18. et

pomaque degenerant sucos oblita priores,

et

glacie cursus frenaret aquarum,

et

mixtaque ridenti colocasia fundit[154] acantho,

et[155]

    est mollis flamma medullas,
interea et tacitum vivit sub pectore vulnus,

et

    udo sub robore vivit
stuppa vomens tardum fumum,

[151] cultusque (*cod.* M[1] *Verg.*)] fructusque *codd. cett. Verg.*
[152] mollire] -te *Verg.* [153] et *ed. Lugd. 1550, om.* ω
[154] fundit] -et *Verg.* [155] et P, *om.* ω

and by cultivation soften your wild ways of life,

and (*G.* 2. 51)

they stripped off their woodland soul,

and (*A.* 11.804)

and driven deep [the arrow] drinks the maiden's
    gore—

as in Homer, concerning a spear (*Il.* 21.168),

eager to eat its fill of flesh—

18. and (*G.* 2.59)

and the fruit deteriorate, forgetting their former
    juices,

and (*G.* 4.136*)

[winter] reins in the galloping streams with ice,

and (*E.* 4.20)

and pours fourth the Egyptian bean mixed with
    smiling acanthus,

and (*A.* 4.66–67)

> Meanwhile, a flame eats at her soft marrow
> and deep in her breast a silent wound is alive,

and (*A.* 5.681–82)

> Beneath the damp oak the tow
> is alive, belching out lingering smoke,

19. et

> saevitque canum latratus in auras,

et

> caelataque amnem fundens pater Inachus urna,

et

> adfixae venis animasque in vulnera ponunt,

et quicquid de apibus dixit in virorum fortium similitudinem, ut adderet quoque mores et studia et populos et proelia, quid plura, ut et Quirites vocaret. 20. dies me deficiet si omnia persequi a Vergilio figurata velim, sed ex his quae dicta sunt omnia similia lector diligens adnotabit.'

7 Cum Servius ista dissereret, Praetextatus Avienum Eustathio insusurrantem videns, 'quin age' inquit 'Eustathi, verecundiam Avieni probi adulescentis iuva et ipse publicato nobis quod immurmurat.' 2. Eustathius; 'iam dudum,' inquit, 'multa de Vergilio gestit interrogare Servium, quorum enarratio respicit officium litteratoris, et tempus indulgeri optat quo de obscuris ac dubiis sibi a doctiore fiat certior.' 3. et Praetextatus, 'probo,' inquit, 'mi Aviene, quod ea de quibus ambigis clam te esse non pateris. unde exoratus sit a nobis doctissimus doctor ut te secum negotium habere patiatur, quia in commune proficient quae desideras audire. ne tu modo ultra cesses aperire Servio viam de Vergilio disserendi.'

---

59 The name used to address the Roman citizen body in formal assembly.

19. and (*A.* 5.257)

> and the dogs' barking rages against the wind,

and (*A.* 7.792)

> and father Inachus, spilling his stream from an
>   engraved urn,

and (*G.* 4.238*)

> stuck fast to the veins [the bees] lay down their lives
>   in the wound,

and his whole account of the bees (*G.* 4.149ff.) that likens them to heroes, even attributing to them customs and focused pursuits and peoples and battles, in short, even calling them "Quirites"[59] (*G.* 4.201*). 20. I'll spend the whole day and more, should I want to give a thorough account of Virgil's figurative language, but from what I've said an attentive reader will remark all the others like them.'

While Servius was holding forth, Praetextatus noticed 7 Avienus whispering to Eustathius and said, 'Come now, Eustathius, make good our fine young friend Avienus' modest restraint and share with us yourself what he's murmuring in your ear.' 2. Eustathius said, 'For a while now he's been dying to ask Servius many questions about Virgil that fall within a teacher's proper sphere, and he hopes he can be allowed the time to be instructed by one more learned than himself on points he finds doubtful and obscure.' 3. And Praetextatus said, 'Good for you, Avienus, for not concealing the things that leave you uncertain. So then, let our most learned teacher be prevailed upon to accept your consultation, since we'll all profit from the things you want to learn: don't be slow, now, to give Servius an opening to talk about Virgil.'

4. Tunc Avienus totus conversus in Servium, 'dicas volo,' inquit, 'doctorum maxime, quid sit quod Vergilius, qui[156] anxie semper diligens fuerit in verbis pro causae merito vel atrocitate ponendis, incuriose et abiecte in his versibus verbum posuit:

> candida succinctam latrantibus inguina monstris
> Dulichias vexasse rates.

"vexasse" enim verbum est levis ac parvi incommodi nec tam atroci casui congruens, cum repente homines a belua immanissima rapti laniatique sint. 5. sed et aliud huiusce modi deprehendi:

> quis aut Eurysthea durum
> aut inlaudati nescit Busiridis aras?

hoc enim verbum "inlaudati" non est idoneum ad exprimendam sceleratissimi hominis detestationem, qui quod homines[157] omnium gentium immolare solitus fuit, non laude indignus, sed detestatione exsecrationeque totius generis humani dignus est. 6. sed nec hoc verbum ex diligentia Vergiliana venire mihi videtur,

> . . . per tunicam squalentem auro:

non enim convenit dicere "auro squalentem" quoniam nitori splendorique auri contraria sit squaloris inluvies.'

[156] qui C: *om.* ω, cum *post* quod R[m]
[157] homines] hospites *Gell.*

4. Then Avienus, turning to face Servius, said,[60] 'Please tell me, best of teachers, why Virgil, who was ever finicky and careful in weighing his words to suit the merits of his subject or their lack, used a word carelessly, just tossing it off, in these lines (*E.* 6.75–76*†),

> girt round her fair groin with baying monsters,
> she harried the ships of Ulysses.

For "harried" is a verb appropriate to a slight and trivial discomfiture, not the horrendous misfortune entailed when people are suddenly seized and torn to bits by an utterly dreadful monster. 5. But there's also another instance of this sort that I've come upon (*G.* 3.4–5*):

> Who does not know of cruel
> Eurystheus or the altars of Busiris, whom none can
> praise?

For saying "whom none can praise" isn't suited to expressing the loathing appropriately felt for the worst sort of criminal, who—seeing that he used to sacrifice people of all nations—was not just unworthy of praise, but worthy of being hated and cursed by the whole human race. 6. For that matter, this word, too, seems inconsistent with Virgil's exacting care (*A.* 10.314*†),

> . . . through his tunic caked with gold:

"caked with gold" is inappropriate, since the filthiness associated with "caking" is the opposite of gold's gleaming splendor.'

---

[60] §§4–19 are based on Gell. 2.6; (D)Serv. offer a parallel discussion of each of the phrases queried.

7. Et Servius: 'de verbo "vexasse" ita responderi posse arbitror: vexasse grave verbum est tractumque ab eo videtur quod est vehere in quo inest iam vis quaedam alieni arbitrii, non enim sui potens est qui vehitur. vexare autem, quod ex eo inclinatum est, vi atque motu procul dubio vastiore est. 8. nam qui fertur et raptatur atque huc et illuc distrahitur, is "vexari" proprie dicitur sicuti "taxare" pressius crebriusque est quam "tangere," unde id procul dubio inclinatum est, et "iactare" multo fusius largiusque est quam "iacere," unde id verbum traductum est, "quassare" etiam quam "quatere" gravius violentiusque est. 9. non igitur quia vulgo dici solet vexatum esse quem fumo aut vento aut pulvere, propterea debet vis vera atque natura verbi deperire, quae a veteribus, qui proprie atque signate locuti sunt, ita ut decuit conservata est. 10. M. Catonis verba sunt ex oratione quam de Achaeis scripsit: "cumque Hannibal terram Italiam laceraret atque vexaret." "vexatam" Italiam dixit Cato ab Hannibale, quando nullum calamitatis aut saevitiae aut immanitatis genus reperiri queat quod in eo tempore Italia non perpessa sit. 11. M. Tullius quarto in Verrem: "quae ab isto sic spoliata atque direpta est, non ut ab hoste aliquo, qui tamen in bello religionem et consuetudinis iura retineret, sed ut a barbaris praedonibus vexata esse videatur."

12. 'De "inlaudato" autem duo videntur responderi posse. unum est eiusmodi: nemo quisquam tam efflictis est

7. Servius said: 'As for the verb "harried," I think a response can be made along these lines: "harry" is a weighty word apparently derived from the verb "carry" [*vehere*], which immediately implies a certain force of another person's will, since one who is carried is not in control of his movements. The derivative verb "to harry" is plainly associated with a much more intense sort of forceful movement. 8. For a person who is borne along, carried off, and pulled this way and that is properly said to be "harried," just as "tag" [*taxare*] involves an action more insistent and repeated than "touch" [*tangere*], from which it is surely derived, and "throw" [*iactare*] is a much broader and larger gesture than "toss" [*iacere*], its source, and "shock" [*quassare*] is more serious and violent than "shake" [*quatere*]. 9. Just because it's commonly said that someone is "harried" by smoke or wind or dust there's no need for us to lose the word's true force and nature, which was appropriately preserved by the ancients, who used language properly and exactly. 10. Here are the words of Marcus Cato, from the speech he wrote on the Achaeans (fr. 187 *ORF*[2]): "And when Hannibal was savaging and harrying the land of Italy." Cato said Italy was "harried" by Hannibal, though no sort of disaster or savagery or inhumanity could be found that Italy did not fully suffer at that time. 11. Marcus Tullius, in the fourth book against Verres (2.4.122): "that scoundrel so despoiled and plundered [the temple] that it seems to have been harried, not by some foreign enemy—who even in war would still have observed religious scruple and traditional rights—but by barbarian free-booters."

12. 'Regarding "whom none can praise," I think there are two possible answers. One goes like this: no one is such

117

moribus quin faciat aut dicat non numquam aliquid quod
laudari queat. unde hic antiquissimus versus vice proverbii
celebratus est:

πολλάκι γὰρ καὶ μωρὸς[158] ἀνὴρ μάλα καίριον[159]
εἶπε.

13. sed enim qui omni in re atque omni tempore laude
omni vacat, is inlaudatus est isque omnium pessimus de-
terrimusque est, ac sicuti omnis culpae privatio incul-
patum facit, inculpatus autem instar est absolutae virtutis, inlaudatus quoque igitur finis est extremae malitiae.
14. itaque Homerus non virtutibus appellandis sed vitiis
detrahendis laudare ampliter solet. hoc enim est:

τὼ δ᾽ οὐκ ἄκοντε πετέσθην

et item illud:

ἔνθ᾽ οὐκ ἂν βρίζοντα ἴδοις Ἀγαμέμνονα δῖον
οὐδὲ καταπτώσσοντ᾽ οὐδ᾽ οὐκ ἐθέλοντα
μάχεσθαι.

15. Epicurus quoque simili modo maximam voluptatem
privationem detractionemque omnis doloris definivit his
verbis: ὅρος τοῦ μεγέθους τῶν ἡδονῶν ⟨ἡ⟩[160] παντὸς τοῦ
ἀλγοῦντος ὑπεξαίρεσις. eadem ratione idem Vergilius
"inamabilem" dixit Stygiam paludem: nam sicut inlauda-
tum κατὰ στέρησιν laudis, ita inamabilem per amoris

---

[158] γὰρ καὶ μωρὸς (om. β₂)] τοι καὶ μωρὸς Stob. 3.4.23,
Diogenianus 7.81: καὶ κηπουρὸς codd. Gell.
[159] μάλα καίριον a Gell. (om. β₂): κατακαίριον Stob., Diogen.
[160] ἡ ex Epicur. supplevi (cf. Gell. 2.9.2)

a desperado that he does not sometimes do or say something that that could be praised. That's why the following very ancient line enjoys the status of a proverb (Aesch. fr. 471 *TGrF* 3:504):

> For often even a foolish man has spoken in a very
>   timely way.

13. But the person entirely bereft of praise in every circumstance and at every moment is someone whom none can praise, the very worst and basest of all; and just as being free of every fault makes one a person whom none can fault—and since being such a one is the image of perfect virtue—being one whom none can praise is therefore the ultimate definition of wickedness. 14. That's why Homer usually expresses the full measure of praise not by naming virtues but by noting the absence of vices: hence we find (*Il.* 5.366 *et al.*)

> the two flew on not unwillingly

and similarly in (*Il.* 4.223–44)

> you would not see brilliant Agamemnon napping
>   there
> nor cowering nor refusing to engage in the battle.

15. Epicurus, too, similarly defined the supreme pleasure as the absence and removal of all pain, in these terms (*Principal Doctrines* 3): "The definition of the magnitude of pleasures is the removal of all that which causes pain." By the same principle Virgil used the term "whom none could love" of the Stygian marsh (*G.* 4.479, *A.* 6.438): just as he expressed his loathing for "one whom none could praise" by depriving such a person of praise, so he did for

119

στέρησιν detestatus est. 16. altero modo inlaudatus ita
defenditur: "laudare" significat prisca lingua nominare ap-
pellareque; sic in actionibus civilibus auctor laudari dicitur, quod est nominari. inlaudatus ergo est quasi inlau-
dabilis, id est numquam nominandus, sicuti quondam a
communi consilio Asiae decretum est uti nomen eius qui
templum Dianae Ephesiae incenderat ne quis ullo in tempore nominaret.

17. 'Tertium restat ex iis quae reprehensa sunt, quod
"tunicam squalentem auri" dixit. id autem significat copiam densitatemque auri in squamarum speciem intexti.
"squalere" enim dictum ab squamarum crebritate aspe-
ritateque, quae in serpentum pisciumve coriis visuntur.
18. quam rem et alii et hic idem poeta locis aliquot demonstrat: "quem pellis," inquit,

aënis

in plumam squamis auro conserta tegebat,

et alio loco:

iamque adeo rutilum thoraca indutus aënis
horrebat squamis.

Accius in Pelopidibus[161] ita scribit:

eius serpentis squamae squalido auro et purpura
praetextae.[162]

161 Pelopidibus (*lapsu nostri*)] Pelopidis *Gell. 2. 6. 23*
162 praetextae] per- *Gell. ibid.*

61 One Herostratus, in 356 BCE: we know his name thanks to
Strabo 14.1.22, prob. drawing on Theopompus (cf. Val. Max. 8.14
(ext.).5).   62 Cf. Non. p. 725.

"one whom none could love" through the removal of love. 16. Here is the second way the epithet *inlaudatus* can be defended. In archaic Latin the verb *laudare* ["to praise"] meant "to name and address": thus in civil trials the person posting a surety is said *laudari*, that is, to be named. Someone who is *inlaudatus*, then, is as it were one who cannot *laudari*, that is, one who is never to be named, just as the joint council of Asia once decreed that no one was ever to speak the name of the man who had burned the temple of Diana at Ephesus.[61]

17. 'The third of the criticisms remains, that fact that he spoke of a "tunic caked with gold." But the phrase conveys the quantity and thickness of the gold that was woven into the tunic, giving the impression of fish-scales: the verb "to be caked" [*squalere*] is derived from the density and roughness of the scales [*squamae*] seen on the skins of snakes and fish.[62] 18. Other authors demonstrate this fact, as does Virgil himself in several passages: "[the horse] was covered," he says (*A.* 11.770–71),

> by a caparison of bronze
> scales stitched with gold in a feather pattern,

and in another passage (*A.* 11.487–88),

> already dressed now in his cuirass, glowing warmly,
> he bristled
> with brazen scales.

Accius in *Pelopides* writes (517–8 SRPF[3] 1:235):

> The serpent's scales were edged with caked gold and
> purple.

19. quicquid igitur nimis inculcatum obsitumque aliqua re erat, ut incuteret visentibus facie nova horrorem, id squalere dicebatur. sic in corporibus incultis squamosisque alta congeries sordium "squalor" appellatur, cuius significationis multo assiduoque usu totum id verbum ita contaminatum est, ut iam "squalor" de re alia nulla quam de solis inquinamentis dici coeperit.'

8   'Gratum mihi est,' Avienus ait,'correctum quod de optimis dictis male opinabar. sed in hoc versu videtur mihi deesse aliquid:

>   ipse Quirinali lituo parvaque sedebat
>   succinctus trabea.

si enim nihil deesse concedimus, restat ut fiat lituo et trabea succinctus, quod est absurdissimum, quippe cum lituus sit virga brevis in parte qua robustior est incurva, qua augures utuntur nec video qualiter lituo possit succinctus videri.'

2. Respondit Servius: 'sic hoc dictum est ut pleraque dici per defectionem solent, veluti cum dicitur "M. Cicero, homo magna eloquentia" et "Roscius, histrio summa venustate." non plenum hoc utrumque neque perfectum est, sed enim pro pleno ac perfecto auditur. 3. ut Vergilius alio in loco:

>   victorem Buten immani corpore—

id est corpus immane habentem—et item alibi:

19. Whatever was packed, then, and thickly covered with some substance so that its strange appearance made those looking at it shudder was said to be "caked": that's why the deep layer of filth that forms on neglected and scaly bodies is called *squalor*, though the constant use of that meaning has so colored the whole word that *squalor* has begun to be used exclusively of impurities.'

'I'm glad,' Avienus said, 'to have my mistaken view of 8 Virgil's excellent verses set straight. But something seems to be lacking in these lines (*A.* 7.187–88):[63]

> He himself [sc. Picus] was seated, girt in his short
> purple
> cloak and the *lituus* of Quirinus.

If we grant that nothing's lacking, we're left with his being girt with a *lituus* and a cloak—and that's silly in the extreme, since a *lituus* is a short staff curved at its thicker end, part of an augur's equipment, and I don't see how he could appear to be "girt" with one.'

2. Servius replied, 'The expression has the form that's usual for expressions that leave something implied, as when we say "Marcus Cicero, a person with great eloquence" or "Roscius, an actor with supreme grace." Neither of these expressions is fully formed and complete, but they're understood as though they were. 3. Compare what Virgil says in another passage (*A.* 5.372),

> the victorious Butes with a monstrous body—

that is, having a monstrous body—and likewise elsewhere (*A.* 5.401*–2),

[63] §§1–6 are based on Gell. 5.8.

123

> in medium geminos immani pondere cestus
> proiecit,

ac similiter:

> domus sanie dapibusque cruentis.

4. sic igitur id quoque dictum videri debet: "ipse Quirinali lituo," id est lituum Quirinalem tenens. quod minime mirandum foret si ita dictum fuisset, Picus Quirinali lituo erat, sicuti dicimus, statua grandi capite erat. et "est" autem et "erat" et "fuit" plerumque absunt cum elegantia sine detrimento sententiae.

5. ʻSed quoniam facta litui mentio est, praetermittendum non est quod posse quaeri animadvertimus, utrum a tuba lituus auguralis appelletur, an tuba a lituo augurum lituus dicta sit. utrumque enim pari forma et pariter in capite incurvum est. 6. sed si, ut quidam putant, tuba a sonitu lituus appellata est, ex illo Homeri versu,

> λίγξε βιός,

necesse est ut virga auguralis a tubae similitudine lituus vocetur. utitur autem vocabulo isto Vergilius et pro tuba, ut ibi:

> et lituo pugnas insignis obibat et hasta.ʼ

7. Subiecit Avienus: "ʻmaturate fugam" quid sit parum mihi liquet. contraria enim videtur mihi fuga maturitati,

---

64 The similarity between the first two letters of *lituus* and Gk. *liggein* ("twang") could satisfy some ancient etymologists that the two were related.   65 §§7–13 are based on Gell. 10.11 (cited by DServ. on G. 1.260), cf. also Non. p. 73.

into the middle of the arena he tossed two gloves
with monstrous mass,

and similarly (A. 3.618):

a house with purulent, bloody banquets.

4. That seems to be the form of expression in the case you
pointed to: "he himself with the *lituus* of Quirinus," that is,
holding the *lituus* of Quirinus. And it would not be at all
strange for it to have been put that way, "There was Picus
with the *lituus* of Quirinus," just as we say, "There was a
statue with a large head." "Is" and "was" and "has been" are
usually omitted, with a delicacy that does not detract from
the thought being communicated.

5. 'But since the *lituus* has come up, I should not let a
possible line of inquiry go by: whether the augur's *lituus* is
so called from the battle-horn of the same name or the
battle-horn is called a *lituus* after the augur's staff—for
both have the same shape, and both are curved at the head.
6. But if, as some suppose, the battle-horn was called a
lituus because of its sound, after this line of Homer
(*Il.* 4.125),

the bow twanged,[64]

then the augur's staff must be called the *lituus* from its re-
semblance to the horn. Furthermore, Virgil uses that word
for the horn, too, as in this case (A. 6.167):

he was going to face battle distinguished by both his
    lituus and his spear.'

7. Avienus interposed,[65] 'The meaning of "Make your
flight *matura*" (A. 1.137*) is not entirely clear to me, for

unde quid de hoc verbo sentiendum sit quaeso me doceas.'
8. Et Servius: 'Nigidius, homo omnium bonarum artium
disciplinis egregius, "mature," inquit, "est quod neque ci-
tius neque serius sed medium quiddam et temperatum
est." bene atque proprie Nigidius. nam et in frugibus et in
pomis "matura" dicuntur quae neque cruda et immitia
sunt neque caduca et nimium cocta sed tempore suo temperate adulta. 9. hanc interpretationem Nigidianam di-
vus Augustus duobus verbis Graecis eleganter exprimebat.
nam et dicere in sermonibus et scribere in epistulis solitum ferunt σπεῦδε βραδέως, per quod monebat ut ad rem
agendam simul adhiberetur et industriae celeritas et tardi-
tas diligentiae, ex quibus duobus contrariis fit maturitas.
10. sic ergo et Vergilius inducit Neptunum discessum ventis imperantem ut et tam cito discedant tamquam fugiant,
et tamen flandi mediocritatem in regressu teneant, tamquam mature id est temperate abeuntes. veretur enim ne
ipso discessu classi noceant dum raptu nimio tamquam per
fugam redeunt. 11. idem Vergilius duo ista verba "maturare" et "properare" tamquam plane contraria scitissime
separavit in his versibus:

frigidus agricolas[163] siquando continet imber,
multa, forent quae mox caelo properanda sereno,
maturare datur.

[163] agricolas] -lam *Verg.*

---

[66] I.e., at *A.* 1.137ff, after the storm has scattered Aeneas'
fleet, where Neptune uses the phrase *maturate fugam* that is this
discussion's starting point.

fleeing seems contrary to the state of being "mature" [*maturitas*]: so please tell me how I ought to make sense of this expression.' 8. Servius replied, 'Nigidius, a man outstandingly learned in all the worthy disciplines, said (fr. 48), "Something that happens 'maturely' happens neither too soon nor too late but achieves a balanced mean," and Nigidius gets it right on the mark. For grains and fruit are said to be "mature" when they're neither hard and unripe nor too soft and ready to fall but have reached a point of balanced ripeness in their proper season. 9. The deified Augustus neatly caught the sense of Nigidius explanation with two Greek words: for they say that in his conversation and correspondence he often said, *speude bradeôs* ["make haste slowly"] (*epist.* fr. 50 Malc.), by which he meant to suggest that to any task one should apply both the speed of serious application and the delay of due diligence, with "maturity" as the product of these two opposing qualities. 10. And that is the way Virgil introduces Neptune when he orders the winds to depart,[66] so that they might leave as quickly as they would if fleeing and yet blow gently while retreating, as though they were going away "maturely," which is to say, temperately—for the god worries that they might harm the fleet by their very departure, if they carried the ships in a retreat that was too much like flight. 11. Virgil also very shrewdly distinguished between "to make mature" [*maturare*] and "to hasten" [*properare*], as direct opposites, in these lines (*G.* 1.259–61):

> Whenever the cold rain keeps the farmer indoors, it
>   is a chance
> to do in good time [*maturare*] many things that will
>   have to be hurried [*properanda*]
> when the weather clears.

12. bene et eleganter duo ista verba divisit. namque in praeparatu rei rusticae per tempestates pluvias, quoniam ex necessitate otium est, maturari potest: per serenas vero, quoniam tempus instat, properari necesse est. 13. sane cum significandum est coactius quid et festinantius factum, rectius hoc dicitur "praemature" factum quam "mature": sicuti Afranius dixit in togata, cui Titulus nomen est:

> adpetis dominatum demens[164] praemature
> praecocem.

in quo versu animadvertendum est quod "praecocem" inquit non "praecoquem," est enim casus eius rectus non "praecoquis" sed "praecox.'"

14. Hic Avienus rursus interrogat: 'cum Vergilius,' inquit, 'Aenean suum tamquam omnia pium a contagione atrocis visus apud inferos vindicaverit, et magis eum fecerit audire reorum gemitus quam ipsa videre tormenta, in ipsos vero campos piorum libenter[165] induxerit, cur hoc tamen[166] versu ostendit illi partem locorum, quibus impii cohibebantur:

> . . . vestibulum ante ipsum primisque in faucibus
> Orci?

qui enim vestibulum et fauces vidit, intra ipsam aedem iam

---

164 demens *Gell. 10. 11. 8*: petens ω (*an lapsu Macrob.?*)
165 libenter *Willis*: licenter ω (*quod defendi potest*)
166 tamen S: tantum ω

---

67 Cf. 6.1.4n., on the *fabula togata*.
68 The adjective *praecox* (> Engl. "precocious") is a compound

12. He drew a very nice distinction between the two words: preparations for farming can be made in good time [*maturari*] during the rainy season, a time of enforced leisure, whereas things must be hurried [*properari*] in fair weather, when time is pressing. 13. Of course, when we have to convey that something was done in too forced and hasty a manner, it's more correct to say that it was done "prematurely" [*praemature*] than "maturely" [*mature*], as Afranius said in his comedy in Roman dress[67] titled *The Tablet* (335 *SRPF*[3] 2:248):

> Madman, you prematurely seek a preposterous
>   mastery—

where we should note that he used the form *praecocem*, not *praecoquem*, since the nominative case is not *praecoquis* but *praecox*.'[68]

14. At this point Avienus put another question:[69] 'Though Virgil protected his perfectly pious Aeneas from being polluted by the underworld's visual horrors—having him hear the groans of the condemned rather than see their torment (*A.* 6.557ff.), while gladly introducing him to the very Fields of the Pious (*A.* 6.638ff.)–why did he nonetheless reveal to him a part of the place where the impious were imprisoned, in this line (*A.* 6.273*):

> . . . before the very reception area, at the opening of
>   Orcus' entryway?

If someone has seen the reception area [*vestibulum*] and

of the prefix *prae-* ("beforehand, ahead") and the verbal root *coqu-* ("cook").   [69] §§14–22 are based on Gell. 16.5, with part of §18 drawn from Gell. 5.12.10; cf. also Non. p. 75.

sine dubitatione successit, aut si quid aliud de vestibuli vocabulo intellegendum est, scire desidero.'

15. Ad haec Servius: 'pleraque sunt vocabula quibus vulgo utimur neque tamen liquido advertimus quid ea ex vera proprietate significent, sicuti est vestibulum in sermonibus celebre atque obvium verbum, non omnibus tamen qui illo facile utuntur liquido spectatum.[167] putant enim vestibulum esse partem domus priorem, quam atrium vocant. 16. sed Caecilius[168] Gallus, vir doctissimus, in libro de significatione verborum quae ad ius civile pertinent secundo, vestibulum dicit esse non in ipsis aedibus neque aedium partem sed locum ante ianuam domus vacuum, per quem de via aditus accessusque ad fores aedium sit. ipsa enim ianua procul a via fiebat, area intersita quae vacaret. 17. quae porro huic vocabulo ratio sit quaeri multum solet, sed quae scripta apud idoneos auctores legi proferre in medium non pigebit. 18. "ve" particula, sicuti quaedam alia, tum intentionem significat tum minutionem. nam "vetus" et "vehemens," alterum ab aetatis magnitudine compositum elisumque est, alterum a nimio impetu et vi mentis instructum. "vecors" autem et "vesanus" privationem significat sanitatis aut cordis. 19. diximus autem superius

---

167 spectatum C *Gell.* (*nisi* exceptum *malis*): ex(s)pectatum ω
168 caecilius ω, *Gell.*: C. Aelius *Pontano apud Gell.*

---

70 M.'s archetype and all but one of the manuscripts of Gellius give the name "Caecilius Gallus" to the jurist of the 1st cent. BCE C. Aelius Gallus: the error was probably already in the copy of Gellius that M. knew.

71 "Used to be" because the style of house M. describes—with the living quarters set back from the street and laid out symmetri-

entryway, he must assuredly have entered the building it-self—or if the word *vestibulum* should be understood differently, I'd like to know it.'

15. Servius replied: 'There are very many words we commonly use whose true and proper meanings we do not clearly apprehend: *vestibulum* is one of them, a word we encounter everywhere in conversation, yet not clearly considered by all who use it casually, under the impression that the *vestibulum* is the first part of the house, which they call the atrium. 16. But Caecilius Gallus,[70] a very learned man, in Book 2 of *On the Meaning of Words Relevant to Civil Law*, says (fr. 23 *IAH* 1:251 = fr. 5 *IAR⁶* = fr. 7 *GRF* 1:547) that the *vestibulum* is not in the building itself nor part of it but is an empty space in front of the house door that provides access to the front doors from the street: the door itself used to be set back some distance from the street, with an empty area left in between.[71] 17. Much effort is often spent in analyzing this word, but I'm not loath to put before you what I've found in the suitable authorities. 18. Like some other particles, *ve* sometime conveys an increase in emphasis, sometimes a decrease: thus in the case of *vetus* ["aged"] and *vehemens* ["forceful, violent"], the former is a compound conveying great age [*ve* + *aetas*] from which a syllable has dropped out, while the other is formed to denote thought [*ve* + *mens*] that is too aggressive and forceful;[72] conversely, *vecors* and *vesanus* convey a deficit of intelligence [*cor*] and sanity [*sanitas*].[73] 19. But as

cally around a long central axis—had passed out of fashion by late antiquity.

[72] Cf. Terent. Scaur. *GL* 7:19.16.

[73] Cf. *LALE* 631 and 639, respectively.

eos qui amplas domos antiquitus faciebant locum ante ianuam vacuum relinquere solitos qui inter fores domus et
viam medius esset. 20. in eo loco qui dominum eius domus salutatum venerant priusquam admitterentur consis-
tebant, et neque in via stabant neque intra aedes erant. ab
illa ergo grandis loci consistione et quasi quadam stabu-
latione vestibula appellata sunt spatia in quibus multum
staretur ab advenientibus priusquam intromitterentur in
domum. 21. alii consentientes vestibula eadem esse quae
diximus, in sensu tamen vocabuli dissentiunt. referunt
enim non ad eos qui adveniunt, sed ad illos qui in domo
commanent, quoniam illic numquam consistunt, sed solius
transitus causa ad hunc locum veniunt exeundo sive re-
deundo. 22. sive igitur ⟨"ve"⟩[169] secundum priores per
augmentum sive per secundos per diminutionem intellegendum est, tamen vestibulum[170] constat aream dici quae
a via domum dividit. fauces autem iter angustum est per
quod ad vestibulum de via flectitur. 23. ergo Aeneas cum
videt fauces atque vestibulum domus impiorum, non est
intra domum nec contactu aedium saevo execrabilique
polluitur, sed de via videt loca inter viam et aedes locata.'

9   '"Bidentes" hostiae quid essent,' inquit Avienus, 'inter-
rogavi quendam de grammaticorum cohorte et ille "biden-

---

[169] ve *addidi*
[170] vestibulum P: -la ω

---

[74] §§1–7 are based on Gell. 16.6.5–14; cf. also Serv. on A. 4.57,
Non. p. 75.

I said above, people who used to build large houses in olden times usually left an empty space in front of the doorway, between the doors and street. 20. People who came to pay their morning respects to the master of the house used to congregate in that space before they were admitted and thus stood neither in the street nor within the house. From the large space devoted to this congregation, as a kind of stable area, the name *vestibula* was given to the spaces where visitors did a lot of standing around [*stare*] before being admitted to the house. 21. Others agree that the *vestibula* are the areas I've described but nonetheless disagree about the meaning of the word, thinking that it applies not to the house's visitors but to its inhabitants, who spend time no time at all standing there but only passing through as they're leaving the house or returning 22. So, then, whether *ve* should be understood here as conveying increased emphasis, as the former hold, or decreased emphasis, as the latter, it is agreed that *vestibulum* is the name given to the space that separates the house from the street. The "opening" [*fauces*], on the other hand, is the narrow passageway that leads from the street to the *vestibulum*. 23. Therefore, when Aeneas sees the "opening" and "reception area" of the impious souls' dwelling, he is not within the dwelling nor is he polluted by contact with the dread and accursed building, but he is looking from the street at the space between the street and the building.'

'I asked one of the general troupe of grammarians,' 9 Avienus said,[74] 'what *bidentes* ["two-toothed"] victims were, and he replied that *bidentes* are sheep, and that is

tes" oves esse respondit idcircoque "lanigeras" adiectum,
ut oves planius demonstrarentur. 2. "esto," inquam, "oves
bidentes dicantur. sed quae ratio huius in ovibus epitheti
scire" inquam "volo." atque ille nihil cunctatus "oves," inquit, "bidentes dictae sunt quod duos tantum dentes ha-
beant." "ubi terrarum quaeso te," inquam, "duos solos per
naturam dentes habere oves aliquando vidisti? ostentum
enim hoc est et factis piaculis procurandum!" 3. tum ille
permotus mihi et inritatus "quaere," inquit, "ea potius
quae a grammatico quaerenda sunt: nam de ovium dentibus opiliones percontator!" facetias nebulonis hominis risi
et reliqui; sed te percontor quasi ipsius verborum naturae
conscium.'

4. Tum Servius: 'de numero dentium, quem ille opina-
tus est, reprehendendus a me non est cum ipse iam riseris,
verum procurandum ne illud obrepat quod bidentes epitheton sit ovium, cum Pomponius, egregius Atellanarum
poeta, in Gallis Transalpinis hoc scripserit:

Mars, tibi voveo facturum, si unquam rediero,[171]
bidente verre.

5. Publius autem Nigidius in libro quem de extis compo-

---

[171] rediero] redierit *Gell. 16.6.7*

---

[75] *laniger* ("wool-bearing") is a fairly common adjective, especially in verse (Virgil uses it five times); but we know that the reference here must be A. 7.93 ("He sacrificed one hundred wool-
bearing *bidentes* in due fashion") because it is the starting point of
the discussion in Gellius that M. is mining.

[76] When a monstrous birth occurred (e.g., a two-headed calf),
it was taken to indicate a disturbance in the "peace of the gods,"

why Virgil added the epithet "wool-bearing" (*A.* 7.93),[75] so that they might more expressly be shown to be sheep. 2. "Very well," said I, "let us take it that sheep are called *bidentes*. But *why* is the epithet used of sheep? That," I said, "is what I want to know." Without missing a beat he replied, "Sheep are called *bidentes* because they have only two teeth." "Where in the world, I ask you," said I, "have you ever seen sheep that naturally have only two teeth? That's a monstrosity demanding expiation!"[76] 3. Quite put out and peeved he was: "Ask me the sort of question a grammarian should be asked," he said, "As for sheeps' teeth, ask the shepherds!" I laughed at the foolish fellow's wisecrack and went off; but now I put the question to you, as one who knows the very nature of words.'

4. Then Servius said: 'I need not criticize the opinion he offered about the number of teeth, since you've already laughed it to scorn, but I should see to it that you are not taken unaware by the view that *bidentes* is an epithet specifically of sheep, since Pomponius, the outstanding author of Atellan farces,[77] wrote this in his *Gauls beyond the Alps* (51–52 *SRPF*[3] 2:279):

> Mars, I vow that if I ever return, I will sacrifice to
> you
> a two-toothed boar.

5. Furthermore, Publius Nigidius, in his book *On Entrails*,

the stable order that proper relations between gods and humans maintained: it was assumed that the disturbance was due to some human misstep, for which expiation had to be offered.
[77] Cf. 1.4.21n.

suit "bidentes" appellari ait non oves solas sed omnes hostias bimas. neque tamen dixit cur ita appellentur. 6. sed in commentariis ad ius pontificium pertinentibus legi "bidennes" primo dictas, d littera ex superfluo, ut saepe adsolet, interiecta. sic pro "reire" "redire" dicitur et pro "reamare" "redamare," et "redarguere," non "rearguere." ad hiatum enim duarum vocalium procurandum interponi solet d littera. 7. ergo "bidennes" primum dictae sunt quasi "biennes" et longo usu loquendi corrupta est vox ex "bidennibus" in "bidentes." Hyginus tamen, qui ius pontificium non ignoravit, in quinto[172] librorum quos de Vergilio fecit "bidentes" appellari scripsit hostias quae per aetatem duos dentes altiores haberent, per quos ex minore in maiorem transcendisse constaret aetatem.'

8. Iterum quaerit Avienus in his versibus,

> frena Pelethronii Lapithae gyrosque dedere
> impositi dorso atque equitem docuere sub armis
> insultare solo et gressus glomerare superbos,

cur Vergilius equi officium equiti dederit. 'nam insultare solo et glomerare gressus equi constat esse, non equitis.' 9. 'bene' inquit Servius 'haec tibi quaestio nata est ex incuria veteris lectionis. nam quia saeculum nostrum ab Ennio

---

[172] quinto] quarto *Gell. 16.6.14*

---

78 §§8–11 are based on Gell. 18.5.4–10; cf. also DServ. on
G. 1.116., Non. p. 152.

said (fr. 81) that not only sheep are called "two-toothed" but all sacrificial victims that are two years old—yet he didn't say why they are so called. 6. But in commentaries relating to pontifical law I read (fr. 2 *IAH* 2.2:566) that they were first called *bidennes* ["two-year"], with a *d* inserted, as often: thus we say *redire* not *reire* ["to go back"], *redamare* not *reamare* ["to love in return"], and *redarguere* not *rearguere* ["to refute"]. The letter *d* is commonly inserted to take care of the gap between two vowels. 7. *bidennes*, then, was first used to convey the idea of *biennes* and then from long usage the word was corrupted from *bidennes* ["two-year"] to *bidentes* ["two-toothed"]. Still, Hyginus, who was not ignorant of pontifical law, wrote in Book 5 of his work on Virgil (fr. 3 *GRF* 1:528) that victims are called "two-toothed" because they are of an age to have two teeth more prominent than the rest, which show that they have passed from a younger to a more mature stage in life.'

8. Again, in connection with these lines (*G.* 3.115–17),

> Bridles and the training course the Pelethronian
>   Lapiths gave us,
> mounted on horseback, and they taught the *eques*
>   under arms
> to bound upon the earth and gallop with proud
>   strides,

Avienus asked why Virgil assigned the function of the horse [*equus*] to the horseman [*eques*]:[78] 'For bounding upon the earth and galloping, as we know, are the horse's job, not the rider's.' 9. 'Of course,' said Servius, 'we have this question because the ancient texts are neglected: since our age has abandoned Ennius and the whole library of an-

et omni bibliotheca vetere descivit,[173] multa ignoramus,
quae non laterent si veterum lectio nobis esset familiaris.
omnes enim antiqui scriptores ut hominem equo insiden-
tem, ita et equum, cum portaret hominem, "equitem" vocaverunt, et "equitare" non hominem tantum sed equum
quoque dixerunt. 10. Ennius libro Annalium septimo ait:

> denique vi magna quadrupes, eques atque elephanti
> proiciunt sese.

numquid dubium est quin equitem in hoc loco ipsum
equum dixerit, cum addidisset illi epitheton quadrupes?
11. sic et "equitare," quod verbum e vocabulo equitis inclinatum est, et homo utens equo et equus sub homine
gradiens dicebatur. Lucilius namque, vir adprime linguae
Latinae scius, equum equitare dicit hoc versu:

> nempe[174] hunc currere equum nos atque equitare
> videmus.

12. ergo et apud Maronem, qui antiquae Latinitatis diligens fuit, ita intellegendum est:

> atque equitem docuere sub armis—

id est, docuerunt equum portando hominem—

---

[173] descivit S (desivit P): disc- ω
[174] nempe] quîs *Gell., Non.*

---

[79] There is some irony in having Servius speak these words,
since his commentary on the *Aeneid* omits many citations of old
Republican poetry that were included in his main source (Aelius
Donatus) and includes many new citations from more recent poets (Lucan, Statius, Juvenal).

cient authors, we are ignorant of many things that would not lie hidden if the ancients' texts were our constant companions.[79] For all ancient writers applied the word *eques* as often to the horse when it carried a rider as to the person riding upon the horse, and they said that not only the person but also the horse "played the *eques*" [*equitare*]. 10. Ennius, in Book 7 of the *Annals*, says (236–7 Sk.):

And then the four-footed ones, *eques* and elephants, violently
hurl themselves forward.

There can be no doubt, can there, that he used *eques* in place of the horse itself, since he applied the epithet "four-footed" to it? 11. So also *equitare*, a verb derived from the noun *eques*, used to be used both of a person riding a horse and of a horse walking along with a person astride it. Lucilius, a man second to none in his knowledge of Latin, uses *equitare* of a horse in this verse (1301):

We see, of course, this horse in its course playing the *eques*.

12. So too in Maro, who was an attentive student of ancient Latin, the usage should be understood in those terms:

and they taught the *eques* under arms—

that is, they taught the horse, in the process of carrying the man—

insultare solo et gressus glomerare superbos.

13. Subiecit Avienus:

'cum iam[175] trabibus contextus acernis
staret equus:

scire vellem in equi fabrica casune an ex industria hoc genus ligni nominaverit. nam licet unum pro quolibet ligno
ponere poeticae licentiae sit, solet tamen Vergilius temeri-
tatem licentiae non amare, sed rationi certae in rerum vel
nominum ele . . .[176]

[175] iam] iam hic *Verg.*
[176] *post* ele *unam lineam vacuam relinquit* α (deest *add.* G),
varie sententiam implent codd. β₂; *subscriptione omnes carent.*

to bound upon the earth and gallop with proud
strides.

13. Avienus interposed (A. 2.112*–13):

'When the horse already stood, woven together
from beams of maple [*acernis*]:

I would like to know whether it was by chance or from de-
sign that he mentioned this kind of wood in speaking of the
horse's construction. Though it's a matter of poetic license
to use one kind of wood to stand for wood of any and every
sort, Virgil nonetheless usually doesn't like the random-
ness that the license encourages but [follows] a specific
plan in [choosing] objects or the labels applied to them
. . .'[80]

[80] The words in square brackets can safely be understood to
supply the sense before the rest of Book 6 is lost in a lacuna.

‹LIBER SEPTIMVS›[1]

1 Primis mensis post epulas iam remotis et discursum va-
riantibus poculis minutioribus Praetextatus, 'solet cibus,'
inquit, 'cum sumitur, tacitos efficere, potus loquaces. at
nos et inter pocula silemus tamquam debeat seriis vel
etiam philosophis carere tractatibus tale convivium.'

2. Et Symmachus: 'verumne ita sentis, Vetti, ut philosophia conviviis intersit et non tamquam censoria quaedam
et plus nimio reverenda materfamilias penetralibus suis
contineatur, nec misceat se Libero, cui etiam tumultus familiares sunt, cum ipsa huius sit verecundiae ut strepitum
non modo verborum, sed ne cogitationum quidem in sa-
crarium suae quietis admittat? 3. doceat nos vel peregrina
institutio et disciplina a Parthis[2] petita, qui solent cum
concubinis, non cum coniugibus, inire convivia, tamquam
has et in vulgus produci et lascivire quoque, illas non nisi
domi abditas tueri deceat tectum pudorem. 4. an ego cen-

---

[1] add. edd. (Incipit Lib. IIII de diversis quaestionibus P,
MACROBII THEODOSII VC ET ILL CONVIVIORVM TER-
TII DIEI INCIPIT Q, silent NGRFAC)
[2] Parthis] Πέρσας Plut.

---

[1] Afternoon of the third day, 19 December.

‹BOOK SEVEN›[1]

When the first course was finished and the tables cleared,   1
as smaller servings of wine were producing a varied bustle,
Praetextatus said, 'Food, when it's taken, usually makes
people quiet, wine makes them talkative—but we're silent
even while we drink, as though a dinner party like this
should abstain from treating serious or even philosophical
topics.'

2. Symmachus said, 'Is that what you really think,
Vettius—that philosophy should attend dinner parties and
not be kept within her own sanctuary, like some severe and
supremely respectable matron, and avoid mingling with
father Liber, that old crony of carouse, though she herself
is a figure of such modest restraint that she bars from her
peaceful shrine all dissonance, not just of words but even
of thoughts?[2] 3. Let even a foreign custom instruct us, a
lesson fetched from the Parthians,[3] who attend dinner parties with their concubines, not their wives, as though it
were proper for the former to be brought forth in public
and even play the wanton, but for wives to uphold their
sheltered modesty only by being shut up at home. 4. Or am

---

[2] §§2–24 are based on Plut. *Mor.* 612F–614D, with some rear-
rangement and supplements in M.'s usual fashion.

[3] In Plutarch, Persians.

seam producendam philosophiam quo rhetorica venire ars
et professio popularis erubuit? Isocrates enim Graecus
orator qui verba prius libera sub numeros ire primus coe-
git, cum in convivio a sodalibus oraretur ut aliquid in medium de eloquentiae suae fonte proferret, hac venia deprecatus est. "quae praesens," inquit, "locus et tempus
exigit ego non calleo, quae ego calleo nec loco praesenti
sunt apta nec tempori.'"

5. Ad haec Eustathius: 'probo, Symmache, propositum
tuum, quo philosophiam ea quam maximam putas obser-
vatione veneraris, ut tantum intra suum penetral aestimes
adorandam. sed si propter hoc a conviviis exulabit, procul
hinc facessant et alumnae eius, honestatem dico et modes-
tiam, nec minus cum sobrietate pietatem. quam enim ha-
rum dixerim minus esse venerabilem? ita fit ut ab huius
modi coetibus relegatus, matronarum talium chorus liber-
tatem conviviorum solis concubinis, id est vitiis et crimini-
bus, addicat. 6. sed absit ut philosophia, quae in scholis suis
sollicite tractat de officiis convivalibus, ipsa convivia re-
formidet, tamquam non possit rebus adserere quae solet
verbis docere, aut nesciat servare modum cuius in omnibus humanae vitae actibus terminos ipsa constituit. neque
enim ita ad mensas invito philosophiam ut non se ipsa moderetur, cuius disciplina est rerum omnium moderationem
docere. 7. ut ergo inter te et Vettium velut arbitrali iudica-

---

4 M. speaks loosely in suggesting that sympotic behavior was
part of the philosophical curriculum: if he does not simply allude
to a general concern for logical and ethical discourse, he perhaps
has in mind passages like Plut. *Mor* 629E (in a chapter imitated at
7.2.1ff.), where "Xenophon the Socratic" is cited for the appropriate sorts of questions to ask when drinking.

I to suppose that philosophy ought to be brought into a setting where rhetoric, wholly a profession of the people, blushed to come? For when the Greek orator Isocrates, who first placed the restraints of rhythm on prose that was previously free, was asked by his companions at a banquet to give them a display from the well-spring of his eloquence, he begged off on the following grounds: "I have no knack for the things this place and time require; the things I have a knack for are not suited to this place and time."'

5. In response Eustathius said, 'I agree with your goal, Symmachus, of paying philosophy the greatest possible respect, which makes you think that she should be worshipped only within her own inner sanctum. But if she will be exiled from banquets for this reason, then let the children she fosters also keep far off—I mean, honorable behavior and restraint, and dutiful devotion along with sobriety: which of these am I to say is less worthy of respect than philosophy? That way the chorus of such reverend matrons, banished from gatherings of this sort, would award the liberty of dinner parties to concubines alone, which is to say, to vices and crimes. 6. But far be it from philosophy—which quite carefully treats in the schools questions of appropriate behavior at banquets[4]—to shrink from banqueting itself, as though it could not make good in fact the lessons it regularly preaches, or would not know how to limit itself when it has itself defined the appropriate boundaries in all spheres of human behavior. Yet if I invite philosophy to the dinner table, I do not mean that she is to abandon self-control, when she is expert at teaching self-control in all things. 7. So, then, to resolve your and Vettius' disagreement by a quasi-judicial decision, I open

145

tione componam, aperio quidem philosophiae triclinio-
rum fores, sed spondeo sic interfuturam, ne mensuram
notae sibi ac sectatoribus suis dispensationis excedat.'

8. Tunc Rufius: 'quia te unicum, Eustathi,' inquit, 'sec-
tatorem philosophiae nostra aetas tulit, oratus sis ut modum dispensationis quam das ei convivanti nobis ipse
patefacias.' 9. Et Eustathius: 'primum hoc eam scio serva-
turam, ut secum aestimet praesentium ingenia conviva-
rum, et si plures peritos vel saltem amatores sui in convivii
societate reppererit, sermonem de se patietur agitari, quia
velut paucae litterae mutae dispersae inter multas vocales
in societatem vocis facile mansuescunt, ita rariores imperi-
ti gaudentes consortio peritorum aut consonant si qua possunt, aut rerum talium capiuntur auditu. 10. si vero plures
ab institutione disciplinae huius alieni sint, prudentibus,
qui pauciores intererunt, sanciet dissimulationem sui, et
patietur loquacitatem maiori parti amiciorem sonare, ne
rara nobilitas a plebe tumultuosiore turbetur.

11. 'Et haec una est de philosophiae virtutibus, quia
cum orator non aliter nisi orando probetur, philosophus
non minus tacendo pro tempore quam loquendo philoso-
phatur. sic ergo pauci qui aderunt doctiores in consensum
rudis consortii salva et intra se quiescente veri notione
migrabunt, ut omnis discordiae suspicio facessat. 12. nec
mirum si doctus faciet quod fecit quondam Pisistratus

the dining rooms' doors to philosophy, but I promise that by her presence she will not overstep the canon of well-regulated behavior familiar to her and her followers.'

8. Then Rufius said, 'Since you are the unrivaled student of philosophy that our generation has produced, Eustathius, please be prevailed on to make plain for us the canon of behavior that *you* set for her at banquet.' 9. Eustathius said, 'First of all, I know that she would observe this rule: she would reflect on the character of the other guests, and if she found that the greater part of the banquet's fellowship were people experienced in her ways, or at least fond of her, she would readily permit herself to be the subject of discussion. For just as a few consonants scattered among many vowels quickly become less dissonant and blend in a kind of vocal alliance, so when those innocent of philosophy are in the minority, they take pleasure in the company of the learned and either chime in as they can or are beguiled by the things they hear. 10. But if the majority have had no philosophical education, then she will permit the well-informed who make up the minority to pretend ignorance of her and will tolerate the chatter that is dearer to the majority's heart, lest the under-represented nobility be harassed by the more rambunctious commons.

11. 'In fact, this is one of philosophy's virtues: whereas an orator is tested only when he speaks, a philosopher practices his wisdom by a timely silence no less than by his speech. So, then, the few learned men who will be present will go along their rude fellows, to banish any hint of discord, while their knowledge of the truth remains unimpaired and placid in their hearts. 12. A learned man will quite plausibly adopt the course once chosen by Pisistra-

Athenaram tyrannus. qui cum filiis suis rectum dando con-
silium non obtinuisset adsensum, atque ideo esset in si-
multate cum liberis, ubi hoc aemulis causam fuisse gaudii
comperit, ex illa discordia sperantibus in domo regnantis
nasci posse novitatem, universitate civium convocata ait
succensuisse quidem se filiis non adquiescentibus patriae
voluntati, sed hoc sibi postea visum paternae aptius esse
pietati, ut in sententiam liberorum ipse concederet. sciret
igitur civitas subolem regis cum patre concordem. 13. hoc
commento spem detraxit insidiantibus regnantis quieti. ita
in omni vitae genere praecipueque in laetitia convivali
omne quod videtur absonum in unam concordiam soni salva innocentia redigendum est. sic Agathonis convivium,
quia Socratas Phaedros Pausanias et Erysimachos habuit,
sic ea cena quam Callias doctissimis dedit, Charmadam
dico, Antisthenen et Hermogenen ceterosque his similes,
verbum nullum nisi philosophum sensit. 14. at vero Alcinoi
vel Didonis mensa quasi solis apta deliciis habuit haec Io-
pam illa Phemium[3] cithara canentes, nec deerant apud
Alcinoum saltatores viri, et apud Didonem Bitias sic hau-
riens merum ut se totum superflua eius effusione prolue-

---

[3] Phemium *Willis*: poliphemum ω

---

[5] An error for "Charmides," Plato's uncle: it is prob. M., not
a scribe, who is responsible for substituting the name of an ad-
herent of the New Academy whom he would have known from
Cicero's *On the Orator* (e.g., 1.45–47; also mentioned in *Orator,
Academica* 2, and *Tusculan Disputations* 1).   [6] That is, the
Symposium of Plato and of Xenophon, respectively.
[7] Cf. *Od.* 8.72–82, 266–366, 469–520 and *A.* 1.740–47; the
comparison is not taken over from Plutarch. M. seems to have

tus, tyrant of Athens. When he gave his sons good advice but could not command their agreement and so quarreled with them, he learned that this was giving comfort to his rivals, who hoped that the royal household's discord would lead to political upheaval. He therefore assembled the whole community and told them that though he had in fact been angry with his sons for refusing to fall in with their father's wishes, he had come to think it more befitting a father's duty that he himself accede to his children's point of view: let the community know, therefore, that the king's offspring were as one with their father. 13. By this contrivance he dashed the hopes of those who were conspiring against their ruler's peace of mind. In every area of life, and especially in the jovial setting of a banquet, anything that seems out of tune should—provided proper means are used—be reduced to a single harmony. That is why Agathon's banquet—with guests like Socrates, Phaedrus, Pausanias, and Eryximachus—and the dinner that Callias served his most learned contemporaries—I mean Charmadas,[5] Antisthenes, Hermogenes, and all the others like them,[6] heard not a single word that did not have to do with philosophy. 14. But Alcinoüs' table, or Dido's, being suited only to frivolity, had Iopas (in the latter case) and Phemius (in the former) singing to the lyre,[7] nor did Alcinoüs lack for male dancers (*Od.* 8.370–80), while at Dido's banquet Bitias drank his unmixed wine so greedily that he drenched himself with the overflow (*A.* 1.738–39).

slipped in calling Demodocus, Alcinous' singer, "Phemius," the name of the bard at Odysseus' home in Ithaca; a scribe subsequently made a further error, transforming him into "Poliphemus," the Cyclops.

ret. nonne si quis aut inter Phaeacas aut apud Poenos sermones de sapientia erutos convivalibus fabulis miscuisset,
et gratiam illis coetibus aptam perderet et in se risum
plane iustum moveret? ergo prima eius observatio erit aestimare convivas.

15. 'Deinde ubi sibi locum patere viderit, non de ipsis
profunditatis suae inter pocula secretis loquetur, nec no-
dosas et anxias, sed utiles quidem, faciles tamen, quaestiones movebit. 16. nam sicut inter illos qui exercitii genus
habent in mediis saltare conviviis, si quis ut se amplius
exerceat vel ad cursum vel ad pugilatum sodales lacessive-
rit, quasi ineptus relegabitur ab alacritate consortii, sic
apud mensam quando licet aptis philosophandum est, ut
crateri liquoris ad laetitiam nati adhibeatur non modo
Nympharum sed Musarum quoque admixtione temperies.
17. nam si, ut[4] fateri necesse est, in omni conventu aut
tacendum est aut loquendum, quaeramus silentiumne
conviviis an et opportunus sermo conveniat. nam si, ut
apud Athenas Atticas Areopagitae tacentes iudicant, ita inter epulas oportet semper sileri, non est ultra quaerendum
inter mensas philosophandum necne sit. si vero non erunt
muta convivia, cur ubi sermo permittitur, honestus sermo
prohibetur, maxime cum non minus quam dulcedo vini hi-

---

[4] si ut F: sicut ω

---

[8] I.e., the water added to the wine.

[9] The sections that follow do not develop the thought of §§15–
16 in a linear fashion but instead look back to the question
whether there is a place for philosophical discussion at all (§17)
and to the point about judging the company (§§18ff); the incon-
cinnity is M.'s doing, not Plutarch's.

If among either the Phaeacians or the Carthaginians someone had mixed recherché remarks about wisdom with the
stories told at those banquets, would he not have both
spoiled the pleasant atmosphere suited to those gatherings
and caused himself to be frankly and justly mocked? Philosophy's first rule, then, is to take the measure of her
fellow guests.

15. 'In the second place, when she's seen that she has an
opening, philosophy will not speak about her profound
mysteries over drinks and will initiate discussion, not of
knotty and finicky questions, but of useful ones that are
still not too taxing. 16. Those (for example) who count it a
kind of exercise to dance in the middle of a banquet will
banish from their cheerful company anyone who's fool
enough to challenge his companions to a footrace or a boxing match just because he wants more exercise: just so,
given the opportunity at table, one should philosophize in
an appropriate way, so that the mixing bowl of the liquid
made for happiness is tempered by the influence not just
of the Nymphs[8] but of the Muses.[9] 17. For if—as must be
acknowledged—in every gathering one must either speak
or be silent, we should ask whether silence is appropriate
to banquets, or conversation too, when it's timely. If—like
the Areopagites of Athens, who rendered their judgment
in silence—diners should properly maintain a constant silence, then there is no point in asking further whether
one should engage in philosophical discussion at table. But
if banquets will not be mute, why, when conversation is
permitted, is honorable conversation forbidden, especially
since words, no less than sweet wine, bring good cheer to a

larent verba convivium? 18. nam si Homeri latentem pru-
dentiam scruteris altius, delenimentum illud quod Helena
vino miscuit—

νηπενθές τ’ ἄχολόν τε, κακῶν ἐπίληθον
  ἁπάντων—

non herba fuit, non ex India sucus, sed narrandi opportunitas quae hospitem maeroris oblitum flexit ad gaudium.
19. Vlixis enim praeclara facinora filio praesente narrabat:

οἷον καὶ τόδ᾽ ἔρεξε καὶ ἔτλη καρτερὸς ἀνήρ.

ergo paternam gloriam et singula eius facta fortia digeren-
do animum filii fecit alacriorem, et ita credita est contra
maerorem vino remedium miscuisse.

20. 'Quid hoc, inquis, ad philosophiam? immo nihil
tam cognatum sapientiae quam locis et temporibus aptare
sermones, personarum quae aderunt aestimatione in medium vocata. 21. alios enim relata incitabunt exempla vir-
tutum, alios beneficiorum, non nullos modestiae, ut et qui
aliter agebant saepe auditis talibus ad emendationem veni-
rent. 22. sic autem vitiis inretitos, si et hoc in conviviis
exegerit loquendi ordo, feriet philosophia non sentientes,
ut Liber pater thyrso ferit per obliquationem circumfusae
hederae latente mucrone, quia non ita profitebitur in
convivio censorem ut palam vitia castiget. 23. ceterum his

---

10 A slip taken over from Plutarch: the speaker is Menelaos,
not Helen.
11 Cf. 1.19.2.

banquet? 18. For should you look more deeply into the wisdom that lurks in Homer, the beguiling element that Helen mixed with the wine (*Od.* 4.221)—

> soothing sorrow and wrath, a means of forgetting all
>   woes—

was not an herb, nor juice from India, but a timely tale that made her guest forget his sorrow and turn joyful: 19. she told of Ulysses' glorious deeds in his son's presence (*Od.* 4.271),[10]

> such things as the mighty man did and endured.

By giving an account, then, of his father's glory and specific heroic deeds she cheered his son and so was believed to have mixed a cure for grief in the wine.

20. 'What does this have to do with philosophy, you say? Why, nothing is as pertinent to philosophy as accommodating one's speech to one's circumstances by considering the character of those present. 21. Some will be stirred by exemplary tales of heroic deeds, others by tales of favors done, some by tales of self-restraint, so that even those whose past behavior was quite different often correct themselves from hearing such stories. 22. But those ensnared by vice, should the conversation in a banquet turn in that direction too, will be struck by philosophy's lash yet not feel it—as father Liber strikes with the thyrsus that has its sharp point hidden beneath a deceptive wreath of ivy[11]—because in a banquet philosophy will not so claim the role of censor as to reprove vices openly. 23. But people under vices' sway will strike back, and guests will be

obnoxii repugnabunt et talis erit convivii tumultus ut sub huius modi invitati videantur edicto:

> quod superest, laeti bene gestis corpora rebus
> procurate, viri, et pugnam sperate parari,

aut ut Homerus brevius et expressius dixit,

> νῦν δ' ἔρχεσθ' ἐπὶ δεῖπνον, ἵνα ξυνάγωμεν ἄρηα.

24. ergo si opportunitas necessariae reprehensionis emerserit, sic a philosopho proficiscetur ut et tecta et efficax sit. quid mirum si feriet sapiens, ut dixi, non sentientes, cum interdum sic reprehendat ut reprehensus hilaretur, nec tantum fabulis suis sed interrogationibus quoque vim philosophiae nihil ineptum loquentis ostendet? 25. hanc ergo nullus honestus actus locusve, coetus nullus excludat, quae ita se aptat ut ubique sic appareat necessaria tamquam abesse illam nefas fuerit.'

2   Et Avienus: 'novas mihi duas disciplinas videris inducere, interrogandi vel etiam reprehendendi ut alacritas utrimque his ad quos sermo est excitetur, cum dolor semper reprehensionem vel iustam sequatur: unde haec quae leviter attigisti fac quaeso enarrando planiora.'

2. 'Primum,' inquit Eustathius, 'hoc teneas volo, non de ea me reprehensione dixisse quae speciem accusationis habet, sed quae vituperationis instar est. hoc Graeci σκῶμμα vocant, non minus quidem amarum quam accu-

---

[12] §§2–15 are based on Plut. *Mor.* 629E–631C.

thrown into such upheaval that they will seem to have been invited in these terms (*A.* 9.157–58),

> As for the rest, take pleasure in what you've
>   accomplished, see to
> your bodies' needs, and wait for battle to be readied,

or as Homer said more briefly and pointedly (*Il.* 2.381),

> but now come to dine, so that we might join battle.

24. If, then, an opportunity for needed reproof should arise, a philosopher will issue it so that it will be both discreet and effective. Why should it seem strange that the vice-ridden, as I said, will not feel the wise man's lash, given that he sometimes leaves the person he criticizes actually feeling cheerful, and will show the power of philosophy, which says nothing off the mark, not just through the parables he tells but also by the questions he asks? 25. Let no honorable dealings or occasion, let no gathering exclude philosophy, which so fits herself to circumstances that her presence seems everywhere necessary, her absence a crime against the gods.'

Avienus said, 'You seem to present me with two new 2 lessons, which have to do with asking questions or even offering criticisms so to leave the recipient feeling cheerful in either case, though anguish often attends criticism, at least when it's just. So please elaborate these points that you've only lightly touched upon.'[12]

2. 'To start with,' Eustathius said, 'please understand that I wasn't referring to the sort of criticism that has the appearance of an accusation but rather the sort that looks like censure. This sort, which the Greeks call *skômma*, is no less galling than an accusation, if it's made inappropri-

satio, si importune proferatur, sed a sapiente sic proferetur ut dulcedine quoque non careat.

3. 'Et ut prius tibi de interrogatione respondeam, qui vult amoenus esse consultor ea interrogat quae sunt interrogato facilia responsu, et quae scit illum sedula exercitatione didicisse. 4. gaudet enim quisquis provocatur ad doctrinam suam in medium proferendam, quia nemo vult latere quod didicit, maxime si scientia quam labore quaesivit cum paucis illi familiaris et plurimis sit incognita, ut de astronomia vel dialectica ceterisque similibus. tunc enim videntur consequi fructum laboris, cum adipiscuntur occasionem publicandi quae didicerant sine ostentationis nota, qua caret qui non ingerit sed invitatur ut proferat. 5. contra magnae amaritudinis est si coram multis aliquem interroges quod non opima scientia quaesivit. cogitur enim aut negare se scire, quod extremum verecundiae damnum putant, aut respondere temere et fortuito se eventui veri falsive committere, unde saepe nascitur inscitiae proditio, et omne hoc infortunium pudoris sui imputat consulenti. 6. nec non et qui obierunt maria et terras gaudent cum de ignoto multis vel terrarum situ vel sinu maris interrogantur libenterque respondent et describunt modo verbis, modo radio loca, gloriosum putantes quae ipsi viderant aliorum oculis obicere. 7. quid duces vel milites? quam fortiter a se facta semper dicturiunt et tamen tacent arrogantiae metu? nonne hi si ut haec referant invi-

ately, but a wise man will make it in such a way that it even has a pleasant aspect.

3. 'Now, to answer you first on the subject of asking questions: the person who wants his inquiry to be pleasant will ask questions that are easy for his interlocutor to answer, on subjects he knows the latter has painstakingly studied and learned. 4. For everyone is glad to be called on to display his learning, because no one wants the fruit of his learning to stay hidden, especially if the knowledge he has laboriously sought is familiar to few and unfamiliar to most, as in the case of astrology, dialectic, and all other such fields. People seem to gain the reward for their labor when they get a chance to share what they've learned without the stigma of showing off, which is avoided when one doesn't thrust his learning forward but offers it up when asked. 5. By contrast, questioning someone before a large audience about a topic on which he has not earned a rich store of knowledge occasions deep bitterness: the person is forced either to say he doesn't know—which people count a blow to their self-respect—or to answer rashly and commit himself blindly to what might turn out to be true or false, which in turn often leads him to betray his ignorance—and he blames his questioner for all the shame that the mischance causes. 6. Similarly, those who have traveled over land and sea are glad to be asked about a topographical feature or gulf unknown to many, answering happily and describing these places now in words, now with a pointer, thinking it glorious to make others see what they have seen for themselves. 7. Why mention generals or soldiers? How eager are they always to tell of their brave exploits—and yet hang back for fear of being thought arrogant? If these men are invited to tell their tales, don't they

tentur, mercedem sibi laboris aestimant persolutam, re-
munerationem putantes inter volentes narrare quae fece-
rant? 8. adeo autem id genus narrationum habet quendam
gloriae saporem ut si invidi vel aemuli forte praesentes
sint, tales interrogationes obstrependo discutiant et alias
inferendo fabulas prohibeant illa narrari quae solent nar-
ranti laudem creare. 9. pericula quoque praeterita vel ae-
rumnas penitus absolutas qui evasit ut referat gratissime
provocatur: nam qui adhuc in ipsis vel paululum detinetur,
horret admonitionem et formidat relatum. ideo Euripides
expressit:

$$ὡς^5 \ ἡδύ \ τοι \ σωθέντα \ μεμνῆσθαι \ πόνων.$$

adiecit enim σωθέντα ut ostenderet post finem malorum
gratiam relationis incipere. et poeta vester adiciendo
"olim" quid aliud nisi post emensa infortunia futuro tempore iuvare dicit memoriam sedati laboris:

> forsan et haec olim meminisse iuvabit.

10. nec negaverim esse malorum genera quae non vult qui
pertulit vel transacta meminisse, nec minus interrogatus
offenditur quam cum in ipsis malis fuit, ut qui carnifices
expertus est et tormenta membrorum, ut qui infaustas per-

---

5 ὡς (*Plut. Mor. 630E, om. β₂*)] ἀλλ' *Stob. 2.39.57*

judge that they've been paid for their toil, reckoning it just compensation to tell a willing audience what they had accomplished? 8. Moreover, that sort of story-telling tastes so strongly of glory that if malicious people or rivals chance to be present, they raise a clamor against the questioning and disrupt it, and by introducing other stories block the telling of those tales that tend to bring credit upon the teller. 9. The person, too, who has emerged from past dangers or from periods of unhappiness that have finally been resolved is very glad to be asked to tell of them, while the person who is still in their grip, even to a slight degree, shrinks back from the thought and dreads telling of them. That is why Euripides said (fr. 133 *TGrF* 5,1:250),

how sweet, once safe, to think back on travail:

he added "once safe" to show that recounting woes begins to have some appeal after they've ended. What point did your poet, too, wish to make by adding "one day," if not to indicate that at some future time, after misfortune has been endured to the end, the memory of toil is pleasing, when it has subsided (*A.* 1.203):

perhaps these things too we will one day be glad to remember.

10. Nor would I deny that there are kinds of misfortune that the victim does not want to recall even when they are past and, if asked, is no less offended than he would have been when he in the midst of his woes, as in the case of one whom the torturer put on the rack, or who suffered sorrowful losses in the family or who once was marked for dis-

tulit orbitates vel cui nota quondam adflicta censoria est.[13] cave interroges, ne videaris obicere.

11. 'Illum saepe, si potes, ad narrandum provoca, qui recitando favorabiliter exceptus est, vel qui libere et feliciter legationem peregit, vel qui ab imperatore comiter affabiliterque susceptus est, vel si quis tota paene classe a piratis occupata seu ingenio seu viribus solus evasit, quia vix implet desiderium loquentis rerum talium vel longa narratio. 12. iuvat si quem dicere iusseris amici sui repentinam felicitatem, quam sponte non audebat vel dicere vel tacere, modo iactantiae modo malitiae metu. 13. qui venatibus gaudet interrogetur de silvae ambitu, de ambage lustrorum, de venationis eventu. religiosus si adest, da illi referendi copiam quibus observationibus meruerit auxilia deorum, quantus illi caerimoniarum fructus, quia et hoc genus religionis existimant, numinum beneficia non tacere, adde quia volunt et amicos se numinibus aestimari. 14. si vero et senex praesens est, habes occasionem qua plurimum illi contulisse videaris, si eum interroges vel quae ad illum omnino non pertinent. est enim huic aetati loquacitas familiaris. 15. haec sciens Homerus quandam congeriem simul interrogationum Nestori fecit offerri:

---

13 When reviewing the citizen-lists under the Republic the censors could place a mark (*nota*) next to the names of those they found morally reprehensible (cf. 2.4.25). Inclusion of the custom in these words of advice is a striking anachronism (it is not in Plutarch): by the time M. was writing more than 450 years had passed since the last censor had been elected, and more than three centuries since an emperor (Domitian) had performed a censor's duties.

grace by the censor.[13] Don't ask about such things, lest you seem to cast it in their teeth.

11. 'You should often call on the person who has given a well-received recitation to tell about it, if you can, or who has completed an embassy without a hitch and with a good outcome, or was given a warm and friendly reception by the emperor, or was the sole survivor, thanks to his cunning or strength, when nearly his whole fleet was seized by pirates, for even a long telling of such events scarcely satisfies the speaker's desire. 12. A person is also glad to be asked to tell of a friend's sudden stroke of good fortune, which on his own he'd hesitate either to mention or to pass over in silence, for fear of seeming boastful, on the one hand, or malicious, on the other. 13. A person who takes pleasure in hunting should be asked how he circled the forest, how he wandered through the animals' haunts, how he succeeded in the hunt. If a devotee of religion is present, give him the chance to tell of the observances that earned him the gods' aid and how he profited from the rituals he performed, because they think that publicizing the gods' benefits is itself a kind of religious observance—and of course they want to be thought to be friends of the gods, too. 14. But if an old man is also present, you have the opportunity of appearing to do him a very great service if you question him even on a subject with which he has no connection whatever, since that time of life is on intimate terms with garrulity. 15. Homer was aware of this when he had a heap of questions, so to speak, presented to Nestor all at once (*Od.* 3.247–49, 251):

ὦ Νέστορ Νηληϊάδη, σὺ δ᾽ ἀληθὲς ἐνίσπες·
πῶς ἔθαν᾽ Ἀτρεΐδης εὐρυκρείων Ἀγαμέμνων;[6]
ποῦ Μενέλαος ἔην; . . .
ἦ οὐκ Ἄργεος ἦεν Ἀχαϊκοῦ . . . ;

tot loquendi semina interrogando congessit ut pruritum
senectutis expleret. 16. et Vergilianus Aeneas gratum se ad
omnia praebens Euandro, varias illi narrandi occasiones
ministrat. neque enim de una re aut altera requirit, sed

> singula laetus
> exquiritque auditque virum monimenta priorum,

et Euander consultationibus captus scitis quam multa nar-
raverit.'

3   Haec dicentem favor omnium excepit. sed mox subiecit
Avienus: 'vos omnes qui doctorum doctissimi adestis, ora-
verim ut hortatu vestro Eustathius quae de scommate paulo ante dixerit animetur aperire.' 2. omnibusque ad hoc
provocantibus ille contexuit: 'praeter κατηγορίαν, quae
ψόγος est, et praeter διαβολήν, quae delatio est, sunt alia
duo apud Graecos nomina, λοιδορία et σκῶμμα, quibus
nec vocabula Latina reperio, nisi forte dicas loedoriam
exprobrationem esse ac directam contumeliam, scomma
enim paene dixerim morsum figuratum, quia saepe fraude
vel urbanitate tegitur ut aliud sonet, aliud intellegas. 3. nec
tamen semper ad amaritudinem pergit, sed non numquam
his in quos iacitur et dulce est. quod genus maxime vel sa-

---

[6] εὐρὺ κρείων Ἀγαμέμνων ed. Colon. 1521 ex Hom.:
ΕΙΡΙΠΕϹ α

14 §§2–7 are based on Plut. Mor. 631C–D.

O Nestor, Nêleus' son, tell me the truth:
how did wide-ruling Agamemnôn, Atreus' son, die?
where was Menelaos? . . .
Was it from Akhaian Argos . . . ?

With his questions he heaped up so many germs of conversation that he satisfied the old man's itch to talk. 16. Virgil's Aeneas, too, while doing everything he can to ingratiate himself with Evander, provides him with various opportunities for telling stories and doesn't just ask about one or two matters but (*A.* 8.311–12)

he gladly asks after the details,
one by one, and hears about the memorials of men of
former days;

and you know the length at which Evander spoke, charmed by these inquiries.'

This presentation was well received all around, before 3 Avienus interposed, 'I ask all of you here—the most learned of the learned—to urge Eustathius to be willing to expand his earlier remarks on the scomma.' 2. And as everyone called on him to do so, Eustathius extended what he had previously said with the following:[14] 'Besides invective—Greek *psogos*—and calumny—*diabolê*—there are two Greek terms—*loidoria* and *skômma*—for which I find no Latin counterparts, unless perhaps you'd say that *loidoria* is a straightforwardly insulting reproach, whereas *skômma* I would almost say is an oblique kind of jibe, since it's often concealed by a deceptive or urbane veneer, so that it sounds like one thing though you hear it as another. 3. Yet it does not always end in bitterness but is sometimes even pleasing to its targets. It is the sort of thing that a wise

piens vel alias urbanus exercet praecipue inter mensas et pocula, ubi facilis est ad iracundiam provocatio. 4. nam sicut in praecipiti stantem vel levis tactus impellit, ita vino vel infusum vel aspersum parvus quoque dolor incitat in furorem. ergo cautius in convivio abstinendum scommate quod tectam intra se habet iniuriam. 5. tanto enim pressius haerent dicta talia quam directae loedoriae, ut hami angulosi quam directi mucrones tenacius infiguntur, maxime quia dicta huius modi risum praesentibus movent, quo velut adsensus genere confirmatur iniuria. 6. est autem loedoria huius modi: oblitusne es quia salsamenta vendebas? scomma autem, quod diximus saepe contumeliam esse celatam, tale est: meminimus quando bracchio te emungebas. nam cum res eadem utrobique dicta sit, illud tamen loedoria est, quod aperte obiectum exprobratumque est, hoc scomma, quod figurate. 7. Octavius, qui natu nobilis videbatur, Ciceroni recitanti ait: "non audio quae dicis." ille respondit: "certe solebas bene foratas habere aures." hoc eo dictum quia Octavius Libys oriundo dicebatur, quibus mos est aurem forare. 8. In eundem Ciceronem Laberius cum ab eo ad consessum non reciperetur, dicentem, "reciperem te nisi anguste sederemus," ait mimus ille mordaciter, "atqui solebas duabus sellis sedere," obiciens tanto viro lubricum fidei. sed et quod Cicero dixit, "nisi anguste sederemus," scomma fuit in C. Caesarem, qui in senatum

---

15 Cf. Anon. *Rhetoric for Herennius* 4.67, Suetonius *Life of Horace* 1.

16 Cf. Plut. *Cic.* 26.4; Octavius here is the future Augustus, whose maternal great-grandfather was alleged by Mark Antony to have been African (Suet. *Aug.* 4.2).

man especially employs, or one who is in other respects so-phisticated, chiefly at table and over drinks, when people are easily provoked to anger. 4. For just as even a slight touch sends someone standing on a cliff-edge headlong, so even a slight grievance stirs to a rage someone who has indulged in wine, whether a little or a lot. At a banquet, then, one must be particularly careful to avoid the carping that conveys a concealed insult. 5. Such things get all the more urgently under the skin than straightforward insults, just as angled hooks pierce and cling more tenaciously than straight blades, especially since witticisms of this sort make the bystanders laugh and add to the insult's force by their apparent agreement. 6. Now, it is a straightforward insult to say, for example, "Do you forget that you were once no better than a peddler of salt-cod?," while it is an oblique insult to say, "I remember when you used to wipe your nose on your sleeve":[15] though the point is the same in both cases, the straightforward insult casts the point in the other's face as an open reproach, the jibe does so obliquely. 7. Octavius, who was taken to be of noble birth, said to Cicero, when he was reciting, "I don't hear what you're saying." Cicero replied, "Surely, you used to have nicely perforated ears" (*dicta* 14)—the point being that Octavius was rumored to have been born in Libya, where pierced ears are the custom.[16] 8. When Laberius was looking for a seat in the theater and Cicero would not have him sit beside him, saying, "I'd make room if the seating weren't so tight," the noted writer of mimes offered the biting rejoinder, "But you used to make a habit of sitting in two seats," reproaching the great man for being more slippery than loyal. But Cicero's own remark, ." . . if the seating weren't so tight," was an oblique insult intended for Gaius Caesar,

passim tam multos admittebat ut eos quattuordecim gradus capere non possent. 9. tali ergo genere, quod fetum contumeliae est, abstinendum sapienti semper, ceteris in convivio est.

10. 'Sunt alia scommata minus aspera, quasi edentatae beluae morsus, ut Tullius in consulem qui uno tantum die consulatum peregit: "solent," inquit, "esse flamines diales, modo consules diales habemus." et in eundem: "vigilantissimus est consul noster, qui in consulatu suo somnum non vidit." eidemque exprobranti sibi quod ad eum consulem non venisset, "veniebam," inquit, "sed nox me comprehendit." 11. Haec et talia sunt quae plus urbanitatis, minus amaritudinis habent, ut sunt et illa de non nullis corporis vitiis, aut parum aut nihil gignentia doloris; ut si in calvitium cuiusquam dicas vel in nasi[7] seu curvam erectionem seu Socraticam depressionem. haec enim quanto minoris infortunii sunt tanto levioris doloris. 12. contra oculorum orbitas non sine excitatione commotionis obicitur. quippe Antigonus rex Theocritum Chium, de quo iuraverat quod ei parsurus esset, occidit propter scomma ab eodem de se dictum. cum enim quasi puniendus ad Antigonum raperetur, solantibus eum amicis ac spem pollicentibus quod omni modo clementiam regis experturus esset, cum ad

---

[7] nasi *Jan*: nasum ω

---

[17] The jest is repeated from 2.3.10, where there is a similar confusion between the seats reserved for knights (Laberius) and those reserved for senators (Cicero): see the n. ad loc.

[18] Cf. 2.2.13, where the witticism is attributed to a different man. [19] Repeated from 2.3.6. [20] Repeated from 2.3.5, where the target is the consul Vatinius.

who admitted so many men indiscriminately to the senate that the first fourteen rows of the theater could not accommodate them all.[17] 9. The wise man should always refrain from remarks of that sort, which are pregnant with insult, while everyone else should refrain from them in the banquet.

10. 'There are other jibes that are less harsh—the bites of a toothless beast—like Tully's remark about the consul who held his office for one day only, "Before this we've had 'daylight priests,' now we have daylight consuls,"[18] and against the same target, "Our consul is the most vigilant of men: he caught not a wink of sleep in his consulship" (*dicta* 24);[19] and when the same man reproached Cicero for not paying a courtesy call on him as consul, Cicero said, "I intended to come, but nightfall overtook me" (*dicta* 32).[20] 11. These remarks and others like them, which are more urbane than bitter, and those that concern some bodily flaws, cause no pain, or very little:[21] for example, if you pass a remark about someone's baldness, or a nose that's a hooked beak or a pug nose like Socrates'. The slight pain such things cause is in direct proportion to the lesser misfortune that they represent. 12. On the other hand, making fun of someone's loss of an eye is bound to stir some feeling. Indeed, though king Antigonus had sworn that he would spare Theocritus of Chios, he had him killed because of the jibe in which he indulged: for when he was being brought hurriedly to Antigonus for punishment, as it seemed, his friends were consoling him and promising him that he had every reason to expect to experience the king's

[21] §§11–12 are based on Plut. *Mor.* 632B–C.

oculos eius venisset, respondit: "ergo impossibilem mihi
dicitis spem salutis." erat autem Antigonus uno orbatus
oculo, et importuna urbanitas male dicacem luce privavit.

13. 'Nec negaverim philosophos quoque incurrisse non
numquam per indignationem hoc genus scommatis. nam
cum regis libertus ad novas divitias nuper erectus philosophos ad convivium congregasset, et inridendo eorum mi-
nutulas quaestiones scire se velle dixisset cur et ex nigra et
ex alba faba pulmentum unius coloris edatur,[8] Aridices
philosophus indigne ferens, "tu nobis," inquit, "absolve cur
et de albis et de nigris loris similes maculae gignantur."

14. 'Sunt scommata quae in superficie habent speciem
contumeliae sed interdum non tangunt audientes, cum eadem, si obnoxio dicantur, exagitant, ut contra sunt quae
speciem laudis habent, et persona[9] audientis efficit contumeliae plena. de priore genere prius dicam. 15. T. Quietus
praetor de provincia nuper reverterat, observata—quod
mireris Domitiani temporibus—praeturae maxima casti-
tate. is cum aeger adsidenti amico diceret frigidas se habere manus, renidens ille ait, "atqui eas de provincia cali-
das paulo ante revocasti." risit Quietus[10] delectatusque est;
quippe alienissimus a suspicione furtorum. contra, si hoc
diceretur male sibi conscio et sua furta recolenti, exacer-

---

[8] edatur *ed. Colon. 1521:* edat ω

[9] persona . . . plena *Jan:* personam . . . plenam ω

[10] T. Quietus . . . Quietus *Wissowa (coll. Plut. Mor. 632A):* L.
Quintus . . . Quintus ω

---

[22] §13 is based on Plut. *Mor.* 634C. Aridices was a pupil of
Arcesilaus (Athen. 420D), head of the Academy from 262 BCE.

[23] §§14–16 are based on Plut. *Mor.* 632A–B.

mercy when he came before his eyes; to which he replied, "Then you're telling me I have no hope of salvation whatever"—because Antigonus had lost one eye. The ill-timed quip ended the life of the maladroit wit.

13. 'Nor would I deny that philosophers too have sometimes fallen to using this sort of jibe out of righteous indignation. When a king's freedman, recently elevated to a position of newfound wealth, had gathered philosophers for a banquet and—making fun of their pedantic inquiries—said he wanted to know why both black beans and white beans made a mash of the same color, the philosopher Aridices, waxing indignant, said, "No, *you* explain to us why white lashes and black produce welts that look alike."[22]

14. 'There are jibes that bear an apparent insult on their surface but sometimes leave their audience unscathed, whereas if the same jibe should be directed at a guilty person they aggravate him;[23] conversely, there are those that appear to offer praise, but the listener's character renders them highly insulting. I'll talk about the first sort first. 15. The praetor Titus Quietus had recently returned from his province, having behaved with the greatest honesty during his tenure—something to cause wonder in the reign of Domitian. When he was sick, he told a friend sitting at his bedside that his hands were cold, and the friend replied, with a grin, "But you brought them back good and warm from your province not long ago." Quietus laughed and was delighted, seeing that he was utterly removed from any suspicion of thievery. On the other hand, if this were said to someone with a bad conscience recalling his

basset auditum. 16. Critobulum famosae pulchritudinis adulescentem Socrates cum ad comparationem formae provocaret, iocabatur, non inridebat. certe si dicas consummatarum divitiarum viro, "tibi excito creditores tuos," aut si nimis casto, "gratae tibi sunt meretrices, quia continua eas largitate ditasti," uterque delectabuntur, scientes his dictis suam conscientiam non gravari. 17. sicut contra sunt quae sub specie laudis exagitant, sicut paulo ante divisi. nam si timidissimo dixero, "Achilli vel Herculi comparandus es," aut famosae iniquitatis viro, "ego te Aristidi in aequitate praepono," sine dubio verba laudem sonantia ad notam vituperationis suae uterque tracturus est.

18. 'Eadem scommata eosdem modo iuvare, modo mordere possunt pro diversitate praesentium personarum. sunt enim quae si coram amicis obiciantur nobis, libenter audire possimus, uxore vero seu parentibus magistrisve praesentibus dici in nos aliquod scomma nolimus, nisi forte tale sit quod illorum censura libenter accipiat: 19. ut si quis adulescentem coram parentibus vel magistris inrideat quod insanire possit continuis vigiliis lectionibusque nocturnis, aut uxore praesente quod stulte faciat uxorium se praebendo nec ullam elegantiam eligendo formarum. haec enim et in quos dicuntur et praesentes hilaritate perfundunt. 20. commendat scomma et condicio di-

---

[24] Xen. *Symp.* 4.19.
[25] §17 is based on Plut. *Mor.* 632D.
[26] §§18–20 are based on Plut. *Mor.* 634A–C.

thefts, it would have annoyed him to hear it. 16. When Socrates challenged Critobulus, a young man famous for his good looks, to a beauty context, he was making a joke, not engaging in mockery.[24] And surely, were you to say to a man whose wealth lacked nothing, "I'm setting your creditors on you," or to an exceedingly chaste man, "You have the whores' gratitude for enriching them with your unflagging bounty," both would be pleased, knowing that these witticisms put no strain on their consciences. 17. Similarly, but conversely, there are those that cause annoyance though they appear to offer praise: this was the distinction I drew not long ago. For if I were to say to a very fearful person, "You should be compared with Achilles or Hercules," or to a man of notorious dishonesty, "I put you ahead of Aristides for fairness," both would doubtless take the words that sound like praise as intended to stigmatize them.[25]

18. 'The same jibes can at different times please or sting the same people, if different witnesses are present.[26] For there are some remarks we're glad hear if they're made about us when friends are present, but when a wife or parents or teachers are present we don't want to be the object of a jibe, unless it's such that their own strict moral sense would be glad to hear: 19. for example, if someone were to make fun of a young man in his parents' or his teachers' presence for risking his mental health by continuously staying up late into the night to read, or if someone were to make fun of a man in his wife's presence for playing the fool by showing his devotion to his wife and never having a choice bit on the side. Both the targets of these remarks and those present to hear them find them quite amusing. 20. The speaker's social circumstances make a jibe accept-

171

centis, si in eadem causa sit: ut si alium de paupertate pauper inrideat, si obscure natum natus obscure. nam Tarseus Amphias cum ex hortulano potens esset et in amicum quasi degenerem non nulla dixisset, mox subiecit: "sed et nos de isdem seminibus sumus," et omnes pariter laetos fecit. 21. illa vero scommata directa laetitia eum in quem dicuntur infundunt, si virum fortem vituperes quasi salutis suae prodigum et pro aliis mori volentem, aut si obieceris liberali quod res suas profundat minus sibi quam aliis consulendo. sic et Diogenes Antisthenen Cynicum, magistrum suum, solebat veluti vituperando laudare. "ipse me," aiebat, "mendicum fecit ex divite, et pro ampla domo in dolio fecit habitare." melius autem ista dicebat quam si diceret, "gratus illi sum quia ipse me philosophum et consummatae virtutis virum fecit."

22. 'Ergo cum unum nomen scommatis sit, diversi in eo continentur effectus. ideo apud Lacedaemonios inter cetera exactae vitae instituta hoc quoque exercitii genus a Lycurgo est institutum, ut adulescentes et scommata sine morsu dicere et ab aliis in se dicta perpeti discerent, ac si quis eorum in indignationem ob tale dictum prolapsus fuisset, ulterius ei in alterum dicere non licebat. 23. cum ergo videas, mi Aviene—instituenda est enim adulescentia tua, quae ita docilis est ut discenda praecipiat—cum videas, inquam, anceps esse omne scommatum genus, suadeo in conviviis, in quibus laetitiae insidiatur ira, ab huius modi dictis facessas et magis quaestiones convivales vel

---

27 M. perhaps misunderstands Plutarch, who says that Amphias was thought to be the son of a gardener.

28 §21 is based on Plut. *Mor.* 632E.

29 §22 is based on (and departs slightly from) Plut. *Mor.* 631F.

able if they are the same as the target's, for example, if one poor man mocks another for his poverty, or one low-born man another: when Amphias of Tarsus, a former gardener,[27] became a great man and passed some comments about a friend's being "of poor stock," he quickly added, "But I too am born from the same seed," and caused equal pleasure on all sides. 21. But jibes that take the form of direct criticism can fill their target with pleasure, for example, if you should criticize a hero for being prodigal of his own well-being and willing to die for others, or a generous man for wasting his estate by being more concerned about others than about himself. That's how Diogenes used to praise his teacher, the Cynic Antisthenes, by appearing to criticize him: "He's the very man," he said, "who made me a beggar, who once was rich, and caused me to live in a clay jar instead of my spacious house." That was more effective than if he were to say, "I'm grateful to him for making me a philosopher and a man of perfect virtue."[28]

22. 'So, then, though "jibe" is a single term, it comprises different effects. That's why among all the other habits of an austere life that Lycurgus established among the Spartans there was this exercise too: young men learned both to offer jibes that lacked a sting and to tolerate jibes directed at them by others, and if any of them became indignant because of such a jibe, he was thereafter forbidden to direct one at another.[29] 23. Since you see, then, my friend Avienus—and it is right that I shape your young mind, which is so readily taught that it anticipates the lessons it should learn—since you see, I say, that every sort of jibe is a two-edged sword, I suggest that in banquets, where anger sets traps for high spirited good humor, you avoid witticisms of this sort and instead propose questions suitable

proponas vel ipse dissolvas. 24. quod genus veteres ita lu-
dicrum non putarunt ut et Aristoteles de ipsis aliqua con-
scripserit et Plutarchus et vester Apuleius, nec contem-
nendum sit quod tot philosophantium curam meruit.'

4   Et Praetextatus: 'hoc quaestionum genus cum et seni-
lem deceat aetatem, cur soli iuveni suadetur? quin agite,
omnes qui adestis, haec apta convivio fabulemur, nec de
cibatu tantum, sed et si qua de natura corporum vel alia,
praesente maxime Dysario nostro, cuius plurimum ad hoc
genus quaestionum poterit ars et doctrina conferre, sortia-
murque, si videtur, ut per ordinem unus quisque propo-
nat quam solvendam aestimat quaestionem.' 2. hic adsensi
omnes Praetextato anteloquium detulerunt, orantes ut
cum ipse coepisset, ceteris ex filo consultationis eius interrogandi constitueretur exemplum. 3. tum ille, 'quaero,' inquit, 'utrum simplex an multiplex cibus digestu sit facilior,
quia multos hunc, non nullos illum sectantes videmus. et
est quidem superba et contumax et velut sui ostentatrix
continentia, contra amoenam se et comem adpetentia vult
videri. cum ergo una censoria sit, delicata altera, scire
equidem velim quae servandae aptior sit sanitati. nec
longe petendus adsertor est cum Dysarius adsit, qui quid
conveniat corporibus humanis non minus callet quam ipsa
natura, fabricae huius auctor et nutrix. dicas ergo velim
quid de hoc quod quaeritur medicinae ratio persuadeat.'

---

30 I.e., the *Problems* falsely attributed to Aristotle and Plutarch's *Questions at Table*, which was among M.'s sources. A similar work by Apuleius is otherwise known only from a reference
to the *Questions at Table* of "the Platonist from Madaura" by
Sidonius Apollinaris, who was born about the time M. was writing
(*Epist.* 9.13, noted by Linke 1880, 56, who argued that Apuleius
was among M.'s sources).

for a banquet, or answer them yourself. 24. The ancients were so far from thinking that activity frivolous that Aristotle wrote some works on the subject and Plutarch and your Apuleius:[30] we should not condemn what so many philosophers thought worthy of their attention.'

Praetextatus said, 'Why is this sort of question urged 4 only on this young man, when it's becoming for the elderly as well? Come now, all of you who are here: let's talk about these topics that befit a banquet, and not just about food, but whatever touches on our physical nature—especially given that our friend Dysarius is here, whose learning and skill will be able to contribute a very great deal to questions of this sort. If it's agreeable, let's draw lots so that each one of us in order might put forward a question that he deems worth answering.' 2. With general agreement on this point they all gave over to Praetextatus the role of starting the discussion, so that once he had begun the rest would have an example to follow in putting their questions as the thread of the discussion unwound. 3. Then Praetextatus said, 'I want to know whether it is easier to digest food that is plain or varied, since I see that many opt for the latter, some for the former. There is in fact a kind of austerity that is proud and defiant, a form of showing off, while a fondness for eating wants to appear pleasant and gracious by contrast. Given, then, that the one is censorious, the other luxurious, I'd like to know which is better suited to maintaining one's health—and there's no need to seek out an authority with Dysarius here, since when it comes to what's right for the human body he's no less skilled than nature herself, the source and support of our physical being. Please tell me, then, what medical science urges on this question.'

4. 'Si me,' Dysarius inquit, 'aliquis ex plebe imperitorum de hac quaestione consuluisset, quia plebeia ingenia magis exemplis quam ratione capiuntur, admonuisse illum contentus forem institutionis pecudum, quibus cum simplex et uniformis cibus sit, multo saniores sunt corporibus humanis, et inter ipsas illae morbis implicantur quibus, ut altiles fiant, offae compositae et quibusdam condimentis variae farciuntur. 5. nec dubitaret posthac cum advertisset animalibus simplici cibo utentibus familiarem sanitatem, aegrescere autem et inter illa quae saginam composita varietate patiuntur, quia constat id genus alimoniae non magis copia quam varietate crudescere. 6. fortasse illum attentiorem exemplo altero fecissem, ut consideraret nullum umquam fuisse medicorum circa curas aegrescentium tam audacis neglegentiae ut febrienti varium et non simplicem cibum daret. adeo constat quam facilis digestu sit uniformis alimonia, ut ei, vel cum infirma est natura, sufficiat. 7. nec tertium defuisset exemplum, ita esse vitandam ciborum varietatem ut varia solent vina vitari. quis enim ambigat eum qui diverso vino utitur in repentinam ruere ebrietatem, necdum hoc potus copia postulante? 8. tecum autem, Vetti, cui soli perfectionem disciplinarum omnium contigit obtinere, non tam exemplis quam ratione tractandum est, quae et me tacente clam te esse non poterit.

9. 'Cruditates eveniunt aut qualitate suci in quem cibus vertitur, si non sit aptus umori qui corpus obtinuit, aut ip-

---

31 §§4–13 are based on Plut. *Mor.* 661A–662A.

4. 'If someone from the uninformed commons had asked me this question,' Dysarius said,[31] 'I mean the sort of people whose wits are engaged more by examples than by rational analysis, I'd have been content to call to mind the way farm animals are raised: since their diet is plain and unvarying, their bodies are much healthier than ours, and those that are dogged by illness are the ones who are fattened by being stuffed with masses of food that combine different kinds and seasonings. 5. Such a person would not be in doubt thereafter when he noticed that animals fed simple food always enjoy good health, while sickness occurs among those who suffer a rich and varied diet, since it's well known that that sort of sustenance causes indigestion by its variety no less than by its abundance. 6. Perhaps, too, I would have used another example, the better to engage such a person's attention, by having him reflect on the fact that no physician has ever been so brazenly negligent in trying to cure his patients as to give someone with a fever not plain but varied food: it is so clearly established how readily digestible a simple diet is that it meets the patient's needs even if he has a frail constitution. 7. Nor would a third example have been lacking: a varied diet ought to be avoided just as we usually avoid mixing wines. Who doubts that a person who drinks different wines succumbs to a sudden drunkenness incommensurate with the amount of wine he's consumed? 8. But in dealing with you, Vettius, who alone have perfect command of all fields of learning, I should use not examples but rational analysis, which will not escape you even if I were silent.

9. 'Bouts of indigestion result either from the kind of juice into which food is converted, if it does not suit the

177

sius cibi multitudine, non sufficiente natura ad omnia quae congesta sunt concoquenda. ac primum de suci qualitate videamus.

10. 'Qui simplicem cibum sumit, facile quo suco corpus eius vel gravetur vel iuvetur usu docente cognoscit. nec enim ambigit cuius cibi qualitate possessus sit, cum unum sumpserit; et ita fit ut noxa cuius causa deprehensa est, facile vitetur. 11. qui autem multiplici cibo alitur, diversas patitur qualitates ex diversitate sucorum, nec concordant umores ex materiae varietate nascentes nec efficiunt liquidum purumve sanguinem, in quem iecoris ministerio vertuntur, et in venas cum tumultu suo transeunt. hinc morborum scaturrigo, qui ex repugnantium sibi umorum discordia nascuntur. 12. deinde quia non omnium quae esui sunt una natura est, non omnia simul coquuntur, sed alia celerius, tardius alia, et ita fit ut digestionum sequentium ordo turbetur. 13. neque enim cibi quem sumimus una digestio est sed, ut corpus nutriat, quattuor patitur digestiones, quarum unam omnes vel ipsi quoque hebetes sentiunt, alias occultior ratio deprehendit. quod ut omnibus liqueat, paulo altius mihi causa repetenda est.

14. 'Quattuor sunt in nobis virtutes quae administrandam alimoniam receperunt, quarum una dicitur καθελκτική, quae deorsum trahit cibaria confecta mandibulis.

---

32 According to the theory of humors, the dominant physiological model of antiquity, human beings have four constituent humors—black bile, blood, yellow bile, and phlegm—which by their varying combinations determine our temperaments and our health.　　33 With §§14–18 cf. [Alex. Aphrod.] *Prob*. 2.60. M. is here following standard doctrine in surveying the 4 "powers" (*dynameis*): cf., e.g., Galen 1:654, 7:63.

body's dominant humor,[32] or from the amount of food itself, when the body's nature is unequal to the task of digesting all that's been heaped up. Let's first consider the
kind of juice.

10. 'Someone who takes plain food easily recognizes
from experience what juice helps his body or causes it distress, and he is in no doubt what kind of food holds sway
over him, because he has eaten only one sort: harm is thus
easily avoided, since its cause is known. 11. On the other
hand, someone who has a varied diet experiences a variety
of juices from the variety of foods; the humors that arise
from this varied material are out of harmony, they produce
blood (into which they are converted by the liver) that is
not clear and pure, and they thus transmit their cacophony
to the veins. As a result, diseases bubble up from the discord of conflicting humors. 12. Furthermore, because all
the things that there are to eat are not of a single nature,
they are digested, not all at the same time, but some more
quickly, some more slowly, so that the orderly sequence of
digestion is thrown into confusion. 13. For the food that we
eat is not digested in a single process but undergoes four
different processes to provide the body with nutrition: one
of these processes everyone, even dullards, perceive, while
a more esoteric analysis is required to detect the others.
The reason for this is something I should go into a bit more
deeply, so that it will be clear to everyone.

14. 'There are in us four special powers that have been
given the task of administering our diet.[33] One of these
powers is the *kathelktikê* [= peristalsis], which draws down
the food after it has been broken down by the jaws: for

179

quid enim tam crassam materiam per faucium angusta ful-
ciret nisi eam vis naturae occultior hauriret? 15. hausta
vero ut non continuo lapsu per omne corpus, succedenti-
bus sibi foraminibus pervium, ad imum usque descen-
dant et talia qualia accepta sunt egerantur, sed salutare
officium digestionis expectent, secundae haec cura virtutis
est, quam Graeci, quia retentatrix est, vocant καθεκτικήν.
16. tertia quia cibum in aliud ex alio mutat, vocatur
ἀλλοιωτική. huic obsequuntur omnes, quia ipsa digestio-
nibus curat. 17. ventris enim duo sunt orificia, quorum superius erectum recipit devorata et in follem ventris recon-
dit. hic est stomachus, qui paterfamilias dici meruit, quasi
omne animal solus gubernans, nam si aegrescat, vita in an-
cipiti est, titubante alimoniae meatu, cui natura tamquam
rationis capaci velle ac nolle contribuit. inferius vero de-
missum intestinis adiacentibus inseritur, et inde via est
egerendis. 18. ergo in ventre fit prima digestio, virtute
ἀλλοιωτικῇ in sucum vertente quicquid acceptum est,
cuius faex retrimenta sunt quae per intestina inferiore
orificio tradente labuntur, et officio quartae virtutis, cui
ἀποκριτκή nomen est, procuratur egestio.

19. 'Ergo postquam in sucum cibus reformatur, hic iam

what could cram such gross matter through the throat's narrow passage were not a more hidden force of nature drawing it in? 15. But to prevent the food that's swallowed from gliding uninterruptedly through the series of bodily openings that provide a passageway, to keep it from reaching bottom and being passed out in the same state in which it was taken in, and to allow it to receive the healthful ministry of digestion—all this is the concern of the second power, which the Greeks call the *kathektikê*, that is, the power of retention. 16. The third power is called the *alloiôtikê* ["transformative"], because it changes the food from one thing into another: all the other powers are subordinate to this one, which itself superintends the processes of digestion. 17. For the belly has two openings. The upper one, which is perpendicular to the belly, receives the food that's been swallowed and deposits it in the belly's sac: this is the stomach, which has deservedly come to be called the "head of the household," on the ground that it governs the whole creature all by itself—for if it falls ill, the creature's life is at risk, as the nutrients' path becomes insecure—and to it nature has assigned the power to signal "stop" or "go" as though it were capable of reason. The lower opening extends downward and into the neighboring intestines and provides the pathway for the matter that is to be expelled. 18. The first digestion, then, takes place in the belly, where the transformative power turns whatever has been ingested into juice: the dregs are the waste products that pass through the intestines by way of the belly's lower opening, and their expulsion is seen to by the good offices of the fourth power, called the *apokritikê* ["secretive"].

19. 'After the food has been reconfigured as juice, then,

iecoris cura succedit. est autem iecur concretus sanguis et ideo habet nativum calorem, quod confectum sucum vertit in sanguinem, et sicut cibum in sucum verti prima est, ita sucum transire in sanguinem secunda digestio est. 20. hunc calor iecoris administratum per venarum fistulas in sua quaeque membra dispergit, parte quae ex digestis frigidissima est in lienem refusa, qui ut iecur caloris ita ipse frigoris domicilium est. 21. nam ideo omnes dexterae partes validiores sunt et debiliores sinistrae, quia has regit calor visceris sui, illae contagione frigoris sinistra obtinentis hebetantur. 22. in venis autem et arteriis, quae sunt receptacula sanguinis et spiritus, tertia fit digestio. nam acceptum sanguinem quodam modo defaecant, et quod in eo aquosum est venae in vesicam refundunt, liquidum vero purumque et altilem sanguinem singulis totius corporis membris ministrant et ita fit ut cum cibum solus venter accipiat, alimonia eius dispersa per universos membrorum meatus ossa quoque et medullas et ungues nutriat et capillos. 23. et haec est quarta digestio, quae in singulis membris fit dum quod uni cuique membro datum est ipsi membro fit nutrimentum. nec tamen huic totiens defaecato retrimenta sua desunt; quae cum membra omnia in sua sunt sanitate, per occultos evanescunt meatus: 24. si qua vero pars corporis aegrescat, in ipsam quasi infirmiorem ultima illa quae diximus retrimenta labuntur, et hinc nascuntur morborum causae quae ῥεύματα medicis vocare mos est. 25. si enim fuerit ultimi suci iusto uberior multitu-

---

34 Cf. Apul. *Apol*. 51 (citing Aristotle's *Problems* = fr. 240 Rose).

it becomes the liver's concern. Now, the liver is congealed blood and for that reason is innately hot: it turns the processed juice into blood, and just as the conversion of food to juice was the first digestion, so the passage of juice into blood is the second. 20. When this process is complete, the liver's heat disperses the blood to each of the limbs through the veins' channels, with the coolest among the digested elements spilling into the spleen, which is the body's cooling center, as the liver is the center of warmth. 21. That's why the whole right side of the body is sturdier, the left weaker: the former is guided by the warmth of the innards on that side, the latter is enfeebled by contact with the cold that grips the left.[34] 22. Now, the third digestion occurs in the veins and arteries, which are the receptacles of blood and breath. For when they've received the blood they filter out the wastes, as it were: the veins deposit in the bladder the part that's watery and serve up to the body's several limbs blood that's clear and pure and rich in nutrients: so it happens that though only the belly takes in food, the food's nutrients are dispersed through all of the limbs' passages and also feed the bones and marrow and nails and hair. 23. This is the fourth digestion: it occurs in the several limbs, as the nutrients given to each become the sustenance for that specific limb. And yet though the material has been filtered so many times, it is not free of waste products, which—when all the limbs are fit and healthy—disappear through invisible passageways. 24. But if some part of the body is ailing, the final waste products I mentioned subside into that very part, as if seeking out the weaker, and this is origin of the diseases that physicians customarily call *rheumata* ["fluxes"]. 25. For if the amount of this final juice is greater than it ought to be, the healthier part

do, hanc a se repellit pars corporis illa quae sanior est, et
sine dubio labitur in infirmam quae vires non habet repel-
lendi, unde alieni receptio distendit locum in quem ceciderit, et hinc creantur dolores. haec est ergo triplex causa
vel podagrae vel cuiuslibet ex confluentia morbi, id est
multitudo umoris, fortitudo membri a se repellentis et re-
cipientis infirmitas.

26. 'Cum igitur adseruerimus quattuor in corpore fieri
digestiones, quarum altera pendet ex altera, et si praece-
dens fuerit impedita, nullus fit sequentis effectus, recurra-
mus animo ad illam primam digestionem quae in ventre
conficitur, et invenietur quid impedimenti ex multiformi
nascatur alimonia. 27. diversorum enim ciborum diversa
natura est, et sunt qui celerius, sunt qui tardius digeruntur.
cum ergo prima digestio vertit in sucum, quia non simul
omnia accepta vertuntur, quod prius versum est, dum alia
tardius vertuntur, acescit; et hoc saepe etiam eructando
sentimus. 28. alia quoque, quibus tarda digestio est, velut
ligna umida quae urgente igne fumum de se creant, sic et
illa imminente igne naturae fumant, dum tardius conco-
quuntur—si quidem nec hoc sensum eructantis evadit.[11]
29. cibus autem simplex non habet controversam moram
dum simul in simplicem sucum vertitur, nec digestio ulla
turbatur dum omnes sibi stata momentorum dimensione
succedunt. 30. si quis autem—quia nihil impatientius im-
peritia—rationes has dedignetur audire, aestimans non
impediri digestionem nisi sola ciborum multitudine, nec
velit de qualitate tractare, hic quoque multiformis alimo-

[11] evadit PA²: -dat ω

of the body expels it, and it naturally subsides into the weak part that doesn't have the strength to repel it: this foreign matter, when it's been received, causes the place into which it has fallen to swell, and the swelling in turn produces pain. This, then, is the threefold cause of gout or of any disease that collected fluids produce: the excess humor, the strength of the limb that rejects it, and the weakness of the limb that receives it.

26. 'So I've shown that four different processes of digestion occur in the body, such that each depends on another, and if an earlier process is blocked, then the one that follows cannot be completed. Let's now think back to the first process that was completed in the belly, and we'll find out what blockage can arise from a varied diet. 27. Different foods have different natures, some being digested more quickly, others more slowly. When the first process is turning food into juice, then, and all that's been ingested is not converted at the same time, the food that's first converted turns acidic while the rest is converted more slowly: we often even perceive this directly when we belch. 28. The foods, too, that are digested slowly, like damp logs that smoke at a fire's urging, produce fumes at the prompting of the body's natural heat while they are being processed more slowly—this too doesn't escape the notice of someone who belches. 29. But plain food, while it is all turned at once into plain juice, entails no delay in conversion, nor is any part of the process disturbed, as one part follows another according to a stable schedule. 30. If anyone, however, should refuse to heed this account (for there's nothing less patient than ignorance) and suppose that only the quantity of food impedes digestion, refusing to consider the kind also, here too a varied diet is caught

nia deprehenditur causa morborum. 31. nam pulmento-
rum varietas recipit varia condimenta, quibus gula ultra
quam naturae necesse est lacessitur, et fit inde congeries,
dum pruritu desiderii amplius vel certe de singulis parva
libantur. 32. hinc Socrates suadere solitus erat illos cibos
potusve vitandos, qui ultra sitim famemve sedandam pro-
ducunt adpetentiam. denique vel propter hoc edendi varietas repudietur, quia plena est voluptatis, a qua seriis et
studiosis cavendum est. quid enim tam contrarium quam
virtus et voluptas? 33. sed modum disputationi facio, ne videar hoc ipsum in quo sumus, licet sobrium sit, tamen quia
varium est accusare convivium.'

5   Haec cum Praetextato et ceteris prona adsensione pla-
cuissent, Evangelus exclamavit: 'nihil tam indignum tole-
ratu quam quod aures nostras Graia[12] lingua captivas tenet
et verborum rotunditati adsentiri cogimur circumventi vo-
lubilitate sermonis, qui ad extorquendam fidem agit in audientes tyrannum. 2. et quia his loquendi labyrinthis im-
pares nos fatemur, age, Vetti, hortemur Eustathium ut
recepta contraria disputatione quicquid pro vario cibo dici
potest velit communicare nobiscum, ut suis telis lingua
violenta succumbat, et Graecus Graeco eripiat hunc plau-
sum, tamquam cornix cornici oculos effodiat.'

3. Et Symmachus: 'rem iucundam, Evangele, amarius
postulasti. vadere[13] enim contra tam copiose et eleganter
inventa res est[14] quae habeat utilem voluptatem, sed non
tamquam ingeniis insidiantes et gloriosis tractatibus invi-

---

[12] Graia *Timpanaro*: gratia α, grata R²FC²Q, Graeca δ
[13] vadere *scripsi*: audire ω, audere C²   [14] est J², *om.* ω

---

[35] Consistent with the Socratic apothegm quoted at 2.8.16.

out as a cause of disease. 31. For a variety of savory dishes requires a variety of seasoning, which stimulate the appetite beyond the demands of nature, and that results in a large accumulation of food: because the appetite is stimulated, too much is consumed, even when small amounts of individual dishes are consumed. 32. That is why Socrates used to advise avoiding food and drink that caused the appetite to persist after hunger and thirst had been satisfied.[35] Finally, a varied diet should be rejected for this reason too: it is laden with pleasure, from which serious and studious people ought to stand aloof. Are any things as opposed as virtue and pleasure? 33. But I'll end the discussion here, lest I appear to indict the present banquet for offering—despite its sobriety—a varied menu.'

When Praetextatus and the rest had, with ready agreement, expressed their satisfaction, Evangelus exclaimed, 'This really is beyond bearing—to have our ears held captive by this Greek and be forced to agree with his orotund pronouncements, fooled by a rapid flow of speech that tyrannizes its listeners to extort their belief. 2. Since we confess that we can't keep up with this labyrinthine discourse, come Vettius, let's urge Eustathius to take up the other side and share with us what can be said on behalf of a varied diet, so that Dysarius, with his linguistic torrent, might be hoist with his own petard—one Greek snatching the applause away from another, like one crow poking out another's eyes.'

3. Symmachus said, 'You've made a pleasant proposal, Evangelus, in quite an unpleasant way: an attack on so substantial and shapely a theory is a thing that could be both useful and enjoyable, but we ought not make the attempt as though we were preparing ambushes in a contest of

dentes hoc debemus expetere. 4. nec abnego potuisse me quoque tamquam palinodiam canere. est enim rhetorica praelusio communes locos in utramvis partem inventorum alternatione tractare. sed quia facilius Graecorum inventionibus a Graecis forte aliis relata respondent, te, Eustathi, oramus omnes ut sensa et inventa Dysarii contrariis repellendo, in integrum restituas exauctoratum conviviorum leporem.'

5. Ille diu hoc a se officium deprecatus ubi tot impellentium procerum, quibus obviandum non erat, hortatui succubuit, 'bellum,' inquit, 'duobus mihi amicissimis cogor indicere, Dysario et continentiae, sed ab auctoritate vestra tamquam ab edicto praetoris impetrata venia gulae patronum, quia necesse est, profitebor.

6. 'In primo speciosis magis quam veris, ut docebitur, exemplis paene nos Dysarii nostri cepit ingenium. ait enim pecudes simplici uti cibo et ideo expugnari difficilius earum quam hominum sanitatem. sed utrumque falsum probabo. 7. nam neque simplex est animalibus mutis alimonia nec ab illis quam a nobis morbi remotiores. testatur unum varietas pratorum quae depascuntur, quibus herbae sunt amarae pariter et dulces, aliae sucum calidum, aliae frigidum nutrientes, ut nulla culina possit tam diversa condire quam in herbis natura variavit. 8. notus est omnibus Eupo-

---

36 Cf. the behavior of the "malicious" described at 7.2.8.

37 Strictly, a "palinode" = a "recantation," though Praetextatus' next remark shows that he means "refutation."

38 At the start of his year in office the urban praetor, who oversaw the city's legal system, issued a statement of the principles that would guide his administration during his term (*edictum perpetuum*). The edict gave the praetor the opportunity both to

wits, out of mere envy for star turns.[36] 4. Nor do I deny that I too could, as it were, have sung a palinode:[37] it's one of the preliminary exercises in the schools of rhetoric to treat general topics by arguing both sides in alternation. But since an account by other Greeks will perhaps more readily respond to the discoveries of Greeks, we all ask you, Eustathius, to refute Dysarius' positions with contrary arguments and thereby reinstate the gaiety of our banquet that was dishonorably dismissed.'

5. Eustathius tried for quite some time to beg off but then gave in to the urging of so many distinguished men, whose insistence was irresistible. 'I am forced to declare war,' he said, 'on two things very dear to me, Dysarius and austerity, but relying on your authority, as though given a waiver by the praetor's edict,[38] I shall present myself as appetite's advocate, since I have no choice.

6. 'First of all, the cleverness of our friend Dysarius took us in with examples—as I shall show—more superficially attractive than valid: for he said that farm animals enjoy a plain diet, and that their health is therefore more resistant to attack than ours. I shall prove that both these propositions are false. 7. For neither is the diet of mute animals plain nor are diseases more foreign to them than to us.[39] As evidence of the first point, consider the variety of the meadows on which they graze: they have sweet and bitter grass alike, some provide warm juice in the forage, some cool—no kitchen could be as varied in its seasonings as nature is in its grasses. 8. Everyone knows of Eupolis,

acknowledge the continued application of old rules and principles and to assert new ones; Eustathius alludes to that authority here.

[39] §§7–32 are based on Plut. *Mor.* 662D–663F.

lis, inter elegantes habendus veteris comoediae poetas. is
in fabula quae inscribitur *Aeges* inducit capras de cibi sui
copia in haec se verba iactantes:

9. βοσκόμεθ' ὕλης ἀπὸ παντοδαπῆς, ἐλάτης,
   πρίνου κομάρου τε
πτόρθους ἁπαλοὺς ἀποτρώγουσαι, καὶ πρὸς
   τούτοισί γε θαλλόν,[15]
κύτισόν τ' ἠδὲ σφάκον εὐώδη, καὶ σμίλακα τὴν
   πολύφυλλον,
κότινον, σχῖνον, μελίαν, λεύκην, ἁλίαν[16] δρῦν,
   κιττόν, ἐρείκην,
πρόμαλον, ῥάμνον, φλόμον, ἀνθέρικον, κισθόν,
   φηγόν, θύμα, θύμβραν.

videturne vobis ciborum ista simplicitas, ubi tot enume-
rantur vel arbusta vel frutices non minus suco diversa
quam nomine? 10. quod autem non facilius morbis homines quam pecudes occupentur, Homero teste contentus
sum qui pestilentiam refert a pecudibus inchoatam, quando morbus, antequam in homines posset inrepere, facilius
captis pecoribus incubuit. 11. sed et quanta sit mutis[17] animalibus infirmitas vitae brevitas indicio est. quod enim eorum quibus notitia nobis in usu est potest annos hominis
aequare nisi recurras forte ad ea, quae de corvis atque cor-
nicibus fabulosa dicuntur? quos tamen videmus omnibus
inhiare cadaveribus universisque seminibus insidiari, fruc-

---

[15] τούτοισί γε θαλλόν *Meineke* (ΤΟΥΤΟΙϹΙΝΕΤΑΛΛΟΗΝ
PF, ΤΟΥΓΟΙϹ- Q), τουτοισιν ἔτ' ἄλλα *Xylander, alii alia*
[16] ἁλίαν] ἀρίαν *Lobeck*   [17] mutis C²J²: multis ω

190

who must be counted among the refined authors of Old Comedy: in his play titled *Goats*, he introduces she-goats who boast of the abundance of their provender in these terms (fr. 14 *PCG* 5:308):

> 9. We graze on every sort of growth, silver fir, holm
>   oak, and arbutus,
> nibbling away at tender shoots, and a green bough to
>   boot,
> tree-medick and fragrant sage-apple, leafy yew too,
> wild olive, mastich, manna ash, white poplar, barren
>   oak, ivy, heath,
> willow, box-thorn, mullein, asphodel, rock-rose,
>   Valonia oak, thyme, savory.

Does that look like a plain diet to you, when so many trees and shrubs are listed, as different in their juices as in their names? 10. As for the fact that humans are no more readily attacked by diseases than animals, I'm content to have Homer as my witness, who tells of a plague that began with cattle (*Il.* 1.50), since the illness found the captive cattle readier targets, before it could spread to humans. 11. Furthermore, their brief life-span shows how infirm mute animals are: which of those with which we are familiar can equal a human span—unless perchance you have recourse to the legends that are told about ravens and crows?[40] Yet we see them eager for dead bodies of all sorts and on the

---

[40] On their proverbial longevity cf. Otto 93.

tus arborum persequi. nam non minus edacitatis habent quam de longaevitate eorum opinio fabulatur.

12. 'Secundum si bene recordor exemplum est solere medicos aegris simplicem cibum offerre, non varium; cum hunc offeratis, ut opinor, non quasi digestu faciliorem, sed quasi minus adpetendum, ut horrore uniformis alimoniae edendi desiderium languesceret, quasi multis concoquendis per infirmitatem non sufficiente natura. ideo si quis aegrescentium vel de ipso simplici amplius adpetat, subducitis adhuc desideranti. ideo vobis commento tali non qualitas sed modus quaeritur. 13. quod autem in edendo sicut in potando suades varia vitari, habet latentis captionis insidias, quia nomine similitudinis coloratur. ceterum longe alia potus, alia ciborum ratio est. quis enim umquam edendo plurimum mente sauciatus est, quod in bibendo contingit? 14. fartus cibo stomachum vel ventrem gravatur, infusus vino fit similis insano, opinor quia crassitudo cibi uno in loco permanens expectat administrationem digestionis, et tunc demum membris sensim confectus illabitur; potus ut natura levior mox altum petit et cerebrum, quod in vertice locatum est, ferit fumi calentis aspergine. 15. et ideo varia vina vitantur ne res, quae ad possidendum caput repentina est, calore tam diverso quam subito consilii sedem sauciet. quod aeque in cibi varietate metuendum nulla similitudo, ratio nulla persuadet.

---

41 M. has, somewhat confusingly, reverted from the topic of longevity to the original point about animals' varied diets.

42 Cf. 7.4.6.

lookout for every kind of seed and eagerly going after fruit on trees: their appetites match the longevity that fable attributes to them.[41]

12. 'Dysarius' second example, if I recall correctly,[42] was that physicians usually give sick people a plain diet, not a varied one: though you people do this, I think, not because it's easier to digest but to restrain appetite, so that the repugnance of the monotonous diet might depress the desire to eat, the thought being that the person's nature is not up to digesting a lot of food because it's enfeebled. That's why when a sick person tries to get more even of the simple food, you take it away while he still wants it: thus it is not the kind but the limited amount that motivates the practice. 13. As for the point you press, to the effect that mixing is avoided in eating as it is in drinking, it involves a trap set by a lurking verbal quibble, since it's made colorable by the use of the same word—"mixing"—in different senses. But the way drink works is very different from the way food works: who ever experienced from overeating the severe impairment of mental capacity that befalls us from drinking? 14. Someone who's stuffed with food feels a burden on his stomach or belly, while someone soaked in wine is like a madman. I think this is because food's density causes it to stay in one place and await the ministrations of digestion, so that only after it's been processed does it seep insensibly into the limbs. Drink, being naturally lighter, soon rises high in the body and strikes the brain, which is located at the highest point, with a scattering of hot fumes. 15. That is why we avoid mixing wines: otherwise something capable of suddenly seizing the brain strikes the seat of reason with a heat that's as varied as it is sudden. No comparison, no explanation makes it plausible that the same danger should be feared from a varied diet.

16. 'In illa vero disputatione, qua digestionum ordinem
sermone luculento et vario digessisti, illa omnia quae de
natura humani corporis dicta sunt et nil nocent propositae
quaestioni, et eloquenter dicta non abnego. illi soli non ad-
sentior quod sucos varios de ciborum varietate confectos
dicis contrarios esse corporibus, cum corpora ipsa de contrariis qualitatibus fabricata sint. 17. ex calido enim et
frigido, de sicco et umido constamus. cibus vero simplex
sucum de se unius qualitatis emittit. scimus autem similibus similia nutriri. dic quaeso unde tres aliae qualitates
corporis nutriantur. 18. singula autem ad se similitudinem
sui rapere testis Empedocles, qui ait,

ὡς γλυκὺ μὲν γλυκὺ μάρπτε, πικρὸν δ' ἐπὶ
    πικρὸν ὄρουσεν,
ὀξὺ δ' ἐπ' ὀξὺ ἔβη, θερμὸν δ' ἐποχεύετο θερμῷ.[18]

19. te autem saepe audio Hippocratis tui verba cum admi-
ratione referentem: εἰ ἓν ἦν ὁ ἄνθρωπος, οὐδέποτ' ἂν
ἤλγεεν·[19] ἀλγεῖ δέ, οὐκ ἄρα ἓν ἐστί.[20] ergo si homo non
unum, nutriendus est non ex uno. 20. nam et deus omnium
fabricator aërem quo circumfundimur et cuius spiramus
haustu non simplicem habere voluit qualitatem, ut aut fri-

18 θερμὸν δ' ἐποχεύετο θερμῷ] δαερὸν δ' ἐποχεῖτο δαηρῷ
Diels, δαλερὸν δαλεροῦ λαβετως Plut.
19 ἤλγεεν] ἤλγει codd. Hippocr.
20 ἀλγεῖ ... ἐστί in codd. Hippocr. desunt

43 The doctrine that everything in the sensible world is a blend
of four elemental qualities (hot, cold, dry, wet) characterizing
four "roots" or "elements" (earth, air, fire, water) goes back to

16. 'Now, in the brilliant and wide-ranging discussion in which you set out the sequence of digestion's processes, all that you said about the nature of the human body does nothing to detract from the position I intend to argue, and that it was all said eloquently I do not deny. I withhold assent only from the statement that the varied juices produced when different sorts of food are processed are inimical to our bodies, and I do so because our bodies themselves are constructed of different sorts of properties. 17. We are a compound of hot and cold, dry and moist,[43] while a plain diet produces from itself juice with one property only. Yet we know that like is nourished by like: please explain, then, where the body's other three properties derive their nourishment. 18. As for the principle that individual elements attract their like, Empedocles is a witness, when he says (fr. 90 D.–K.),

> Thus sweet fastened on sweet, bitter sought after
> bitter,
> tart lighted upon tart, warm coupled with warm.

19. Moreover, I often hear you repeating the words of your Hippocrates with warm approval (*On Human Nature* 2), "If the human being were a single thing, he would never feel pain; but he does feel pain and therefore is not a single thing." It follows that if the human being is not a single thing, his nourishment should not be a single thing. 20. God, too, the creator of all things, did not want the air that surrounds us and that we draw in with our breathing to have a single property—always cold or always hot—nor

---

Empedocles of Acragas (b. ca. 492; cf. §18); accepted by Aristotle, it became the dominant view in antiquity.

gidus sit semper aut caleat, sed nec continuae siccitati nec perpetuo eum addixit umori, quia una nos non poterat qualitate nutrire de permixtis quattuor fabricatos. ver ergo calidum fecit et umectum, sicca est aestas et calida, autumnus siccus et frigidus, hiems umida pariter et frigida est. 21. sic et elementa, quae sunt nostra principia, ex diversitatibus et ipsa constant et nos nutriunt. est enim ignis calidus et siccus, aër umectus et calidus, aqua similiter umecta sed frigida, terra frigida pariter et sicca. cur ergo nos ad uniformem cibum redigis cum nihil nec in nobis nec circa nos nec in his de quibus sumus uniforme sit? 22. quod autem acescere vel non numquam fumare in stomacho cibum vis adsignare varietati, ut credamus, pronunties oportet aut semper eum qui vario cibo utitur haec pati aut numquam illum pati qui simplicem sumit. si vero et qui mensa fruitur copiosa hoc vitium saepe non sentit, et qui se uno cibo adficit saepe sustinet quod accusas, cur hoc varietati et non modo edacitatis[21] adsignas? nam et de simplici avidus noxam patitur cruditatis, et in vario moderatus digestionis commodo fruitur.

23. '"At," inquies, "ipsa immoderatio ex ciborum varietate nascitur titillante gula et adsumenda plura quam necesse est provocante." 24. rursus ad ea quae iam dixi revolvor, cruditates de modo, non de qualitate provenire. modum vero servat qui sui potens est et in mensa Sicula vel

---

21 edacitatis *scripsi*: -ti ω

---

44 Cf. *Comm.* 1.6.60.   45 Cf. *Comm.* 1.6.27.

46 "Asia" [= Asia minor] was proverbially a place of luxury, and "the varied delicacies of Sicily" were a byword already for Plato (*Rep.* 404D, cf. Hor. *Odes* 3.1.17–19, Otto 321).

did he determine that it would be continually dry or always damp, since a single property could not support us, who are compounded of four mingled properties. So he made the spring warm and damp, while the summer dry and hot, the autumn dry and cold, the winter both damp and cold.[44] 21. So too the elements that are our basic constituents themselves consist of different qualities and sustain us thereby: fire is hot and dry, air is hot and damp, water is likewise damp but cold, earth is both cold and dry.[45] Why, then, do you restrict us to a simple diet when nothing around us or in us or in the things of which we're composed is simple? 22. As for your attempt to attribute to a varied diet the fact that food in the stomach turns acidic or sometimes gives off fumes, you have to claim either that a person who enjoys a varied diet always suffers these symptoms or that a person who has a plain diet never suffers them. But if someone who enjoys an abundant meal often escapes this problem and someone who treats himself with a plain diet often does suffer the condition you censure, why do you attribute this to the variety of food and not the proper limit placed on consumption? For a greedy consumer of plain food suffers the ill of indigestion, and a moderate partaker of varied food enjoys the benefit of good digestion.

23. "'But," you'll say, "loss of self-control itself arises from taking a range of different foods, as the appetite is stimulated and urges consumption of more than is necessary." 24. I return again to my earlier statement: indigestion results from the amount, not the character, of the food. Someone with self-control observes a proper limit even at a meal of Sicilian or Asian proportions,[46] while a

Asiana, excedit impotens[22] et si solis olivis aut olere vesca-
tur. et tam ille copiosus si moderationem tenuit sanitatis
compos est, quam insanus fit ille cui merus sal cibus est, si
hoc ipsum voraciter invaserit. 25. postremo si in his quae
sumimus varietatem noxiam putas, cur potionum remedia
quae per os humanis visceribus infunditis ex tam contrariis
ac sibi repugnantibus mixta componitis? 26. suco papaveris admiscetis euphorbium, mandragoram aliasque herbas
conclamati frigoris pipere temperatis, sed nec monstrosis
carnibus abstinetis, inserentes poculis testiculos castorum
et venenata corpora viperarum, quibus admiscetis quicquid nutrit India, quicquid devehitur herbarum quibus
Creta generosa est. 27. cum ergo ad custodiam vitae hoc
faciant remedia quod cibus, si quidem illa eam revocent,
iste contineat, cur illis providere varietatem laboras, istum
squalori uniformitatis addicis?

28. 'Post omnia in voluptatem censura cothurnati sermonis invectus es, tamquam voluptas virtuti semper inimica sit et non cum in luxum spreta mediocritate prolapsa
est. quid enim agit ipse serius non edendo nisi cogente
fame nec potando praeter sitim nisi ut de utroque ca-
piat voluptatem? ergo voluptas non mox nomine ipso in-
famis est, sed fit modo utendi vel honesta vel arguenda.

---

[22] impotens *Willis*: impatiens ω

---

[47] Beavers were thought to castrate themselves to escape cap-
ture, aware how eagerly their inguinal glands (*castorea*) were
sought for medicinal purposes (Phaedr. *Fables* 30.1–9, Pliny *Natural History* 32.26, Juvenal 12.36–38, Serv. on *G.* 1.58); for a pre-
scription of wide-ranging efficacy combining *castoreum*, poppy,
and mandrake see Cels. *On Medicine* 5.25.3.

person without self-control exceeds that limit even if he's dining on olives or greens. And just as the one who enjoys an abundantly varied meal holds onto his good health if he has observed a proper limit, so a man who eats mere salt become unhealthy, should he fall upon it greedily. 25. Finally, if you think variety in the things we consume is harmful, why do you compound from such contrary and conflicting ingredients the potable medicines that you administer by mouth, for people to dose their innards? 26. You mix euphorbium with poppy juice and balance mandrake and other herbs of a disastrously cold nature with pepper, and you even use horrendous kinds of animal tissue, putting beavers' testicles[47] and poisonous snake's flesh in your potions and mingling with them all the produce of India, all the imported herbs in which Crete is so fertile. 27. Since when it comes to life's safe-keeping, then, medicine does in restoring it what food does in maintaining it, why do you take the trouble to make sure that medicines are complex while you condemn food to a dismal uniformity?

28. 'To top it all off, you launched an attack on pleasure in a censorious aria, as though pleasure is always virtue's enemy and not just when it rejects moderation and lapses into luxury. For that matter, what does your Mr. Sobersides do, in not eating beyond the demands of hunger and in drinking only when thirsty, but take pleasure from both? Pleasure, then, is not instantly disreputable just because of its very name, it becomes something to respect or condemn according to the limit placed on its enjoyment.

29. parum est si excusata sit et non etiam laudetur voluptas. nam cibus qui cum voluptate sumitur, desiderio tractus in ventrem reconditur patula expectatione rapientem:
et dum animose fruitur, mox eum concoquit, quod non
ex aequo cibis evenit quos nulla sui dulcedo commendat.
quid ergo accusas varietatem quasi gulae irritamentum
cum salus sit hominis vigere adpetentiam, qua deficiente
languescit et periculo fit propior? 30. nam sicut in mari gu-
bernatores vento suo etiam si nimius sit, contrahendo in
minorem modum vela praetervolant et flatum cum est
maior coercent, sopitum vero excitare non possunt, ita et
adpetentia cum titillatur et crescit, rationis gubernaculo
temperatur, si semel ceciderit, animal extinguitur.[23] 31. si
ergo cibo vivimus et cibum appetentia sola commendat,
elaborandum nobis est commento varietatis ut haec semper provocetur, cum praesto sit ratio qua intra moderatio-
nis suae terminos temperetur. 32. memineritis tamen lepi-
do me convivio adesse, non anxio; nec sic admitto
varietatem ut luxum probem, ubi quaeruntur aestivae ni-
ves et hibernae rosae et, dum magis ostentui quam usui
servitur, silvarum secretum omne lustratur et peregrina
maria sollicitantur. ita enim fit ut etiam si sanitatem su-
mentium mediocritas observata non sauciet, ipse tamen
luxus morum sit aegritudo.'

33. His favorabiliter exceptis Dysarius: 'obsecutus es,'
inquit, 'Eustathi, dialecticae, ego medicinae. qui volet eli-

---

[23] extinguitur S: -guit ω

---

[48] The Romans' sole source of cooling for drinks, and a favor-
ite target of moralists as a luxury item.
[49] I.e., Eustathius' arguments were exercises in logic, unsup-
ported by medical knowledge.

29. But it's not enough just to offer an excuse for pleasure: it should be praised, too. For food that's consumed with pleasure is drawn down eagerly and put away in a belly that receives it readily in open anticipation; and while the belly enjoys it energetically, it digests it promptly, which does not happen in the same way to foods that have no allure of their own to commend them. Why, then, do you accuse a varied diet of stimulating appetite when a vigorous appetite is healthy for a human being, who languishes when it fails and is imperiled? 30. Pilots fly ahead with a following wind even if it's too strong, and they check its force when it grows too great, but they cannot raise it when it falls. Just so, reason, our pilot, tempers appetite when it is stimulated and grows, but once it has fallen off, the living creature is snuffed out. 31. If, then, our life is sustained by food and only appetite makes us receptive of it, we must take pains always to stimulate our appetite by devising a varied diet, since reason is on hand to keep it balanced and poised within moderation's proper limits. 32. Still, bear in mind that I'm a guest at a pleasant banquet, not one that's finicky, nor do I grant such free rein to variety as to approve luxury, which looks for snow[48] in summer and roses in winter and which, in the interest of display more than utility, scours every hidden place in the woods and troubles foreign seas. Thus, even though the proper mean, when it's observed, does not harm diners' health, luxury itself is still a moral sickness.'

33. When these remarks had been well received, Dysarius said, 'You've followed the precepts of dialectic, Eustathius, I of medicine:[49] the person who wants to

gere sequenda usum consulat, et quid sit utilius sanitati experientia docebit.'

6   Post haec Flavianus: 'et alios quidem medicos idem dicentes semper audivi, vinum inter calida censendum; sed et nunc Eustathius cum causas ebrietatis attingeret, praedicabat vini calorem. mihi autem saepe hoc mecum reputanti visa est vini natura frigori propior quam calori, et in medium profero quibus ad hoc aestimandum trahor, ut vestrum sit de mea aestimatione iudicium. 2. vinum, quantum mea fert opinio, sicut natura frigidum est, ita capax vel etiam appetens fit caloris, cum calidis fuerit admotum. nam et ferrum cum tactu sit frigidum—

ψυχρὸν δ' ἔλε χαλκὸν ὀδοῦσιν—

si tamen solem pertulerit, concalescit et calor advena nativum frigus expellit. hoc utrum ita esse ratio persuadeat requiramus. 3. vinum aut potu interioribus conciliatur, aut fotu, ut superficiem curet, adhibetur. cum infunditur cuti, quin frigidum sit nec medici infitias eunt, calidum tamen in interioribus praedicant, cum non tale descendat sed admixtum calidis concalescat. 4. certe respondeant volo cur stomacho in lassitudinem degeneranti ad instaurandas constrictione vires offerant aegrescenti vinum, nisi frigore suo lassata cogeret et colligeret dissoluta? et cum lasso, ut

---

[50] §§1–13 are based on Plut. *Mor.* 651F–653A.

choose a course to follow should give thought to what's proved useful, and experience will show what is more useful to health.'

Flavianus then said, 'I've always heard other doctors 6 too making this same point, that wine should be counted among the things that are naturally warm; and just now Eustathius, too, in touching on the causes of drunkenness, mentioned wine's warmth. But when I've pondered the question, as I often have, I've formed the impression that wine is by nature more nearly cool than warm: I'll put before you the reasons that lead me to this assessment, so that you can pass judgment on it.[50] 2. As far as I can see, wine is on the one hand cool by nature but is on the other hand capable of taking on warmth, or even seeks it out when it has been brought near sources of heat. For though metal too is cold to the touch (*Il.* 5.75)—

he gripped the cold bronze with his teeth—

it nonetheless grows warm when it's received the sunlight, and the warmth, though a new arrival, drives out the native chill. Let's ask, then, whether reason urges that the same is true of wine. 3. Wine is either introduced to the body's inner regions by drinking or is applied as a poultice to treat the body's surface. Not even physicians are going to deny that it is cool when it is poured on the skin, yet they assert that it is warm inside the body—though it is not warm as it goes down but becomes warm when it mingles with sources of heat. 4. I would certainly like them to explain why they give wine to a sick person whose gut has become inactive, to restore its powers with wine's astringent effect, if wine's cool nature does not gather and bind up what has become weak and loose. And since, as I said, they apply

203

dixi, stomacho nihil adhibeant calidum, ne crescat ulterius lassitudo, a vini potu non prohibent, defectum in robur hac curatione mutantes.

5. 'Dabo aliud indicium accidentis vino quam ingeniti caloris. nam si quis aconitum nesciens hauserit, non nego haustu eum meri plurimi solere curari. infusum enim visceribus trahit ad se calorem et veneno frigido quasi calidum iam repugnat. si vero aconitum ipsum cum vino tritum potui datum sit, haurientem nulla curatio a morte defendit. 6. tunc enim vinum natura frigidum admixtione sui frigus auxit veneni nec in interioribus iam calescit, quia non liberum sed admixtum alii, immo in aliud versum, descendit in viscera. 7. sed et sudore nimio vel laxato ventre defessis vinum ingerunt, ut in utroque morbo constringat meatus. insomnem medici frigidis oblinunt, modo papaveris suco, modo mandragora vel similibus, in quibus est et vinum; nam vino somnus reduci solet, quod non nisi ingeniti frigoris testimonium est. 8. deinde omnia calida Venerem provocant et semen excitant et generationi favent, hausto autem mero plurimo fiunt viri ad coitum pigriores, sed nec idoneum conceptioni serunt,[24] quia vini nimietas ut frigidi facit semen exile vel debile. 9. hoc vero vel manifestissimam aestimationis meae habet adsertionem, quod quaecumque nimium algentibus, eadem contingunt

[24] conceptioni serunt *ed. Paris. 1585* (conceptionis erunt α): conceptioni ferunt β₂

---

[51] M. mistranslates Plutarch's "hemlock" (κώνειον = Lat. *cicuta*) as "aconite" (*aconitum*); on wine as an antidote to hemlock, cf. Pliny *Natural History* 25.152.

[52] Cf. Cels. *On Medicine* 3.18.12, 5.25.2.

nothing warm to an inactive stomach, lest it become still more inactive, they don't forbid the drinking of wine, turning weakness into strength by this application.

5. 'I'll give a piece of evidence that warmth is a contingent, not an essential, trait of wine. If someone unknowingly drinks aconite,[51] I acknowledge that he is usually cured by drinking wine unmixed with water: that's because when the wine has been instilled in the internal organs, it takes on their warmth and, once rendered warm itself, counteracts the cold poison. But if aconite is administered by being dissolved in wine and drunk, no remedy can save the drinker from death. 6. For in that case wine, being cool by nature, increases the poison's chill by being mixed with it, since it doesn't reach the internal organs in an independent state but mixed with the other, or rather turned into that other. 7. But they even force wine on people worn out from excessive sweating or loose bowels, so that in both cases it might bind up the passageways. When someone cannot sleep, physicians treat him with cool substances, now poppy juice, now mandrake or the like, including wine:[52] wine usually restores sleep, which can only be evidence of its innate coolness. 8. Furthermore, all naturally warm substances stir sexual desire, stimulate production of seed, and promote procreation, yet when they've drunk a very great deal of unmixed wine men become less eager for intercourse and also do not sow seed suitable for conception, for the excess wine, being a cool substance, makes the seed thin and weak. 9. But here's the thing that offers most obvious confirmation of my assessment: all the things that happen to people who are too cool also happen to peo-

ebriis. fiunt enim tremuli, graves, pallidi, et saltu tumultuantis spiritus artus suos et membra quatiuntur. idem corporis torpor ambobus, eadem linguae titubatio. multis autem et morbus ille quem παράλυσιν Graeci vocant sic nimio vino, ut multo algore, contingit. 10. respicite etiam quae genera curationis adhibeantur ebriis. nonne cubare sub multis operimentis iubentur ut exstinctus calor refoveatur? non et ad calida lavacra ducuntur? non illis unctionum tepore calor corporis excitatur? 11. postremo qui fiunt crebro ebrii ‹alii›[25] cito senescunt, alii ante tempus competentis aetatis vel calvitio vel canitie insigniuntur, quae non nisi inopia caloris eveniunt. 12. quid aceto frigidius, quod culpatum vinum est? solum enim hoc ex omnibus umoribus crescentem flammam violenter extinguit, dum per frigus suum calorem vincit elementi. 13. nec hoc praetereo, quod ex fructibus arborum illi sunt frigidiores, quorum sucus imitatur vini saporem, ut mala seu simplicia seu granata vel cydonia, quae cotonea vocat Cato.

14. 'Haec ideo dixerim, quod me saepe movit et exercuit mecum disputantem, quia in medium proferre volui, quid[26] de vino aestimaverim sentiendum. ceterum consultationem mihi debitam non omitto. te enim, Dysari, convenio ut quod quaerendum mihi occurrit absolvas. 15. legisse apud philosophum Graecum memini—ni fallor, ille Aristoteles fuit in libro quem de ebrietate composuit—

---

[25] alii *add. Willis* (*sed post* senescunt)
[26] quid *ed. Ven. 1472*: quod ω

---

[53] Called *contonium* at 3.19.2; both forms are attested.
[54] §§14–21 are based on Plut. *Mor.* 650A–F.

ple who are drunk. They shake, they become sluggish and pale, and their joints and limbs are wracked with their uneven breathing. Both experience physical sluggishness and uncertain speech. Many, furthermore, even lapse into the disease the Greeks call *paralysis*, from too much wine as from a deep chill. 10. Consider, too, the kinds of cures used for drunks. Aren't they told to sleep under numerous blankets, so that the warmth that's been extinguished can be rekindled? Aren't they also given warm baths? Aren't warm ointments used to excite their bodies' warmth? 11. Finally, some people who get drunk frequently become old before their time, while others become prematurely bald or gray, which happens only out of a deficit of warmth. 12. What has a cooler nature than vinegar, which is wine that's gone off? Of all liquids vinegar alone forcefully extinguishes a growing fire, as its own chill overcomes that element's heat. 13. There's also this: among the fruits that trees produce, those are by nature cooler whose juice imitates the flavor of wine, for example apples or pomegranates or quinces, which Cato calls *cotonea* (*Agr.* 7.3).[53]

14. 'I've made these remarks because I wanted to put before you the view of wine I think should be adopted, something that has much exercised me in my musings.[54] I'm not giving up the chance I have coming to put a question;[55] but I turn to you, Dysarius, to answer one that it occurs to me should be asked. 15. I recall reading in a Greek philosopher—the great Aristotle, if I'm not mistaken, in

[55] A reference to the agreement to take turns questioning Dysarius, established at 7.4.1–2.

mulieres raro in ebrietatem cadere, crebro senes; nec causam vel huius frequentiae vel illius raritatis adiecit. et quia ad naturam corporum tota haec quaestio pertinet, quam nosse et industriae tuae et professionis officium est, volo te causas rei quam ille sententiae loco dixit, si tamen philosopho adsentiris, aperire.'

16. Tum ille: 'recte et hoc Aristoteles ut cetera, nec possum non adsentiri viro cuius inventis nec ipsa natura dissentit. mulieres, inquit, raro ebriantur, crebro senes. rationis plena gemina ista sententia, et altera pendet ex altera. nam cum didicerimus quid mulieres ab ebrietate defendat, iam tenemus quid senes ad hoc frequenter impellat. contrariam enim sortita naturam sunt muliebre corpus et corpus senile. 17. mulier umectissimo est corpore. docet hoc et levitas cutis et splendor, docent praecipue adsiduae purgationes superfluo exonerantes corpus umore. cum ergo epotum vinum in tam largum ceciderit umorem, vim suam perdit et fit dilutius nec facile cerebri sedem ferit fortitudine eius extincta. 18. sed et haec ratio iuvat sententiae veritatem, quod muliebre corpus crebris purgationibus deputatum pluribus consertum est foraminibus, ut pateat in meatus et vias praebeat umori in egestionis exitum confluenti, per haec foramina vapor vini celeriter evanescit. 19. contra senibus siccum corpus est, quod probat

---

56 I.e., Aristotle's *Symposium* (fr. 99–110 Rose): M. draws the title *On Drunkenness* from Plutarch.

57 I.e., menstruation, as is made clear at 7.7.4.

58 The supposedly spongier quality of women's flesh was used to explain a number of traits: cf. Dean-Jones 1994, 55–57.

the book that he wrote on drunkenness[56]—that women become inebriated rarely, old men frequently, but he didn't include the reason either for the latter frequency or the former rarity. Since this whole question is relevant to our physical nature, which you ought to know, given both your diligence and your profession, please reveal the reason for the facts that he stated in rather gnomic form—if, at any rate, you agree with the philosopher's statement.'

16. Dysarius replied, 'Aristotle was right about this as about all else, nor could I fail to agree with a man whose discoveries nature herself finds agreeable. Women (he said) become drunk rarely, old men frequently. That two-part formulation is entirely reasonable, and each part depends on the other: when we've learned what protects women from drunkenness, we'll at the same time grasp what frequently drives old men to it—for the female body and the body of an aged male are allotted natures that are exact opposites. 17. A woman has the most moist sort of body: this is shown by their smooth and radiant skin and above all by their constant purgings,[57] which relieve the body of water. When, therefore, the wine they've drunk spills into such a large collection of moisture, it loses its force, becomes diluted, and cannot readily impinge on the brain's settled state when its strength has been snuffed out. 18. Further support for the truth of Aristotle's statement comes from the fact that the female body, which has to perform frequent purgings, has been constructed with a rather large number of cavities that open out into channels and provide the passageways for the moisture that gathers to be discharged:[58] wine's fumes quickly dissipate through these cavities. 19. By contrast, an old man's body is dry, as the roughness and dullness of his skin show. That's also

asperitas et squalor cutis. unde et haec aetas ad flexum fit
difficilior, quod est indicium siccitatis. intra hos vinum nec
patitur contrarietatem repugnantis umoris et integra vi
sua adhaeret corpori arido, et mox loca tenet quae sapere
homini ministrant. 20. dura quoque esse senum corpora
nulla dubitatio est, et ideo ipsi etiam naturales meatus in
membris durioribus obserantur, et hausto vino exhalatio
nulla contingit, sed totum ad ipsam sedem mentis ascendit. 21. hinc fit ut et sani senes malis ebriorum laborent,
tremore membrorum, linguae titubantia, abundantia loquendi, iracundiae concitatione, quibus tam subiacent iu-
venes ebrii quam senes sobrii. si ergo levem pertulerint
impulsum vini, non accipiunt haec mala sed incitant, quibus aetatis ratione iam capti sunt.'

7   Probata omnibus Dysarii disputatione subiecit Symmachus: 'ut spectata est tota ratio quam de muliebris ebrietatis raritate Dysarius invenit, ita unum ab eo praetermissum
est, nimio frigore quod in earum corpore est frigescere
haustum vinum et ita debilitari ut vis eius quae elanguit
nullum possit calorem, de quo nascitur ebrietas, excitare.'
2. Ad haec Horus: 'tu vero, Symmache, frustra opinaris fri-
gidam mulierum esse naturam, quam ego calidiorem virili,
si tibi volenti erit, facile probabo. 3. umor naturalis in corpore, quando aetas transit pueritiam, fit durior et acuitur
in pilos. ideo tunc et pubes et genae et aliae partes corporis
vestiuntur. sed in muliebri corpore hunc umorem calore
siccante fit inopia pilorum, et ideo in corpore sexus huius
manet continuus splendor et levitas. 4. est et hoc in illis in-

---

59 §§1–12 are based on Plut. *Mor.* 650F–651F.

why people at this stage in life are less flexible, which is evidence of dryness. In old men wine does not encounter a contrary moisture to oppose it, so it fastens onto the dry body with its strength intact and quickly occupies the places that provide a person with good sense. 20. There's also no doubt that old men's bodies are hard, so that the natural passageways become occluded in their harder limbs, and the wine they've drunk has no chance to dissipate but instead rises undiminished to the seat of the mind. 21. That's why even healthy old men suffer from the same ills as drunks: their limbs shake, their tongues are unsteady, they talk a lot and are prone to anger—conditions to which drunk young men are as subject as sober old men. Once they've borne wine's onslaught in even a slight form, these woes, by which they're already beset because of their age, are not merely experienced, they're exacerbated.'

When all had expressed approval of Dysarius' account, 7 Symmachus added, 'The whole account that Dysarius devised to explain the rarity with which women become drunk is tested and true, yet there is one point that was left out: the wine that is drunk is chilled by their bodies' extreme coolness and is so weakened that its force become feeble and cannot arouse the heat from which drunkenness emerges.'[59] 2. In response, Horus said, 'Symmachus, you're wrong to think that women's nature is cool: if you're agreeable, I'll easily demonstrate that it's warmer than a man's. 3. The natural moisture in a body past childhood hardens and is sharpened into bristles: that's why at that age the pubic area, the cheeks, and other parts of the body take on a coating of hair. But in a woman's body the warmth dries this moisture and results in a dearth of hair, and that's why the female body remains smooth and radiant. 4. There

dicium caloris, abundantia sanguinis cuius natura fervor est, qui ne urat corpus, si insidat, crebra purgatione subtrahitur. quis ergo dicat frigidas, quas nemo potest negare plenas caloris quia sanguinis plenae sunt? 5. deinde licet urendi corpora defunctorum usus nostro saeculo nullus sit, lectio tamen docet eo tempore quo igni dari honor mortuis habebatur, si quando usu venisset ut plura corpora simul incenderentur, solitos fuisse funerum ministros denis virorum corporibus adicere singula muliebria, et unius adiutu quasi natura flammei et ideo celeriter ardentis cetera flagrabant. 6. ita nec veteribus calor mulierum habebatur incognitus. nec hoc tacebo quod, cum calor semper generationis causa sit, feminae ideo celerius[27] quam pueri fiunt idoneae ad generandum quia calent amplius. nam et secundum iura publica duodecimus annus in femina et quartus decimus in puero definit pubertatis aetatem. 7. quid plura? nonne videmus mulieres quando nimium frigus est, mediocri veste contentas, nec ita operimentis plurimis involutas ut viri solent, scilicet naturali calore contra frigus quod aër ingerit repugnante?'

8. Ad haec renidens Symmachus, 'bene,' inquit, 'Horus noster temptat videri orator ex Cynico, qui in contrarium vertit sensus quibus potest muliebris corporis frigus probari. nam quod pilis ut viri non obsidentur, inopia caloris est. calor est enim qui pilos creat, unde et eunuchis desunt,

27 celerius J[2]S: celeriter ω (om. P)

---

60 Inhumation, long the norm in the Greek-speaking east, replaced cremation in the Latin-speaking west by the 3rd century CE.   61 Cf. *Digest* 28.1.5 (Ulpian).

62 With §8 cf. [Alex. Aphrod.] *Prob*. 1.6, *Suppl. Prob*. 2.4.

is in their bodies also this further indication of warmth: the abundance of blood, which is by nature hot and is drawn off by frequent purgings, lest it burn the body were it to become settled. Who, then, would maintain that they're cool, when no one can deny that they're warm because they're full of blood? 5. Furthermore, though we no longer follow the practice of burning the dead,[60] we learn from our reading that in the period when cremation was considered a way of honoring the dead, if it ever turned out that a number of corpses were to be burned at the same time, the funeral attendants usually added one female corpse for every ten male corpses: with the addition of this one corpse—fiery by nature, as it were, and therefore quick to burn—all the rest caught fire. 6. Thus the ancients too were aware of women's innate warmth. I'll add this point too: since heat is always the cause of procreation, women become suitable for that purpose more quickly than boys, because they are naturally warmer: according to public law, too, the twelfth year marks puberty in the case of a woman, the fourteenth in the case of a boy.[61] 7. No need to go on, I think: don't we observe that when it's very cold women can make do with a moderate amount of clothing and they're not wrapped in blankets as men usually are, because (of course) their innate warmth combats the chill that the air lets loose upon them?

8. Smiling in response, Symmachus said, 'Our friend Horus bids fair to appear an orator instead of a Cynic, turning on their heads the perceptions that could be taken to prove the innate coolness of women's bodies. In fact it's lack of warmth that causes them to be less hairy than men.[62] It's heat that produces hair, and that's why eunuchs also lack it, since no one would deny that their nature is

213

quorum naturam nullus negaverit frigidiorem viris, sed et in corpore humano illae partes maxime vestiuntur quibus amplius inest caloris. leve autem est mulierum corpus quasi naturali frigore densetum, comitatur enim algorem densitas, levitas densitatem. 9. quod vero saepe purgantur, non multi sed vitiosi umoris indicium est. indigestum est enim et crudum quod egeritur, et quasi infirmum effluit nec habet sedem, sed natura quasi noxium et magis frigidum pellitur. quod maxime probatur quia mulieribus cum purgantur etiam algere contingit, unde intellegitur frigidum esse quod effluit, et ideo in vivo corpore non manere quasi inopia caloris extinctum. 10. quod muliebre corpus iuvabat ardentes viros, non caloris erat sed pinguis carnis et oleo similioris, quod non illis contingeret ex calore. 11. quod cito admonentur generationis, non nimii caloris sed naturae infirmioris est, ut exilia poma celerius maturescunt, robusta serius. sed si vis intellegere in generatione veram rationem caloris, considera viros longe diutius perseverare in generando quam mulieres in pariendo, et hoc tibi sit indubitata probatio in utroque sexu vel frigoris vel caloris. nam vis eadem in frigidiore corpore celerius extinguitur, in calidiore diutius perseverat. 12. quod frigus aëris tolerabilius viris ferunt, facit hoc suum frigus, similibus enim similia gaudent. ideo ne corpus earum frigus horreat, facit consuetudo naturae quam sortitae sunt frigidiorem.

13. 'Sed de his singuli ut volent iudicent. ego vero ad

cooler than men's; also, those parts of the human body where there's more warmth are most coated by hair. But women's bodies are smooth because they're made dense by their innate coolness: density accompanies chilliness, and smoothness density. 9. Further, their frequent purgings are the sign not of a large quantity of moisture but of its poor quality. That which is expelled is raw and undigested: as a feeble thing, it flows out and has no settled resting place but is driven out as though naturally harmful and cooler. The clearest token of this is the fact that women tend also to become chilled when they're purging, and from that we can infer that the effluent is cool and so does not remain in the living body, inasmuch as it perishes from lack of warmth. 10. The fact that a woman's corpse helped men's corpses to burn was a function not of its warmth but of its rich and oily flesh, a condition male corpses lack because of their innate warmth. 11. The fact that women are quickly put in mind of procreation is a result of their weaker nature, not their excessive warmth, as scrawny fruits ripen first, the sturdier more slowly. If you want to grasp the real place of warmth in procreation, consider the fact that men continue to play that role far longer than women continue to bear children: let that be an absolutely certain demonstration of the coolness or warmth present in each sex, since the same power is more quickly extinguished in the cooler body and continues longer in the warmer. 12. As for the fact that they tolerate cold air more.than men, that's a product of their own cool nature: like takes pleasure in like, and the habituation of the cooler nature that is their lot causes their bodies not to dread the cold.

13. 'But let each person judge these matters as he

sortem venio consulendi, et quod scitu dignum aestimo, ab
eodem Dysario quaero et mihi usque ad affectum nimium
amico et cum in ceteris tum in his optime docto. 14. nuper
in Tusculano meo fui, cum vindemiales fructus pro annua
sollemnitate legerentur. erat videre permixtos rusticis ser-
vos haurire vel de expresso vel de sponte fluente mustum
nec tamen ebrietate capi. quod in illis praecipue admira-
bar, quos impelli ad insaniam parvo vino noveram. quaero
quae ratio de musto ebrietatem aut tardam fieri faciat aut
nullam?'

15. Ad haec Dysarius: 'omne quod dulce est cito satiat
nec diuturnam desiderii sui fidem tenet, sed in locum sa-
tietatis succedit horror. in musto autem sola dulcedo est,
suavitas nulla. nam vinum cum in infantia est, dulce; cum
pubescit, magis suave quam dulce est. 16. esse autem ha-
rum duarum rerum distantiam certe Homerus testis est,
qui ait,

$$\mu\acute{\epsilon}\lambda\iota\tau\iota \ \gamma\lambda\upsilon\kappa\epsilon\rho\hat{\omega} \ \kappa\alpha\grave{\iota} \ \mathring{\eta}\delta\acute{\epsilon}\ddot{\iota} \ o\ddot{\iota}\nu\omega.$$

vocavit enim mel dulce et vinum suave. mustum igitur
cum necdum suave est sed tantum modo dulce, horrore
quodam tantum sumi de se non patitur quantum sufficiat
ebrietati. 17. addo aliud, naturali ratione ebrietati dulcedinem repugnare, adeo ut medici eos qui usque ad pericu-
lum distenduntur vino plurimo cogant vomere, et post vo-
mitum contra fumum vini qui remansit in venis panem

---

63 §§14–20 are based on Plut. *Mor.* 655E–656B.

wishes: I come now to the place allotted to me for asking a question—something I think worth knowing, which I put to Dysarius again, someone I'm almost too fond of, a man of supreme learning both in all other matters and in the matter before us. 14. I was recently on my estate in Tusculum, when the grapes were being picked at vintage-time according to the annual custom.[63] One could see the mingled crowd of slaves and peasants drinking the must as it was pressed from the grapes or flowed freely from them, and yet they didn't become drunk: I was especially surprised in the case of those whom I knew to become crazy drunk from a little wine. My question is, why does must produce drunkenness either slowly or not at all?'

15. Dysarius replied, 'Everything sweet quickly leaves one feeling he's had enough and doesn't long create the impression that one wants more; instead, revulsion takes the place of satisfaction. Must, however, is merely sweet without being pleasant: wine in its infancy is sweet, while as it grows into maturity it's more pleasant than sweet. 16. Homer testifies to the difference between the two qualities when he says (*Od.* 20.69),

with sweet honey and pleasant wine,

calling honey sweet [*glykeros*] and wine pleasant [*hêdys*]. Must, then, which is not yet pleasant but merely sweet, doesn't allow enough of itself to be consumed to cause drunkenness, because of a certain repugnance. 17. I can add another point: sweetness is so naturally resistant to drunkenness that physicians force people whose stomachs are dangerously swollen to vomit by giving them a great deal of wine, and after they've vomited they give them bread smeared with honey as an antidote to the fumes of

offerunt melle inlitum, et ita hominem ab ebrietatis malo dulcedo defendit. ideo ergo non inebriat mustum in quo est sola dulcedo.

18. 'Sed et hoc de idonea ratione descendit, quod mustum grave est et flatus et aquae permixtione et pondere suo cito in intestina delabitur ac profluit, nec manet in locis obnoxiis ebrietati, delapsum vero relinquit sine dubio in homine ambas qualitates naturae suae, quarum altera in flatu, altera in aquae substantia est. 19. sed flatus quidem quasi aeque ponderosus in ima delabitur, aquae vero qualitas non solum ipsa non impellit in insaniam sed et, si qua vinalis fortitudo in homine resedit, hanc diluit et extinguit. 20. inesse autem aquam musto vel hinc docetur quod cum in vetustatem procedit fit mensura minus sed acrius fortitudine, quia exhalata aqua qua molliebatur, remanet vini sola natura cum fortitudine sua libera, nulla diluti umoris permixtione mollita.'

8   Post haec Rufius Albinus: 'ego quoque pro virili portione Dysarium nostrum inexercitum non relinquo. dicas quaeso quae causa difficile digestu facit isicium, quod ab insectione "insicium" dictum amissione n litterae postea quod nunc habet nomen obtinuit, cum multum in eo digestionem futuram iuverit tritura tam diligens, et quicquid grave erat carnis absumpserit[28] consummationemque eius multa ex parte confecerit.'

---

[28] absumpserit CS: ass- ω

---

[64] Cf. Aristotle fr. 220 Rose, cited by Plut. *Mor*. 656B.
[65] With §§1–3 cf. [Alex. Aphrod.] *Prob*. 1.22.
[66] Cf. Varro *Latin Language* 5.110; the Greek name for the

the wine that remains in their veins, the sweetness thus protecting the person from the evil of drunkenness. That, then, is why must, which is merely sweet, does not make someone drunk.

18. 'But appropriate analysis produces this consideration also: must is heavy, and because of its mixture of gas and water and its own weight it quickly settles into the intestine and is expelled.[64] It does not stay in the areas of the body subject to drunkenness, but after it has departed it naturally leaves behind in a person the two qualities that are essential to it, gas and water. 19. Now, gas is no less heavy and so settles into the nether regions, whereas water not only doesn't drive one senseless but even dilutes and quenches any remnant of wine's residual strength. 20. That water is present in must is shown, moreover, by the fact that when must ages, its volume decreases while its strength increases, since the water that made it milder has evaporated and only the essence of the wine remains, strong and unimpeded, with no admixture of water to dilute it and make it mild.'

After these remarks Rufius Albinus said, 'I too will do   8
my best not to leave our friend Dysarius idle.[65] Please explain why it's hard to digest a mincemeat croquette—I mean the dish that got the name *insicium* from the process of mincing [*insectio*],[66] then lost the *n* to get the name it now has [*isicium*]—even though the thorough grinding involved in its preparation should have done a lot to aid in its digestion by removing whatever was heavy in the meat and largely completing the process of breaking it down.'

dish was the same, *isikos* or dimin. *isikion*. For the various forms of the dish, cf. Apicius 2.1.

2. Et Dysarius: 'inde hoc genus cibi difficile digeritur unde putas ei digestionem ante provisam. levitas enim quam tritura praestat facit ut innatet udo cibo quem in medio ventris invenerit, nec adhaereat cuti ventris de cuius calore digestio promovetur. 3. sic et mox tritum atque formatum[29] cum in aquam coicitur, natat. ex quo intellegitur quod idem faciens in ventris umore subducit se digestionis necessitati, et tam sero illic coquitur quam tardius conficiuntur quae vapore aquae quam quae igne solvuntur. deinde dum instantius teritur, multus ei flatus involvitur, qui prius in ventre consumendus est, ut tum demum conficiatur quod remansit de carne iam liberum.'

4. 'Hoc quoque scire aveo,' Rufius inquit, 'quae faciat causa non nullos carnes validiores facilius digerere quam tenues. nam cum cito coquant offas bubulas, in asperis piscibus concoquendis laborant.' 5. 'in his,' Dysarius ait, 'huius rei auctor est nimia in homine vis caloris: quae si idoneam materiem suscipit, libere congreditur et cito eam in concertatione consumit; levem modo praeterit ut latentem, modo in cinerem potius quam in sucum vertit, ut ingentia robora in carbonum frusta lucentia igne vertuntur, paleae si in ignem ceciderint, mox solum de eis cinerem

---

29 formatum *ed. Paris. 1585*: firm- ω

---

67 With §§4–6 cf. [Alex. Aphrod.] *Prob.* 1.52, 2.17, and see also §6n.

68 *asperis* ("coarse, rough, unrefined") probably represents M.'s attempt to render Greek *petraious* (sc. *ikhthyas*: so pseudo-Alexander) after failing to recognize it as the name of a species, "rock-fish." If the error happens to be a scribe's, however, we might think that M. wrote *apuis piscibus* (as Peter White sug-

2. Dysarius replied, 'The thing that causes you to suppose that this food's digestion is cared for in its preparation is just what makes it difficult to digest. For the lightness that the grinding produces causes it to float in the moist food it encounters in the middle of the belly, preventing it from sticking to the belly's surface, which promotes digestion with its warmth. 3. So too, when it's tossed in water right after it's been ground and shaped, it floats: from that you can gather what it does in the stomach's moisture as it distances itself from the necessity of digestion; so digestion is then delayed, just as things that are steamed are broken down more slowly than those that are seared. Furthermore, while the meat is ground quite energetically a lot of gas becomes wrapped up in it, and the belly has to dispose of that first, so that what remains of the meat can finally be digested when it's free of the gas.'

4. 'Here's another thing I very much want to know,' Rufius said.[67] 'Why is it that some people find it easier to digest more robust forms of meat than those that are delicate? For example, though they quickly digest chunks of beef, they have a hard time digesting coarse fish.'[68] 5. 'In these cases,' Dysarius said, 'the source of the problem is the person's excessive warmth. If it encounters an appropriate substance, it freely comes into contact with it, grapples with it, and quickly finishes it off. But in the case of insubstantial material, at one time it bypasses it as though it failed to see it, at another it turns it into ash rather than juice, just as fire turns massive oaks into glowing lumps of charcoal, whereas if wheat chaff falls into a fire, only its

gested to me), which offers a sense—"small fry"—more in line with the logic of the passage.

221

restat videri. 6. habes et hoc exemplum non dissonum quod potentior mola ampliora grana confringit, integra illa quae sunt minutiora transmittit: vento nimio abies aut quercus avellitur, cannam nulla facile frangit procella.'

7. Cumque Rufius delectatus enarrantis ingenio plura vellet interrogare, Caecina se Albinus obiecit: 'mihi quoque desiderium est habendi paulisper negotii cum tam facunda Dysarii doctrina. dic, oro te, quae facit causa ut sinapi et piper, si adposita cuti fuerint, vulnus excitent et loca perforent, devorata vero nullam ventris corpori inferant laesionem.' 8. et Dysarius, 'species,' inquit, 'et acres et calidae superficiem cui adponuntur exulcerant, quia integra virtute sua sine alterius rei admixtione utuntur ad noxam. sed si in ventrem receptae[30] sint,[31] solvitur vis earum ventralis umoris alluvione, qua fiunt dilutiores, deinde prius vertuntur in sucum ventris calore quam ut integrae[32] possint nocere.'

9. Caecina subiecit: 'dum de calore loquimur, admoneor rei quam semper quaesitu dignam putavi, cur in Aegypto, quae regionum aliarum calidissima est, vinum non calida sed paene dixerim frigida virtute nascatur.' 10. ad hoc Dysarius: 'usu tibi, Albine, compertum est, aquas quae vel de altis puteis vel de fontibus hauriuntur fumare hieme, aestate frigescere. quod fit non alia de causa nisi quod aëre qui nobis circumfusus est propter temporis ra-

---

[30] receptae *Jan*: -ta ω   [31] sint R²ε: sunt Gβ₂, est P
[32] integrae *Jan*: integra ω

---

[69] The parable of the oak and the reed appears as *Fable* 16 in the collection dedicated to M. by the fabulist Avianus (or Avienus: see Introd. §1).

ashes soon remain to be seen. 6. Here's another suitable analogy: the more powerful sort of millstone breaks down larger grains of wheat but passes over smaller grains, leaving them intact; an exceedingly strong wind uproots a silver fir or oak tree, but no gale easily breaks a reed.'[69]

7. And though Rufius wanted to ask more questions, delighted as he was by his interlocutor's cleverness, Caecina Albinus intervened:[70] 'I too am eager to engage Dysarius' fluent learning for a bit. Tell me, please: why do mustard and peppercorn raise a welt and pierce the skin when they're placed on it but do no damage to the belly's tissue when they're swallowed?' 8. Dysarius replied, 'Spices, being both sharp and hot, wound a surface they're placed against because they use their power, which is strong and unmixed with any other substance, to do harm. But when they've been taken into the belly, their strength's undone as they're bathed in the belly's fluid, which dilutes them, and then they're turned into juice by the belly's warmth before they can do the sort of harm they do when whole.'

9. Caecina added, 'While we're talking about warmth, I'm put in mind of something I've always thought deserved to be looked into:[71] why is it that in Egypt, the hottest of any land, wine is produced that has, not an essential heat, but I'd almost venture to say an essential coldness?' 10. Dysarius replied, 'I'm sure you've had the experience of seeing water drawn from deep wells or springs smoking in the winter, though they're cold in the summer. This happens precisely because when the air that surrounds us is

70 With §§7–8 cf. [Alex. Aphrod.] *Prob.* 1.30, 67.
71 With §§9–11 cf. [Alex. Aphrod.] *Prob.* 1.56–57.

tionem calente, frigus in terrarum ima demergitur et aquas inficit quarum in imo est scaturrigo, et contra cum aër hiemem praefert, calor in inferiora demergens aquis in imo nascentibus dat vaporem. 11. quod ergo ubique alternatur varietate temporis, hoc in Aegypto semper est, cuius aër semper est in calore. frigus enim ima petens vitium radicibus involvitur, et talem dat qualitatem suco inde nascenti. ideo regionis calidae vina calore caruerunt.'

12. 'Tractatus noster,' Albinus inquit, 'semel ingressus calorem non facile alio digreditur. dicas ergo volo cur qui in aquam descendit calidam, si se non moverit, minus uritur; sed si agitatu suo aquam moverit, maiorem sentit calorem et totiens aqua urit amplius, quotiens novus ei motus accesserit.' 13. et Dysarius, 'calida,' inquit, 'quae adhaeserit nostro corpori, mox praebet tactum sui mansuetiorem, vel quia cuti adsuevit vel quia frigus accepit a nobis. motus vero aquam novam semper ac calidam[33] corpori applicat et cessante adsuetudine de qua paulo ante diximus semper novitas auget sensum caloris.' 14. 'cur ergo,' Albinus ait, 'aestate cum aër calidus flabro movetur, non calorem sed frigus adquirit? eadem enim ratione et in hoc fervorem deberet motus augere.' 15. 'non eadem ratio,' Dysarius inquit, 'in aquae et aëris calore. illa enim corporis solidioris est, et crassa materies cum movetur, integra vi sua superficiem cui admovetur invadit; aër motu in ventum solvitur

---

[33] aquam novam semper ac calidam G: aquam novam semper ac novam PF, aquam novam γ

---

[72] With §§12–15 cf. [Alex. Aphrod.] *Prob.* 1.112–13.

warm because of the season, the cold sinks down into the earth's deepest recesses and chills the waters that bubble up in the depths; conversely, when the air is wintry, the heat descends to the nether regions and makes the water steam as it arises in the depths. 11. Accordingly, a phenomenon that alternates with the seasons everywhere else is always the same in Egypt, where the air is always hot: as it seeks the depths, the cold becomes wrapped up in the roots of the vines and so gives that property to the juice produced there. That's why the wines of a hot region are free of heat.'

12. 'Having once entered on the topic of heat,' Albinus said, 'our line of inquiry is not finding it easy to head in a different direction.[72] Please tell me why a person who enters a hot bath is burned less if he doesn't move but feels the heat more if he stirs the water with his own motion, as the water burns more intensely every time it is moved.' 13. Dysarius said, 'Hot water that adheres to our body soon feels milder, either because the skin has become acclimated to it or because it is cooled by contact with us. But motion constantly brings new hot water into contact with the body, the acclimatization I just referred to fails to occurs, and the constant supply of new water increases the sensation of heat.' 14. 'Why, then,' Albinus said, 'when the hot air is moved by a breeze in the summer, does it feel not hotter but cooler? By the same principle motion should increase the burning sensation in this case too.' 15. 'The same principle is not at work in the warmth of water and the warmth of air,' Dysarius said. 'The substance of water is more solid, and when dense matter is moved against some surface, it attacks it with its force undiminished. When air is moved it's dispersed as wind: having become

225

et liquidior se factus agitatu flatus efficitur. porro ut flatus illud removet quod circumfusum nobis erat, erat autem circa nos calor, remoto igitur per flatum calore restat ut advenam sensum frigoris praestet agitatus.'

9   Interpellat Evangelus pergentem consultationem et 'exercebo,' inquit, 'Dysarium nostrum si tamen minutis illis suis et rorantibus responsionibus satisfaciet consulenti. 2. dic, Dysari, cur qui ita se vertunt ut saepe in orbem rotentur, et vertiginem capitis et obscuritatem patiuntur oculorum, postremo, si perseveraverint, ruunt, cum nullus alius motus corporis hanc ingerat necessitatem.'

3. Ad haec Dysarius, 'septem,' inquit, 'corporei motus sunt. aut enim accedit priorsum aut retrorsum recedit, aut in dexteram laevamve devertitur, aut sursum promovet aut deorsum, aut orbiculatim rotatur. 4. ex his septem motibus unus tantum in divinis corporibus invenitur, sphaeralem dico, quo movetur caelum, quo sidera, quo cetera moventur elementa. terrenis animalibus illi sex praecipue familiares sunt, sed non numquam adhibetur et septimus. sed sex illi ut directi, ita et innoxii; septimus, id est qui gyros efficit, crebro conversu turbat et umoribus capitis involvit spiramentum quod animam cerebro quasi omnes corporis sensus gubernanti ministrat. 5. hoc est autem spiramen-

---

73 On the metaphor, see 5.17.7n.

74 With §§2–7 cf. [Alex. Aphrod.] *Prob.* 1.131, which lacks the doctrine of the seven bodily motions (next n.).

75 Cf. *Comm.* 1.6.81, Philo *On the Craftsmanship of the Universe* 122, Iambl.(?) *Theology of Arithmetic* p.55.10–11, John Lydus *On the Months* 2.11.

76 The principle of psychic "breath" (Lat. *spiramentum* = Gk. *pneuma*) is central to the physiological model developed by

more fluid than it formerly was, it's turned into a breeze when it's stirred up. Furthermore, as a breeze it removes what surrounded us; but since what surrounded us was heat, once the heat has been removed by the breeze, it gives us a new feeling of cool when it's stirred.'

Evangelus interrupted the ongoing questioning and said, 'I'll give our friend Dysarius a workout, if he'll but satisfy his questioner with those "small and dewy"[73] answers of his. 2. Tell me, Dysarius, why people who turn repeatedly in a circle experience dizziness and darkened vision and finally fall down, if they continue, though no other bodily motion has this inevitable effect.'[74]

3. Dysarius replied, 'The body knows seven motions: it moves forward or back, or it turns right or left, or it goes up or down, or it spins in a circle.[75] 4. Only one of these seven motions is found in divine bodies, the circular one, which is the motion of the heavens, the stars, and all the other elements. The other six are chiefly the ones best known to earth-bound animals, but sometimes the seventh also comes into play. But those six, being unidirectional, are harmless; the seventh, the one that causes circular motion, produces confusion by constantly turning upon itself and mingles cranial fluids with the breath that provides the life-principle to the brain, the pilot, as it were, of all the body's senses.[76] 5. This breath, moreover, in circling the

9

Erasistratus (3rd cent. BCE): some of the air that we breathe is transmitted from the lungs to the heart, where it is converted to "vital breath" before being transmitted from the heart to the brain; there it is further purified as the "psychic breath" that is the source of all sensation and motion, distributed to the body by the nerves that M. describes in §§19ff.

tum quod ambiens cerebrum singulis sensibus vim suam
praestat; hoc est quod nervis et musculis corporis fortitu-
dinem praebet. ergo vertigine turbatum et simul agitatis
umoribus oppressum languescit et ministerium suum deserit. 6. inde fit his qui raptantur in gyros hebetior auditus,
visus obscurior, postremo, nervis et musculis nullam ab eo
virtutem quasi deficiente sumentibus, totum corpus, quod
his sustinetur et in robur erigitur, desertum iam fulcimen-
tis suis labitur in ruinam. 7. sed contra haec omnia consuetudo, quam secundam naturam pronuntiavit usus, illos iuvat qui in tali motu saepe versantur. spiramentum enim
cerebri quod paulo ante diximus, adsuetum rei iam non
sibi novae, non pavescit hunc motum nec ministeria sua
deserit. ideo consuetis etiam iste agitatus innoxius est.'

8. 'Inretitum te iam, Dysari, teneo et si vere opinor,
nusquam hodie effugies. et alios enim in arte tibi socios et
ipsum te audivi saepe dicentem, cerebro non inesse sensum, sed ut ossa ut dentes ut capillos, ita et cerebrum esse
sine sensu. verumne est haec vos dicere solitos, an ut falsum refelles?' 9. 'verum,' ait ille. 'ecce iam clausus es. ut
enim concedam tibi praeter capillos in homine aliquid esse
sine sensu, quod non facile persuasu est, tamen cur sensus
omnes paulo ante dixisti a cerebro ministrari, cum cerebro
non inesse sensum ipse fatearis? potestne excusare huius
contrarietatis ausum vel vestri oris nota volubilitas?'

10. Et Dysarius renidens: 'retia quibus me involutum

brain, gives the several senses their power and furnishes the sinews and muscles with strength. When it is disturbed by dizziness and at the same time is overwhelmed by the cranial fluids that have been stirred up, it grows faint and ceases to perform its proper function. 6. That's why people who are turned rapidly in circles have dulled hearing and darkened vision; finally, when the sinews and muscles get no power from the fainting breath, the whole body, which those sinews and muscles support and keep upright like a tree trunk, is bereft of its props and collapses. 7. But habit, which experience has called our second nature, helps those who are frequently turned in a circle to counter these effects: the brain's breath, which I mentioned a short time ago, becomes accustomed to it, regards it as familiar and not fearful, and does not cease to perform its proper function. Thus that sort of agitation is harmless to those who become habituated to it.'

8. 'I have you in my snare now, Dysarius, and if I'm not mistaken, you'll make no escape today (cf. E. 3.49). I have often heard other physicians, and you yourself, saying that the brain lacks sensation, but just like bones, like teeth, like hair, the brain is without feelings. Is it true that you lot are accustomed to saying this, or will you reject that as false?' 9. 'True,' said he. 'Aha—now you're trapped. Suppose I grant you that there is something in human beings other than hair that lacks sensation—a point that is difficult to make credible—still, why did you say just now that all the senses are served by the brain, when you yourself acknowledge that there is no sensation in the brain? Can even the well-known fluency of that mouth of yours excuse this brazen contradiction?'

10. Dysarius said, with a smile, 'The net in which you

tenes nimis rara sunt, nimis patula: ecce me, Evangele, sine nisu inde exemptum videbis. 11. opus naturae est ut sensum vel nimium sicca vel nimium umecta non capiant. ossa, dentes cum unguibus et capillis nimia siccitate ita denseta sunt ut penetrabilia non sint effectui animae qui sensum ministrat; adeps medulla et cerebrum ita in umore atque mollitie sunt, ut eundem effectum animae quem siccitas illa non recipit mollities ista non teneat. 12. ideo tam dentibus unguibus ossibus et capillis quam adipi medullis et cerebro sensus inesse non potuit. et sicut sectio capillorum nihil doloris ingerit, ita si secetur vel dens vel os seu adeps seu cerebrum seu medulla, aberit omnis sensus doloris. 13. "sed videmus," inquies, "tormentis adfici quibus secantur ossa, torqueri homines et dolore dentium." hoc verum esse quis abneget? sed ut os secetur, omentum quod impositum est ossi cruciatum, dum sectionem patitur, importat. quod cum medici manus transit, os iam cum medulla quam continet habent indolentiam sectionis similem capillorum. et cum dentium dolor est, non os dentis in sensu est, sed caro quae continet dentem. 14. nam et unguis quantus extra carnem crescendo pergit sine sensu secatur, qui carni adhaeret iam facit si secetur dolorem, non suo sed sedis suae corpore; sicut capillus dum superior secatur nescit dolorem: si avellatur, sensum accipit a carne quam deserit. et cerebrum quod tactu sui hominem vel torquet vel frequenter interimit, non suo sensu sed vestitus sui, id est omenti, hunc importat dolorem.

77 With §§11–14 cf. Arist. *On the Soul* 1.5 410a30–b2, *Parts of Animals* 2.5 651b4–7, 2.7 652b5–7, 2.10 656a23–25, Alex. Aphrod. *Commentary on "On Sensation" CAG* 3,1:39, *On the Soul CAG* Suppl. 2,1:75, 97, Nemesius *On Human Nature* p. 63.18–19.

hold me ensnared is exceedingly loose-knit and has very large gaps: just watch, Evangelus, and you'll see me effortlessly escape. 11. It is nature's doing that things either exceedingly dry or exceedingly wet have no feeling.[77] Bones, teeth, fingernails, hair—they're all so densely composed of very dry material as to be impenetrable to that effect of the life-principle which provides sensation; fat, marrow, and the brain are so moist and soft that their softness fails to retain the same effect of the life-principle that the dryness I referred to fails to receive. 12. For that reason sensation could no more be present in teeth, nails, bones, and hair than it was in fat, marrow, and the brain. And just as cutting hairs causes no pain, so if a tooth or bone or fat or the brain or marrow should be cut, there would be absolutely no pain. 13. "But," you say, "we see people in agony when their bones are cut, people tormented by toothache, too." Who would deny that's the case? But when bone is cut, it's the sheath covering the bone that introduces the feeling of agony while it suffers the cutting; once the physician's hand has got past that, the bone and the marrow it contains are as free from pain when they're cut as hairs are. And when teeth hurt, it's not the tooth's bony tissue that's in pain but the flesh that holds the tooth. 14. Take the fingernail too: all of it that grows clear of flesh is cut with no sensation, the part that adheres to the flesh cause pain if it's cut, not from its own tissue from that of its base. So too hair: while its upper part is cut, it feels no pain; if it's torn out, it acquires a sensation from the flesh it leaves behind. The brain, too, which torments a person or even kills him when it's touched, brings on this pain not from its own capacity for feeling but from that of its covering, that is, the caul.

15. 'Ergo diximus quae in homine sine sensu sint et quae hoc causa faciat indicatum est. reliqua pars debiti mei de eo est cur cerebrum, cum sensum non habeat, sensus gubernet. sed de hoc quoque temptabo, si potero, esse solvendo.

16. 'Sensus de quibus loquimur quinque sunt: visus, auditus, odoratus, gustus et tactus. hi aut corporei sunt aut circa corpus, solisque sunt caducis corporibus familiares. nulli enim divino corpori sensus inest, anima vero omni corpore, vel si divinum sit, ipsa divinior est. ergo, si dignitas divinorum corporum sensum dedignatur, quasi aptum caducis, multo magis anima maioris est maiestatis quam ut sensu egeat. 17. ut autem homo constet et vivum animal sit, anima praestat, quae corpus inluminat. porro inluminat inhabitando et habitatio eius in cerebro est. sphaeralis enim natura et ad nos de alto veniens, partem in homine et altam et sphaeralem tenuit et quae sensu careat, qui non est animae necessarius. 18. sed quia necessarius animali est, locat in cavernis cerebri spiramentum de effectibus suis: cuius spiramenti natura haec est ut sensus et ingerat et gubernet. 19. de his ergo cavernis, quas ventres cerebri nostra vocavit antiquitas, nascuntur nervorum septem συ-ζυγίαι. cui rei nomen quod ipse voles Latinum facito. nos

---

[78] Cf., e.g., Arist. *On the Soul* 3.1 424b22–23, *History of Animals* 4.8 532b32–33, Chrysippus fr. 836 *SVF* 2:227, Philo *On the Craftsmanship of the Universe* 62, Galen 7:56, 18,1:222, [Alex. Aphrod.] *Prob.* 2.61.   [79] Cf. Pl. *Timaeus* 44D.

[80] Cf. *Comm.* 1.14.9.   [81] Cf. §4n. above.

[82] Pairs of cranial nerves had been recognized through dissection by Herophilus of Alexandria (ca. 330–260 BCE), but the doctrine that there were exactly 7 pairs is owed to the anatomist

15. 'I've spoken, then, about the parts of a human being that are without feeling and have indicated why that is so. It remains for me to discharge my obligation by explaining why the brain governs the senses while being without sensation itself. I will try to dispose of this question too.

16. 'The senses we're speaking of are five in number: sight, hearing, smell, taste, and touch.[78] These are located either in or around the body and are known only to bodies destined to die: no divine body possesses sensation, whereas the soul is itself more divine than any body, even if the body is a god's. If, then, the gods with their lofty standing regard bodily sensation as unworthy of themselves, on the ground that it is something suited to mortals, so much more is the soul's majesty too great to stand in need of sensation. 17. The soul, which gives the body the light of life, causes a human being to continue to exist and be a living creature. Furthermore, it gives the body the light of life by dwelling in it, and its dwelling is the brain: being spherical in nature and coming to us from on high,[79] it has occupied the part of the human being that is high and spherical and that lacks sensation, for which the soul has no use.[80] 18. But because a creature needs sensation, the soul locates in the brain's cavities the breath that is one of its effects, and this breath by its nature provides and governs the senses.[81] 19. From these cavities, which our ancestors called the brain's ventricles, there are seven *syzygiai* ["pairs"] of nerves:[82] you can use whatever Latin term you

Marinus (early 2nd cent. CE), cf. Herophilus fr. 82–83 (Galen thought that in the case of the 5th pair Marinus might have conflated two pairs in one, but he continued to use the terminology: 2:837, *On Anatomical Procedures* 14.4).

enim συζυγίαν nervorum vocamus, cum bini nervi pariter emergunt et in locum certum desinunt. 20. septem ergo nervorum συζυγίαι de cerebri ventre nascentes vicem implent fistularum, spiramentum sensificum ad sua quaeque loca naturali lege ducentes, ut sensum vicinis et longe positis membris animalis infundant.

21. 'Prima igitur συζυγία nervorum talium petit oculos et dat illis agnitionem specierum et discretionem colorum; secunda in aures se diffundit per quam eis innascitur notitia sonorum; tertia naribus inseritur vim ministrans odorandi; quarta palatum tenet quo de gustatibus iudicatur; quinta vi sua omne corpus implet, omnis enim pars corporis mollia et aspera, frigida et calida discernit. 22. sexta de cerebro means stomachum petit, cui maxime sensus est necessarius, ut quae desunt adpetat, superflua respuat et in homine sobrio se ipse moderetur. septima συζυγία nervorum infundit sensum spinali medullae, quae hoc est animali quod est navi carina, et adeo usu aut dignitate praecipua est ut longum cerebrum a medicis sit vocata. 23. ex hac denique, ut ex cerebro, diversi nascuntur meatus, virtutem tribus animae propositis ministrantes. tria sunt enim quae ex animae providentia accipit corpus animalis: ut vivat, ut decore vivat et ut immortalitas illi successione quaeratur. 24. his tribus propositis, ut dixi, animae per spinalem me-

---

[83] That the spine is continuous with the brain was known to Aristotle (*Parts of Animals* 2.7 652a26–27), but the term "long brain" (*enkephalos makros*) seems not to be otherwise attested before Theophilus Protospatharius *On the Construction of the Human Body* (4.9, 5.3) of the 9th or 10th cent.

wish, but we Greeks refer to a *syzygia* of nerves when two nerves arise together and terminate at a specific point. 20. The seven *syzygiai* of nerves, then, arise from the brain's ventricle and serve as channels that conduct, each to its own terminus, the sense-bearing breath according to the law of nature, infusing the creature's limbs—the nearby and farther removed alike—with sensation.

21. The first *syzygia* of these nerves, then, has the eyes as its target and allows them to perceive sights and distinguish colors; the second spills into the ears, which thereby are able to recognize sounds; the third insinuates itself into the nostrils and provides the ability to smell; the fourth occupies the palate, which discerns tastes; the fifth fills the whole body with its power—for every part of the body distinguishes soft and rough, cold and hot. 22. The sixth passes from the brain and makes for the stomach, which stands in greatest need of sensation, so that it can seek out what it needs, reject what it doesn't, and act in a balanced way in a sober person. The seventh *syzygia* of nerves infuses with sensation the spine's marrow—for a creature, the equivalent of a ship's keel—and is so much the most useful and important *syzygia* that physicians have called it the "long brain."[83] 23. From this *syzygia*, as from the brain, passages emerge and extend in different directions, empowering the soul to pursue the three chief aims that a creature's body has, thanks to the soul's providence: that it remain alive, that it live in a fitting way,[84] and that it seek immortality through its posterity. 24. The soul's influence where these three aims are concerned is channeled, as I

[84] I.e., in a way appropriate to it not just as a living creature but as a creature of a specific kind.

dullam praebetur effectus. nam cordi et iecori et spirandi ministeriis, quae omnia ad vivendum pertinent, vires de spinalibus quos dixi[34] meatibus ministrantur. nervis etiam manuum pedum aliarumve partium, per quas decore vivitur, virtus inde praestatur, et ut successio procuretur, nervi ex eadem spinali medulla pudendis et matrici, ut suum opus impleant, ministrantur. 25. ita nulla in homine pars corporis sine spiramento, quod in ventre cerebri locatum est, et sine spinalis medullae beneficio constat. sic ergo fit ut cum ipsum cerebrum sensu careat, sensus tamen a cerebro in omne corpus proficiscatur.'

26. 'εὖγε! Graeculus noster,' Evangelus ait, 'tam plane nobis ostendit res opertu naturae tectas ut quicquid sermone descripsit oculis videre videamur. 27. sed Eustathio iam cedo, cui praeripui consulendi locum.' Eustathius: 'modo vel vir omnium disertissimus Eusebius vel quicumque volent alii ad exercitium consultationis accedant, nos postea liberiore otio congrediemur.'

10   'Ergo,' ait Eusebius, 'habendus mihi sermo est, Dysari, tecum de aetate cuius ianuam iam paene ambo pulsamus. Homerus cum senes πολιοκροτάφους vocat, quaero utrum ex parte poetico more totum caput significari velit, an ex aliqua ratione canos huic praecipue parti capitis adsignet?' 2. et Dysarius: 'et hoc divinus ille vates prudenter ut cetera. nam pars anterior capitis umidior occipitio est, et inde crebro solet incipere canities.' 'et si pars anterior,' ait

---

[34] dixi P: -imus Gβ_2 (an recte?)

[85] With §§1–10 cf. [Alex. Aphrod.] *Prob.* 1.1–4; with §5 cf. [Alex. Aphrod.] *Suppl. Probl.* 2.80.

said, through the spine's marrow: the heart, the liver, and the organs that support breathing—all of them relevant to the goal of remaining alive—receive their energy from what I've called the spinal passages. That is also the source of strength for the nerves of the hands, feet, or other parts that allow one to live in a fitting way; and to provide offspring the nerves from the same spinal marrow serve the genitals and womb and allow them to perform their proper function. 25. Thus every part of a human being's body enjoys the breath that is located in the brain's ventricle and benefits from the spine's marrow. That is why, then, sensation begins from the brain and extends throughout the entire body even though the brain itself is without sensation.'

26. 'Hats off to our little Greek,' Evangelus said, 'for revealing to us things nature has kept hidden so clearly that we seem to see every detail he described. 27. But now I yield to Eustathius, whose turn I took in asking my question.' Eustathius said, 'Let that most learned of all men, Eusebius, or any of the others who wish step forward to ask a question, and I'll engage with Dysarius later, at a more relaxed interlude.'

'Well then,' said Eusebius, 'I should speak with you, Dysarius, about the time of life on whose door we're both now nearly knocking.[85] I wonder whether, when Homer speaks of old men as "gray at the temples" (*Il.* 8.518), he intends the whole head to be meant from mention of a part—as poets often do—or is there some reason he assigns gray hair to this part of the head especially?' 2. Dysarius replied, 'On this point, as on all others, that god-like poet spoke shrewdly: the front of the head has more moisture than the back and graying is frequently accustomed to start from that point.' 'And if the front of the

10

ille, 'umidior est, cur calvitium patitur quod non nisi ex siccitate contingit?' 3. 'opportuna,' inquit Dysarius, 'obiectio:
sed ratio non obscura est. partes enim priores capitis fecit
natura rariores, ut quicquid superflui aut fumei flatus circa
cerebrum fuerit, evanescat per plures meatus. unde videmus in siccis defunctorum capitibus velut quasdam sutu-
ras quibus hemisphaeria, ut ita dixerim, capitis illigantur.
quibus igitur illi meatus fuerint ampliores, umorem siccitate mutant et ideo tardius canescunt sed non calvitio carent.' 4. 'si ergo siccitas calvos efficit et posteriora capitis
sicciora esse dixisti, cur calvum occipitium numquam videmus?' 5. ille respondit: 'siccitas occipitii non ex vitio sed
ex natura est. ideo omnibus sicca sunt occipitia. ex illa autem siccitate calvitium nascitur, quae per malam tempe-
riem, quam Graeci δυσκρασίαν solent vocare, contingit.
6. inde capillos[35] crispi, quia ita temperati sunt ut capite
sicciore sint, tarde canescunt, cito in calvitium transeunt.
contra qui capillo sunt rariore, non eo facile nudantur, nu-
triente umore quod φλέγμα vocitatur; sed fit illis cita canities. nam ideo albi sunt cani quia colorem umoris quo nutriuntur imitantur.' 7. 'si ergo senibus abundantia umoris
capillos in canitiem tinguit, cur senecta opinionem exactae
siccitatis accepit?' 8. 'quia senecta,' inquit ille, 'extincto per
vetustatem naturali calore fit frigida, et ex illo frigore gelidi
et superflui nascuntur umores. ceterum liquor vitalis longaevitate siccatus est; inde senecta sicca est inopia naturalis umoris, umecta est abundantia vitiosi ex frigore pro-

---

[35] capillos β_2: capilli sunt α (inde *post* capilli *add*. G), capillo
R²ε, capilli FᵐA²

---

[86] Cf. 7.4.9n.

head has more moisture,' Eusebius said, 'why does it experience baldness, which only dryness produces?' 3. 'Your objection is to the point,' Dysarius said, 'but the reason is clear. Nature made the anterior parts of the head more porous, so that any superabundant or vaporous fumes around the brain could dissipate through more passages. That's why we see in the dried skulls of the dead what look like sutures, which bind together the two hemispheres, so to speak, of the head. People with more generous passages swap moisture for dryness and therefore turn gray more slowly, though they're subject to baldness.' 4. 'If dryness makes people bald, then, and the back of the head is drier, why do we never see the back of the head bald?' 5. The other replied, 'The dryness of the back of the head is a natural condition, not a flaw: everyone's occipital region is dry. Baldness, on the other hand, arises from the sort of dryness that occurs as the result of an imbalance—what the Greeks call *dyskrasia*. 6. So curly-headed people, whose balance is such that their heads are drier, are late turning gray but make an early transition to baldness; on the other hand, those with thinner hair don't readily lose it, since the humor called phlegm[86] nourishes it, but they become gray early. Hairs turn white in imitation of the color of the humor by which they're nourished.' 7. 'If, then, an abundance of that humor colors old men's hair gray, why has old age come to be thought of as a time of extreme dryness?' 8. 'Because old age,' Dysarius said, 'turns cold when the passage of time extinguishes the natural warmth, and from that cold there arise chill and superfluous humors; but longevity makes the life-giving humor dry up. As a result, old age is dry and lacking in natural humors, but it is damp with a superabundance of the unnatural humor produced

creati. 9. hinc est quod et vigiliis aetas gravior afficitur, quia somnus, qui maxime ex umore contingit, de naturali nascitur, sicut est multus in infantia, quae umida est abundantia non superflui sed naturalis umoris. 10. eadem ratio est quae pueritiam canescere non patitur cum sit umectissima, quia non ex frigore nato phlegmate umida est sed illo naturali et vitali umore nutritur. ille enim umor qui aut de aetatis frigore nascitur aut cuiuslibet vitiositatis occasione contrahitur, ut superfluus, ita et noxius est.

11. 'Hunc videmus in feminis, nisi crebro egeratur, extrema minitantem, hunc in eunuchis debilitatem tibiis ingerentem, quarum ossa quasi semper in superfluo umore natantia naturali virtute caruerunt et ideo facile intorquentur, dum pondus superpositi corporis ferre non possunt, sicut canna pondere sibi imposito curvatur.' 12. Et Eusebius: 'quoniam nos a senectute usque ad eunuchos traxit superflui umoris disputatio, dicas volo cur ita acutae vocis sunt ut saepe mulier an eunuchus loquatur, nisi videas, ignores.' 13. id quoque facere superflui umoris abundantiam ille respondit. 'ipse enim ἀρτηρίαν, per quam sonus vocis ascendit, efficiens crassiorem angustat vocis meatum et ideo vel feminis vel eunuchis vox acuta est, viris gravis, quibus vocis transitus habet liberum et ex integro patentem meatum. 14. nasci autem in eunuchis et in feminis ex pari frigore parem paene importuni umoris abundantiam etiam hinc liquet, quod utrumque corpus saepe pinguescit, certe ubera prope similiter utrique grandescunt.'

---

[87] With §§11–14 cf. [Alex. Aphrod.] *Prob.* 1.7–8, 97, 2.24; with §13 cf. also [Alex. Aphrod.] *Suppl. Probl.* 2.5.

by its coolness. 9. That is why this more burdened time of life is also afflicted with insomnia: sleep, which is chiefly the result of humor, depends on natural humor, of the sort that's generously present in infancy, which abounds in humor that's natural, not superfluous. 10. The same principle prevents graying in childhood, even though it's a very moist time of life: it is not moist with the phlegm that cold produces but is nourished by a natural and life-giving humor. The humor that either arises from the coldness of old age or is contracted from some chance defect is superfluous and so also harmful.

11. 'We see this humor endangering women's extremities, if it is not purged frequently,[87] we see it weakening eunuch's lower legs, where the bones lack their natural strength from being constantly bathed in excess humor and so are easily twisted: they cannot bear the burden of the body they prop up, like a reed that bends under a weight set upon it.' 12. Eusebius said, 'Since discussion of excess humor has taken us from old age all the way to eunuchs, please explain why their voices are so high-pitched that you often cannot know whether a woman or a eunuch is speaking unless you take a look.' 13. Dysarius answered that an abundance of excess humor caused that condition too: 'It thickens the *artêria* [= windpipe] through which the sound of the voice rises, making the voice's passageway narrow: that's why high-pitched voices belong to women or eunuchs, deep voices to men, whose voice passes through a passageway that is unencumbered and entirely open. 14. That an equal coolness produces an almost equal abundance of misplaced humor in eunuchs and women is apparent from this point too: both often become plump, and both surely have breasts that are enlarged in almost similar ways.'

11   His dictis cum ad interrogandum ordo Servium iam vocaret, naturali pressus ille verecundia usque ad proditio-
nem coloris erubuit. 2. et Dysarius, 'age Servi, non solum
adulescentium qui tibi aequaevi sunt sed senum quoque
omnium doctissime, commascula frontem et sequestrata
verecundia, quam in te facies rubore indicat, confer nobiscum libere quod occurrerit, interrogationibus tuis non minus doctrinae collaturus quam si aliis consulentibus ipse
respondeas.' 3. cumque diutule tacentem crebris ille hor-
tatibus excitaret: 'hoc,' inquit Servius, 'ex te quaero quod
mihi contigisse dixisti, quae faciat causa ut rubor corpori
ex animi pudore nascatur?'

    4. Et ille, 'natura,' inquit, 'cum quid ei occurrit honesto
pudore dignum, imum petendo penetrat sanguinem, quo
commoto atque diffuso cutis tinguitur, et inde nascitur
rubor. 5. dicunt etiam physici quod natura pudore tacta
ita sanguinem ante se pro velamento tendat, ut videmus
quemque erubescentem manum sibi ante faciem frequenter opponere. nec dubitare de his poteris cum nihil aliud
sit rubor nisi color sanguinis.' 6. addit Servius: 'et qui gaudent cur rubescunt?' et Dysarius, 'gaudium,' inquit, 'extrinsecus contingit; ad hoc animoso occursu natura festi-
nat, quam sanguis comitando quasi alacritate integritatis
suae compotem tinguit cutem, et inde similis color nascitur.' 7. idem refert: 'contra qui metuunt, qua ratione pal-
lescunt?' 'nec hoc,' Dysarius ait, 'in occulto est. natura
enim cum quid de extrinsecus contingentibus metuit, in

---

88 §§1–9: on the blush see Gell. 19.6 (citing Arist. fr. 243
Rose), [Alex. Aphrod.] *Prob.* 1.12–15.

After these remarks, when the sequence of question-   11
ing was now calling on Servius, he was restrained by his innate modesty, to the point of blushing.[88] 2. Dysarius said,
'Come now, Servius—most learned not just among your
young contemporaries but among the old too—put a bold
face on, set aside the modesty that your blushing betrays in
you, and contribute whatever occurs to you—a contribu-
tion that will teach as much by the questions you ask as
your answers would if others were questioning you.' 3. And
when, as he remained silent a bit longer, the other roused
him with repeated encouragements, Servius said, 'My
question has to do with my condition, as you remarked:
what causes a blush to appear on the body as a result of the
mind's sense of shame?'

4. Dysarius replied, 'When one's nature encounters
something that should cause a decent person shame, it
seeks the depths and pervades the blood, which becomes
disturbed and dispersed, thus coloring the skin and producing a blush. 5. Physical scientists also say that when
one's nature has been touched by shame, it holds the blood
out before itself like a veil, as we see someone who blushes
often holding a hand up in front of his faith. You'll have no
ground for doubt on these matters, since a blush is merely
the color of blood.' 6. Servius added, 'And people who re-
joice—why do they blush?' Dysarius replied, 'Joy arises
from some external stimulus, which our nature hastens
spiritedly to approach: blood follows along and, as though
by its own excitement, imparts to the skin the tint of its
own essence, and that is why the color like blood arises.'
7. Servius rejoined, 'Conversely, those who feel fear—why
do they grow pale?' 'This too is not obscure,' Dysarius said.
'When our nature fears something happening outside us, it

243

altum tota demergitur, sicut nos quoque cum timemus la-
tebras et loca nos occulentia quaerimus. 8. ergo tota des-
cendens ut lateat, trahit secum sanguinem quo velut curru
semper vehitur. hoc demerso umor dilutior cuti remanet,
et inde pallescit. ideo timentes et tremunt, quia virtus
animae introrsum fugiens nervos relinquit quibus teneba-
tur fortitudo membrorum, et inde saltu timoris agitantur.
9. hinc et laxamentum ventris comitatur timorem, quia
musculi quibus claudebantur retrimentorum meatus, fugientis introrsum animae virtute deserti, laxant vincula
quibus retrimenta usque ad egestionis[36] opportunitatem
continebantur.' 10. Servius his dictis venerabiliter adsensus opticuit.

12   Tunc Avienus, 'quia me ordo,' ait, 'ad similitudinem
consultationis adplicat, reducendus mihi est ad convivium
sermo qui longius a mensa iam fuerat evagatus et ad alias
transierat quaestiones. 2. saepe adposita salita carne quam
laridum vocamus, ut opinor quasi "large aridum," quae-
rere mecum ipse constitui qua ratione carnem ad diuturni-
tatem usus admixtio salis servet. hoc licet aestimare mecum possim, malo tamen ab eo qui corporibus curat certior
fieri.'

3. Et Dysarius: 'omne corpus suapte natura dissolubile
et marcidum est et, nisi quodam vinculo contineatur, facile
defluit. continetur autem, quam diu inest, anima recipro-
catione aëris, qua vegetantur conceptacula spiritus, dum
semper novo spirandi nutriuntur alimento. 4. hoc cessante

---

[36] egestionis *Willis*: dig- ω

[89] Differently [Arist.] *Prob.* 27.10 948b–949a.

withdraws wholly into the depths of our being, just as we also look for cover and places of concealment when we're afraid. 8. So then, as it descends entirely to its hiding place, it draws along the blood that's always carrying it along as though in a chariot: once it has hit bottom, the skin retains a thinner sort of humor, and that's the source of its pallor. That's the reason people also tremble in fear: by fleeing inward the soul's strength abandons the sinews that keep the limbs sturdy, and so they're shaken by the jumpiness of fear. 9. And it is also why fear is accompanied by a loosening of the bowels: the muscles that had been keeping the waste products' passage shut are bereft of the soul's strength, as it flees inward, and loosen the bonds that had been holding the waste products in until it was time to expel them.'[89] 10. Servius expressed his respectful agreement with this account and fell silent.

Then Avienus said, 'Since the sequence gives me the   12 task of putting a question—or at least appearing to—I should bring the conversation back to our banquet, after it had wandered rather far from the table and passed over to other lines of inquiry. 2. Often when I've been served the preserved meat we call bacon [*laridum*]—I suppose, because it is largely dried [*large aridum*]—I've begun to ask myself why adding salt preserves meat for long-term use. Though I might be able to work this out on my own, I'd rather be informed by one who cares for our bodies.'

3. Dysarius said, 'Every body is naturally liable to dissolution and rot and it quickly melts away if there is no bond to hold it together. However, as long as the soul is resident, it holds the body together through the intake and expulsion of air, which keeps the breath's receptacles healthy, as they are constantly nourished by a new intake. 4. When

per animae discessum membra marcescunt, et omne pondere suo conflictum corpus obteritur. tum sanguis etiam, qui quam diu fuit compos caloris, dabat membris vigorem, calore discedente versus in saniem, non manet intra venas sed foras exprimitur, atque ita laxatis spiramentis effluit tabes faeculenta. 5. id fieri sal admixtus corpori prohibet. est enim natura siccus et calidus, et fluxum quidem corporis calore contrahit, umorem vero siccitate vel coercet vel exsorbet. certe umorem sale differri sive consumi fit hinc cognitu facile quod, si duo panes pari magnitudine feceris, unum sale aspersum, sine sale alterum, invenies indigentem salis pondere propensiorem, scilicet umore in eo per salis penuriam permanente.'

6. 'Et hoc a Dysario meo quaesitum volo: cur defaecatum vinum validius fit viribus sed infirmius ad permanendum, et tam bibentem cito permovet quam ipsum, si manserit, facile mutatur?' 7. 'quod cito,' inquit Dysarius, 'permovet haec ratio est, quia tanto penetrabilius efficitur in venas bibentis, quanto fit liquidius faece purgata. ideo autem facile mutatur, quod nullo firmamento nixum undique sui ad noxam patet. faex enim vino sustinendo et alendo et viribus sufficiendis quasi radix eius est.'

8. 'Et hoc quaero,' Avienus ait, 'cur faex in imo subsidit omnium nisi mellis, mel solum est quod in summum faecem expuat? ad hoc Dysarius, 'faecis materia ut spissa atque terrena ceteris laticibus pondere praestat, melle vin-

---

90 Cf. [Arist.] *Prob*. 21.5 927a–b; in fact this is the opposite of what an empirical test would show.

91 Contrast Plut. *Mor*. 692D.

this stops at the soul's departure, the limbs wither, and the entire body is annihilated by the pressure of its own weight. Then the blood too, which gave strength to the limbs as long as it retained its warmth, turns to pus when that warmth is lost and does not remain within the veins but forces its way out, and with the body's openings thus relaxed a thick slime of decay flows out. 5. Salt mixed with the body keeps this from happening, because being naturally dry and warm it restricts the body's dissolution with its warmth and blocks or absorbs the moisture with its dryness. Certainly, the fact that moisture is dispersed or consumed by salt is easily seen if you make two loaves of bread of equal size and sprinkle one with salt while leaving the other without salt: you'll find that the salt-free loaf is heavier, obviously because the lack of salt causes it to retain moisture.'[90]

6. 'I'd like to ask Dysarius this question also: why does wine that's been filtered become stronger in its effect[91] but have less staying power in storage, affecting the drinker as quickly as it itself is affected—by turning to vinegar—if it's kept?' 7. 'It quickly affects the drinker,' Dysarius said, 'because the clearer it's made by filtering out the dregs, the more able it is to penetrate the drinker's veins. It turns quickly, however, because it has nothing to give it body and is vulnerable to harm on every side: the dregs are, in effect, the wine's roots, supporting it, nourishing it, and giving it strength.'

8. 'Here's another question,' Avienus said. 'Why do the impurities of all liquids save honey sink to the bottom, while honey alone sends its impurities up to the surface?' Dysarius replied, 'In all other liquids the impure material, being dense and earthy, is heavier, but it's lighter than

247

citur. ideo in illis gravitate devergens ad fundum decidit, in melle vero ut levior de loco victa sursum pellitur.'

9. 'Quoniam ex his quae dicta sunt ingerunt se similes quaestiones, cur, Dysari, ita mel et vinum diversis aetatibus habentur optima, mel quod recentissimum, vinum quod vetustissimum? unde est et illud proverbium quo utuntur gulones, mulsum quod probe temperes miscendum esse novo Hymettio et vetulo Falerno.' 10. 'propterea,' inquit ille, 'quia inter se ingenio diversa sunt. vini enim natura umida est, mellis arida. si dicto meo addubitaveris, medicinae contemplator effectum. nam quae udanda sunt corporis, vino foventur, quae siccanda sunt melle detergentur. igitur longinquitate temporis de utroque aliquid exsorbente vinum meracius fit, mel aridius et ita mel suco privatur ut vinum aqua liberatur.'

11. 'Nec hoc quod sequetur dissimile quaesitis est: cur si vasa vini atque olei diutule semiplena custodias, vinum ferme in acorem corrumpitur, oleo contra sapor suavior conciliatur?' 12. 'utrumque,' Dysarius ait, 'verum est. in illud enim vacuum quod superne liquido caret aër advena incidit, qui tenuissimum quemque umorem elicit et exorbet, eo siccato vinum quasi spoliatum viribus, prout ingenio imbecillum aut validum fuit, vel acore exasperatur vel austeritate restringitur, oleum autem supervacuo umore siccato velut mucore qui in eo latuit absterso adquirit novam suavitatem saporis.'

---

92 With §§9–10 cf. [Alex. Aphr.] *Suppl. Prob.* 3.22 (diff. [Alex. Aphr.] *Prob.* 2.70).   93 Hor. *Satires* 2.2.15, cf. Pliny *Natural History* 22.113.   94 With §§11–12 cf. Arist. fr. 224 Rose, Plut. *Mor.* 701E–702C, [Alex. Aphrod.] *Suppl. Prob.* 3.9.

95 This description is not obviously consistent with the effect attributed to air in §14.

honey: in the former, then, it sinks of its own weight and falls to the bottom, but in honey it's forced upward, dislodged from its place because it is lighter.'

9. 'Since questions similar to what's been said are occurring to me, Dysarius, why is it that honey and wine are considered best at very different ages, honey when it's very fresh, wine when it's very old?[92] For that's the source of the proverb that gourmands employ: to strike the right balance in your honeyed wine, you should mix new honey from Hymettus with an old Falernian wine.'[93] 10. 'The reason,' Dysarius said, 'is that they are opposite in character: wine is essentially moist, honey dry. If you doubt what I'm saying, consider the effect of medicine: parts of the body that need to be moistened are bathed with wine, those that need to be dried are wiped down with honey. As the passage of time draws off something from both, wine becomes more concentrated, honey becomes drier: honey loses its juice, wine its water.'

11. 'The next question I'm going to ask is not unlike the others:[94] if you keep containers of wine and olive oil half full for a while, why does the wine almost always turn sour while the oil, by contrast, takes on a more pleasant flavor?'
12. 'Correct on both counts,' Dysarius said. 'Air from the outside enters the empty space above the level of the liquid, drawing off and absorbing all the finest particles of moisture. This drying effect in a sense strips wine of its strength, causing it to be more harshly sour or more astringently dry, according to whether it was naturally weak or robust.[95] In the case of oil, by contrast, the drying of the excess moisture has the effect of clearing out the mustiness that was lurking in it, giving the oil a new, pleasant flavor.'

13. Rursus ait Avienus: 'Hesiodus cum ad medium dolii perventum est, compercendum et ceteris eius partibus ad satietatem dicit abutendum, optimum vinum sine dubio significans quod in dolii medietate consisteret. sed et hoc usu probatum est, in oleo optimum esse quod supernatat, in melle quod in imo est. quaero igitur cur oleum quod in summo est, vinum quod in medio, mel quod in fundo, optima esse credantur.'

14. Nec cunctatus Dysarius ait, 'mel quod optimum est reliquo ponderosius est. in vase igitur mellis pars quae in imo est utique praestat pondere, et ideo supernante pretiosior est. contra in vase vini pars inferior admixtione faecis non modo turbulenta, sed et sapore deterior est; pars vero summa aëris vicinia corrumpitur, cuius admixtione fit dilutior. 15. unde agricolae dolia, non contenti sub tecto reposuisse, defodiunt et operimentis extrinsecus inlitis muniunt, removentes in quantum fieri potest a vino aeris contagionem, a quo tam manifeste laeditur ut vix se tueatur in vase pleno et ideo aëri minus pervio. 16. ceterum si inde hauseris et locum aëris admixtioni patefeceris, reliquum quod remansit omne corrumpitur. media igitur pars quantum a confinio summi utriusque tantum a noxa remota est, quasi nec turbulenta nec diluta.'

17. Adiecit Avienus, 'cur eadem potio meracior videtur ieiuno quam ei qui cibum sumpsit?' et ille: 'venas inedia vacuefacit, saturitas obstruit. igitur cum potio per inanitatem penitus influit, quia non obtusas cibo venas invenit,

---

96 §§13–16 are based on Plut. *Mor.* 701D–702A.

97 Hesiod does not specify that he is speaking of wine; M. follows Plutarch in the assumption.

13. Once more Avienus:[96] 'Hesiod says that when you reach the middle of a wine-jar, you should save up what's there, though you should drink your fill of the rest (*Op.* 368–69),[97] no doubt meaning to say that the best wine settles in the middle of the jar. But it's also shown by experience that the best olive oil floats on top, while the best honey is at the bottom. Why is it, then, that the best oil is believed to be at the top, the best wine in the middle, and the best honey at the base of the jar?'

14. Without hesitation, Dysarius replied, 'The best honey is heavier than the rest, and so the portion of honey at the bottom of the jar is obviously heavier and therefore more valuable than that above it. In a wine-jar, by contrast, the admixture of dregs not only makes the lower portion murkier but also makes it taste worse, while the upper is spoiled by its contact with the air, which mingles with it and makes it more diluted. 15. That's why farmers are not content just to store wine-jars indoors but actually bury them and fortify them by smearing the outside with a sealant, doing everything they can to keep the wine out of contact with the air, which so plainly harms the wine that it scarcely retains its freshness in a vessel that's full and therefore more impervious to the air. 16. But if you draw from it and leave room for the air the mix in, all that remains becomes spoiled. The wine in the middle, then, is protected from harm in direct proportion to its distance from the two extremes, being neither murky nor diluted.'

17. Avienus added, 'Why does the same drink seem more potent to someone who's been fasting than to someone who's eaten?' Dysarius said, 'Fasting empties the veins, being full closes them up: so when a drink flows straight into the empty veins, since it doesn't find them

251

neque fit admixtione dilutior et per vacuum means gustatu fortiore sentitur.'

18. 'Hoc quoque sciendum mihi est,' Avienus ait, 'cur qui esuriens biberit aliquantulum famem sublevat, qui vero sitiens cibum sumpserit non solum non domat sitim sed magis magisque cupidinem potus accendit?' 19. 'nota est,' inquit Dysarius, 'causa. nam liquori quidem nihil officit quin sumptus ad omnes corporis partes quoquo versus permanet et venas compleat, et ideo inedia quae inanitatem fecerat, accepto potus remedio, quasi iam non in totum vacua recreatur. cibatus vero utpote concretior et grandior in venas non nisi paulatim confectus admittitur. ideo sitim quam repperit nullo solatio sublevat, immo quicquid foris umoris nactus est exorbet et inde penuria eius, quae sitis vocatur, augetur.'

20. 'Nec hoc mihi,' Avienus ait, 'ignoratum relinquo: cur maior voluptas est cum sitis potu extinguitur quam cum fames sedatur cibo?' et Dysarius: 'ex praedictis hoc quoque liquet. nam potionis totus haustus in omne corpus simul penetrat et omnium partium sensus facit unam maximam et sensibilem voluptatem, cibus autem exiguo subministratu paulatim penuriam consolatur. ideo voluptas eius multifariam comminuitur.'

21. 'Hoc quoque si videtur addo quaesitis: cur qui avidius vorant facilius satias capit[37] quam qui eadem quietius

---

[37] capit *ed. Lugd. Bat. 1597*: capiunt ω

---

[98] §§18–19 are based on Plut. *Mor.* 689A–690B.

blocked with food, it is not diluted by any admixture and is perceived as being stronger as it passes through the empty space.'

18. 'Here's something else I need to know,' Avienus said.[98] 'Why does someone who drinks when he's hungry relieve his hunger a little, whereas someone who eats when he's thirsty does not just leave his thirst unquenched but actually becomes even more eager to drink?' 19. 'The reason is well known,' Dysarius said. 'Nothing keeps liquid from seeping through all parts of the body and filling the veins, wherever it turns when it is taken in, and so the fasting that produced the emptiness is relieved by the antidote of drink, as though the emptiness was partly filled. But food, being larger and more solid, is received by the veins only gradually when it has been processed and so offers no relief or consolation to the thirst it encounters—rather, it absorbs whatever external moisture it encounters, and so the lack of moisture that we call thirst increases.'

20. 'Here's another thing I don't want to remain ignorant of,' Avienus said. 'Why do we experience more pleasure from quenching thirst with a drink than from soothing hunger with food?' Dysarius replied, 'The answer here too is clear from what I've said before: all that's taken in by drinking goes to all the body's recesses at once and the sensation of all its parts produces one very great and perceptible feeling of pleasure. Food, by contrast, being distributed very meagerly, only gradually assuages the feeling of deprivation: its pleasure is therefore diminished in a number of ways.'

21. 'I also want to add this to the questions I've asked: why does a feeling of satiety more readily come over those who eat greedily than those who eat the same food more

253

ederint?' 'brevis est,' inquit, 'illa responsio. nam ubi avide devoratur, tunc multus aër cum edulibus infertur propter hiantium rictus et crebritatem respirandi. igitur ubi aër venas complevit, ad obiciendum fastidium pro cibo pensatur.'

22. 'Ni molestus tibi sum, Dysari, patere plus nimio ex discendi cupidine garrientem, et dicas quaeso cur edulia satis calida facilius[38] comprimimus ore quam manu sustinemus et si quid eorum plus fervet quam ut diutius mandi possit, ilico devoramus et tamen alvus non perniciose uritur.' 23. et ille: 'intestinus calor qui in alvo est quasi multo maior vehementiorque quicquid calidum accipit magnitudine sua circumvenit ac debilitat. ideo praestat si quid ori fervidum admoveris, non ut quidam faciunt hiare, ne novo spiritu fervori vires ministres, sed paulisper labra comprimere, ut maior calor qui de ventre etiam ori opitulatur comprimat minorem calorem. manus autem, ut rem fervidam ferre possit, nullo proprio iuvatur calore.'

24. 'Iamdudum,' inquit Avienus, 'nosse aveo cur aqua quae obsita globis nivium perducitur ad nivalem rigorem minus[39] in potu noxia est quam ex ipsa nive aqua resoluta. scimus enim quot quantaeque noxae epoto nivis umore nascantur.' 25. Et Dysarius: 'addo aliquid a te quaesitis. aqua enim ex nive resoluta, etiam si igne calefiat et calida bibatur, aeque noxia est ac si epota sit frigida. ergo non solo

---

[38] facilius S: satis facilius ω
[39] minus *ed. Lugd. Bat. 1597*: non minus ω

---

99 §§24–27 are based on Gell. 19.5.5–9; the quotation in §26 is a slightly free rendering of Aristotle fr. 214 Rose, quoted in Greek at Gell. 19.5.9.

sedately?' 'My reply can be brief,' Dysarius said. 'When someone swallows food down greedily, he ingests a lot of air with the food because his jaws are wide open and he's breathing rapidly: when air has filled his veins, it serves in the place of food in producing the sort of repugnance born of satiety.'

22. 'If I'm not annoying you, Dysarius, please put up with me as I gabble along out of an excessive desire to learn: please tell me why we more easily hold food that's quite hot in our mouths than in our hands, and why if we immediately swallow some food that's too hot to chew any longer, our bellies aren't seriously burned.' 23. Dysarius said, 'The belly's internal heat, being much greater and more forceful, envelops in its own intensity any hot thing it receives and weakens it. That's why, if you put something very hot in your mouth, it's better not to open your jaws wide as some people do—so you don't make the hot thing hotter with a fresh breath of air—but to briefly close your lips, so that greater heat can come to the mouth even from the belly and overwhelm the lesser heat. The hand, by contrast, has no heat of its own that enables it to carry a hot object.'

24. 'I've long been eager to know,' Avienus said, 'why water that's filled with chunks of snow and is made as cold as snow is less harmful to drink than water from melted snow—for we know how many kinds of serious harm come from drinking snow melt.'[99] 25. Dysarius said, 'I'll add a further point to your question: even if water from melted snow is heated over a fire and drunk hot, it's no less harmful than if it's drunk cold. Water from snow, then, is dan-

rigore nivalis aqua perniciosa est, sed ob aliam causam,
quam non pigebit aperire auctore Aristotele, qui in physi-
cis quaestionibus suis hanc posuit et in hunc sensum ni
fallor absolvit. 26. "omnis aqua," inquit,

> habet in se aeris tenuissimi portionem quo salutaris
> est, habet et terream faecem qua est corpulenta post
> terram. cum ergo aeris frigore et gelu coacta coales-
> cit, necesse est per evaporationem velut exprimi ex
> ea auram illam tenuissimam, qua discedente conve-
> niat in coagulum, sola terrea in se remanente natu-
> ra. quod hinc apparet quia cum fuerit eadem aqua
> solis calore resoluta, minor modus eius reperitur
> quam fuit antequam congelasceret, deest autem
> quod evaporatio solum in aqua salubre consumpsit.

27. nix ergo quae nihil aliud est quam aqua in aëre denseta,
tenuitatem sui, cum denseretur, amisit et ideo ex eius reso-
lutae potu diversa morborum genera visceribus insemi-
nantur.'

28. 'Nominatum gelu veteris, quae me solebat agitare,
admonuit quaestionis, cur vina aut numquam aut rarenter
congelascant, ceteris ex magna parte umoribus nimietate
frigoris cogi solitis? num quia vinum semina quaedam in
se caloris habet—et ob eam rem Homerus dixit αἴθοπα
οἶνον, non ut quidam putant propter colorem[40]—an alia

---

[40] colorem *ed. Colon. 1521*: calorem ω

---

[100] §§28–31 are based on Gell. 17.8.9–16; cf. also [Alex.
Aphrod.] *Prob*. 1.128.

[101] The Homeric scholia are divided between regarding the
epithet as = "black" (Σ D *Il*. 4.259) or as = "blazing" (Σ *Od*. 10.152,

gerous not just because it is very cold but for another reason, which I'll reveal relying on the authority of Aristotle,
who posed it in his *Inquiries in Physics* and presented his
solution, if I'm not mistaken, in these terms: 26. "All water," he says,

> contains a certain amount of very rarefied air that
> makes it healthy, but it also contains earthy impuri-
> ties that give it body, though less body than the
> earth. When it is compacted by cold air and frigid
> weather, then, and congeals, the very rarefied air is
> inevitably expelled, as it were, by evaporation, and
> with that air's departure it freezes solid, left with
> only its earthy nature. This is apparent from the fact
> that when the same water is melted by the sun's
> heat, less of it is left than there was before it froze,
> while it lacks the only healthy element in the water,
> which the evaporation removed.

27. Snow, which is merely water that has condensed in the
atmosphere, loses its rarefied element by being condensed
and therefore plants in our innards the seeds of a wide
range of diseases when it is melted and drunk.'

28. 'Mention of frigid weather reminded me of an old
question that used to exercise me:[100] why do wines never or
rarely freeze, though most all other liquids usually are
made to congeal by excessive cold? Is it because wine contains some germs of heat—leading Homer to speak of
"gleaming wine" (*Il.* 1.462 *et al.*) for that reason, not (as
some suppose) because of its color[101]—or is there some

following Aristarchus' correct derivation from the verb *aithein*)
or both (Σ D *Il.* 1.462 "black, or hot").

quaepiam causa est? quam quia ignoro scire cupio.'

29. Ad haec Dysarius: 'esto vina naturali muniantur calore, num oleum[41] minus ignitum est aut minorem vim in corporibus calefactandis habet? et tamen gelu stringitur. certe si putas ea quae calidiora sunt difficilius congelascere, congruens erat nec oleum concrescere et ea quae frigidiora sunt facile gelu cogi, acetum autem omnium maxime frigorificum est atque id tamen numquam gelu stringitur. 30. num igitur magis oleo causa est coaguli celerioris quod et levigatius et spissius est? faciliora enim ad coeundum videntur quae levatiora densioraque sunt, vino autem non contingit tanta mollities, et est quam oleum multo liquidius, acetum vero et liquidissimum est inter ceteros umores et tanto est acerbius ut sit acore tristificum; et exemplo marinae aquae, quae ipsa quoque amaritudine sui aspera est, numquam gelu contrahitur. 31. nam quod Herodotus historiarum scriptor contra omnium ferme qui haec quaesiverunt opinionem scripsit, mare Bosporicum, quod et Cimmerium appellat, earumque partium mare omne, quod Scythicum dicitur, id gelu constringi et consistere, aliter est ac putatur. 32. nam non marina aqua contrahitur, sed quia plurimum in illis regionibus fluviorum est et paludum in ipsa maria influentium, superficies maris, cui dulces aquae innatant, congelascit et incolumi aqua marina videtur in mari gelu, sed de advenis undis coactum. 33. hoc et in Ponto fieri videmus, in quo frusta quaedam et, ut ita dixerim, prosiciae gelidae feruntur, contractae de

---

[41] num oleum *ed. Ven. 1472*: ne oleum ω

other reason? Since I'm ignorant of the reason, I want to know.'

29. In response Dysarius said, 'Granted that wines are fortified by their essential warmth: is olive oil of a less fiery nature, or is it less capable of warming our bodies? And yet it congeals in frigid weather. Surely, if you suppose that things that are innately warmer freeze less readily, it would be consistent for olive oil not to harden and for things that are innately colder to freeze readily in frigid weather—yet vinegar, the foremost coolant among liquids, never congeals in frigid weather. 30. Is it the case, then, that oil congeals more quickly because it is both smoother and thicker? Fluids that are smoother and denser seem to congeal more readily, but wine doesn't have that syrupy quality and is much more fluid than oil, while vinegar is the most fluid of all liquids and is so much harsher that its sour quality makes it distressing; and there's the example of sea water, which is also harsh because of its bitterness and never freezes in frigid weather. 31. As for the fact that the historian Herodotus wrote—against the virtually unanimous opinion of those who have looked into these matters—that the Bosporus (which he also calls the Cimmerian Sea) and all the seas in the region called Scythia freeze in frigid weather and come to a standstill (4.28), that is contrary to what is generally thought. 32. Sea water doesn't freeze; however, because there are very many rivers and marshes in those regions that flow into the sea, the fresh water floats on the sea's surface and congeals, and though the seawater is unaffected, there seems to be ice in the sea, though it's really formed from the inflowing water. 33. We see this happen in the Black Sea too: some chunks and, so to speak, slabs of ice are borne along, solidified out of a

259

fluvialium vel palustrium undarum multitudine, in quas licet frigori, quasi levatiores marina. 34. plurimum autem aquarum talium influere Ponto et totam superficiem eius infectam esse dulci liquore, praeter quod ait Sallustius, "mare Ponticum dulcius quam cetera est," hoc quoque testimonio, quod si in Pontum vel paleas vel ligna seu quaecumque natantia proieceris, foras extra Pontum feruntur in Propontidem atque ita in mare quod adluit Asiae oram, cum constet in Pontum influere maris aquam, non effluere de Ponto. 35. meatus enim qui solus de Oceano receptas aquas in maria nostra transmittit, in freto est Gaditano quod Hispaniam Africamque interiacet; et sine dubio inundatio ipsa per Hispaniense et Gallicanum litora in Tyrrhenum prodit, inde Hadriaticum mare facit, ex quo dextra in Parthenium, laeva in Ionium et directim in Aegaeum pergit, atque ita ingreditur in Pontum. 36. quae igitur ratio facit ut rivatim aquae de Ponto effluant cum foris influentes aquas Pontus accipiat? sed constat utraque ratio. nam superficies Ponti propter nimias aquas quae de terra dulces influunt, foras effluit; deorsum vero intro pergit influxio. 37. unde probatum est natantia quae, ut supra dixi, iaciuntur in Pontum foras pelli, si vero columna deciderit, introrsum urinari.[42] et hoc saepe usu probatum est,

---

[42] urinari *Rodgers*: minari ω, innare *ed. Colon. 1521*

---

[102] There is in fact a double current in the Bosporus, as the lighter, less saline water of the Black Sea flows on the surface out into the Sea of Marmara while a swifter, deeper current of denser, saltier water flows in.

[103] I.e., the Strait of Gibraltar.

[104] I.e., the eastern Mediterranean, cf. Amm. Marc. 14.8.10.

great mass of river and marsh water that's at the mercy of the cold, since it's smoother than sea water. 34. As evidence that a very great amount of such water flows into the Black Sea, whose entire surface is imbued with fresh water, we have not only Sallust's statement (*Histories* fr. 3.65)—"The Black Sea is fresher than all others"—but also the fact that if you throw wheat chaff or sticks or any floating material in the Black Sea, they're carried beyond the Black Sea and into the Sea of Marmara and from there into the sea that washes the coast of Asia Minor—though it's well known that the sea's water flows into the Black Sea, not out of it.[102] 35. For the only passage that transmits water from Ocean into our seas is the Strait of Cadiz[103] that lies between Spain and Africa: that influx itself most assuredly advances along the coasts of Spain and Africa to the Tyrrhenian Sea, then forms the Adriatic, from which it extends on the right to the Parthenian Sea,[104] on the left to the Ionian, and straight ahead to the Aegean, from which it enters the Black Sea. 36. Why, then, does water flow like a river from the Black Sea, when the Sea receives water that flows in from beyond it? Both the following explanations hold true: the Black Sea's surface water flows out because of the exceedingly large amount of fresh water that enters it from the land; but the water flowing in follows a path that runs at a greater depth. 37. Hence it can be regarded as established that floating things that are tossed into the Black Sea are forced out, but if a column[105] falls in, it floats inward. It has also been shown by experience that all the heavier ob-

[105] I.e., an object heavier than the "floating material" like chaff or sticks mentioned in §34.

ut graviora quaeque in fundo Propontidis ad Ponti interiora pellantur.'

38. 'Adiecta hac una consultatione reticebo: cur omne dulcium magis dulce videtur cum frigidum est quam si caleat?' respondit Dysarius: 'calor sensum occupat, et gustatum linguae fervor interpedit. ideo exasperatione oris praeventa suavitas excluditur. quod si caloris absit iniuria, tum demum potest lingua incolumi blandimento dulcedinem pro merito eius excipere. praeterea sucus dulcis per calorem non impune penetrat venarum receptacula et ideo noxa minuit voluptatem.'

13   Successit Horus et, 'cum multa,' inquit, 'de potu et cibatu quaesisset Avienus, unum maxime necessarium, sponte an oblitus ignoro, praetermisit, cur ieiuni magis sitiant quam esuriant. hoc in commune nobis, Dysari, si videtur, absolve.'

2. Et ille: 'rem tractatu dignam,' inquit, 'Hore, quaesisti sed cuius ratio in aperto sit. cum enim animal ex diversis constet elementis, unum est de his quae corpus efficiunt quod aut[43] solum aut maxime ultra cetera aptum sibi quaerat alimentum, calorem dico, qui liquorem sibi exigit ministrari. 3. certe de ipsis quattuor elementis extrinsecus videmus nec aquam nec aërem neque terram aliquid quo alatur aut quod consumat exigere nullamque noxam vicinis vel adpositis sibi rebus inferre, solus ignis alimenti perpetui desiderio quicquid offendit absumit. 4. inspice

---

[43] aut *Jan dubitanter*: et ω

---

[106] Cf. [Arist.] *Prob.* 22.12 931a.
[107] §§1–5 are based on Plut. *Mor.* 686E–687B.
[108] Cf. 7.5.17n.

jects that end up in the depths of the Sea of Marmara are driven into the inner reaches of the Black Sea.'

38. 'If I can add this one further question, I'll be quiet: why do all sweet things seem sweeter when cold than when hot?'[106] Dysarius replied, 'Heat engrosses the senses, and great warmth impedes the tongue's faculty of taste: hence the pleasant sensation is blocked when the mouth has first been irritated. But if heat is not present to do harm, then— and only then—can the tongue register the appropriate degree of sweetness, its attractive quality being diminished. Furthermore, sweet juice cannot pass through the heat and be received by the veins unimpaired, and that impairment diminishes the pleasure.'

Taking his turn next, Horus said, 'Though Avienus 13 asked many questions about food and drink, he omitted a critical one, whether intentionally or by oversight I don't know: why do people who fast become more thirsty than hungry? If you wish, Dysarius, please do us all the benefit of answering this question.'[107]

2. Dysarius replied, 'You've asked a question worthy of consideration, Horus, but one with an obvious answer. Though a creature is composed of diverse elements, there's one form among those that constitute the body that either uniquely or to a degree beyond all the rest seeks sustenance that is suited to its own nature: I mean heat, which demands that it be provided with liquid. 3. We certainly see that of the four elements,[108] when they exist in the world outside us, neither water nor air nor earth needs something to sustain it or to consume, and they do no harm to nearby things even when they're placed in contact with them: only fire has a constant need to be fed, consuming whatever it encounters. 4. Consider, too, how much food

et primae aetatis infantiam, quantum cibum nimio calore
conficiat, et contra senes cogita facile tolerare ieiunium
quasi exstincto in ipsis calore qui nutrimentis recreari solet. sed et media aetas, si multo exercitio excitaverit sibi na-
turalem calorem, animosius cibum adpetit. consideremus
et animalia sanguine carentia, quae nullum cibum quae-
rant penuria caloris. 5. ergo si calor semper in adpetentia
est, liquor autem proprium caloris alimentum est, bene in
nobis cum ex ieiunio corpori nutrimenta quaeruntur, praecipue calor suum postulat, quo accepto corpus omne recreatur et patientius expectat cibatum solidiorem.'

6. His dictis Avienus anulum de mensa rettulit qui illi
de brevissimo dexterae manus digito repente deciderat,
cumque a praesentibus quaereretur cur eum alienae manui[44] et digito, et non huic gestamini deputatis potius in-
sereret, ostendit manum laevam ex vulnere tumidiorem.
7. hinc Horo nata quaestionis occasio et, 'dic,' inquit, 'Dysari—omnis enim situs corporis pertinet ad medici notio-
nem, tu vero doctrinam et ultra quam medicina postulat
consecutus es—dic, inquam, cur sibi communis adsensus
anulum in digito qui minimo vicinus est, quem etiam me-
dicinalem vocant, et manu praecipue sinistra gestandum
esse persuasit?'

8. Et Dysarius: 'de hac ipsa quaestione sermo quidam
ad nos ab Aegypto venerat, de quo dubitabam fabulamne
an veram rationem vocarem, sed libris anatomicorum pos-

---

[44] alienae manui *ed. Colon. 1521*: aliena manu ω

---

[109] Acc. to Arist. *Parts of Animals* 4.5 678a27–32, cephalo-
pods, crustacea, testacea, and insects are without blood and viscera.   [110] Cf. Alex. Trall. *Therapeutica* 2:585.

we consume in the first stage of life, infancy, because of our excessive heat, and reflect, on the other hand, that old men easily tolerate fasting, as though the warmth within them, which is usually renewed by being fed, has been damped down. But even middle-aged people who rouse their natural warmth with a lot of exercise have a more spirited appetite for food. Let us also consider bloodless creatures,[109] which for lack of warmth seek no food. 5. If warmth is always present in appetite, then, and if liquid is the suitable sustenance of warmth, then appropriately, in our case, when nourishment is sought for a body that has been fasting, warmth above all seeks its own proper nourishment: when it's been received, the whole body is refreshed and awaits more solid food more patiently.'

6. After these remarks, Avienus retrieved from the table a ring that had just fallen from the pinky of his right hand, and when those present asked him why he had put it on the wrong hand and finger, not the hand and finger intended for ring-wearing, he showed that his left hand was quite swollen from a wound. 7. Taking this as an opportunity to ask a question, Horus said, 'Tell me, Dysarius—for a physician should know the whole layout of the body, and you've achieved a degree of knowledge even beyond that demanded by your profession—tell me, I say, why as a matter of common agreement we are convinced that a ring should be worn on the finger next to the pinky, which people also call the "medicinal finger,"[110] and particularly on the left hand?'

8. Dysarius said, 'Some talk bearing on this question had reached me from Egypt, though I was in doubt whether I should call it a fable or a true account—but when I later consulted anatomists' texts, I discovered it

tea consultis verum repperi, nervum quendam de corde
natum priorsum pergere usque ad digitum manus sinistrae
minimo proximum, et illic desinere implicatum ceteris
eiusdem digiti nervis; et ideo visum veteribus ut ille digitus
anulo tamquam corona circumdaretur.'

9. Et Horus, 'adeo,' inquit, 'Dysari, verum est ita ut dicis Aegyptios opinari, ut ego sacerdotes eorum, quos pro-
phetas vocant, cum in templo vidissem circa deorum simulacra hunc in singulis digitum confectis odoribus inlinere
et eius rei causas requisissem, et de nervo quod iam dictum est principe eorum narrante didicerim et insuper
et de numero qui per ipsum significatur. 10. complicatus
enim senarium numerum digitus iste demonstrat, qui om-
nifariam plenus perfectus atque divinus est, causasque cur
plenus sit hic numerus ille multis adseruit, ego nunc ut
praesentibus fabulis minus aptas relinquo. haec sunt quae
in Aegypto, divinarum omnium disciplinarum compote,
cur anulus huic digito magis inseratur agnovi.'

11. Inter haec Caecina Albinus, 'si volentibus vobis
erit,' inquit, 'in medium profero quae de hac eadem causa
apud Ateium Capitonem, pontificii iuris inter primos peri-
tum, legisse memini. qui cum nefas esse sanciret deorum formas insculpi anulis, eo usque processit ut et cur in

___

111 §8 is based on Gell. 10.10.   112 M. refers to a system
of signifying numbers, recorded by the Venerable Bede (*On the
Reckoning of Time* 1), in which the number six is registered by
bending the ring finger of the left hand to meet the palm; cf.
1.9.10, on the statue of Janus that signifies the number 300 with
the fingers of one hand and the number 65 with the fingers of the
other.   113 A "perfect number" is a positive integer that is
the sum of the positive integers, other than itself, that are its divi-

was true: a certain nerve that arises in the heart runs forward all the way to the finger next to the pinky on the left hand and ends there, entangled with all the other nerves of that finger. For that reason the ancients decided to surround that finger with a ring, as though with a crown.'[111]

9. Horus replied, 'Indeed, it's true, as you say, that the Egyptians hold that opinion: when I saw in one of their temples that this finger on each of the gods' images was anointed with specially prepared perfumes, I asked their priests, whom they call prophets, for an explanation, and I learned from their leader the account you've already given about the nerve, and also learned about the number that the finger signifies. 10. For when it's bent,[112] it symbolizes the number six, which is in every way complete, perfect, and divine:[113] he explained at length why the number is complete, though I now pass over the reasons as unsuited to the present conversation. This is the account I received in Egypt, the mistress of all divine branches of learning, as to why the ring tends to be placed on this finger more often.'

11. In the midst of this discussion Caecina Albinus said, 'If you're all agreeable, I can contribute what I recall reading on this same explanation in Ateius Capito, one of the foremost scholars of pontifical law. Holding that it was against divine law for rings to be carved on images of the

sors: 6 (= 1+2+3) and three other such numbers—28, 496, and 8128—were known to ancient mathematics (Euclid derived a formula for generating them: *Elements* 9.36); cf. *Comm.* 1.6.12–16, Vitruv. 3.1.6. Christians further saw the number's perfection in the 6 days of creation: Aug. *On the City of God* 11.30, *On the Trinity* 4.7, *Literal Meaning of Genesis* 4.2–3.

hoc digito vel in hac manu gestaretur anulus non taceret.
12. "veteres," inquit,

> non ornatus sed signandi causa anulum secum cir-
> cumferebant. unde nec plus habere quam unum li-
> cebat nec cuiquam nisi libero, quos solos fides dece-
> ret quae signaculo continetur. ideo ius anulorum
> famuli non habebant. imprimebatur autem sculptu-
> ra materiae anuli, seu ex ferro seu ex auro foret, et
> gestabatur ut quisque vellet, quacumque manu
> quolibet digito. 13. postea (inquit) usus luxuriantis
> aetatis signaturas pretiosis gemmis coepit insculp-
> ere, et certatim haec omnis imitatio lacessivit, ut
> de augmento pretii quo sculpendos lapides paras-
> sent gloriarentur. hinc factum est ut usus anulorum
> exemptus dexterae, quae multum negotiorum gerit,
> in laevam relegaretur, quae otiosior est, ne crebro
> motu et officio manus dexterae pretiosi lapides fran-
> gerentur. 14. electus autem (inquit) in ipsa laeva
> manu digitus minimo proximus, quasi aptior ceteris
> cui commendaretur anuli pretiositas. nam pollex,
> qui nomen ab eo quod pollet accepit, nec in sinistra
> cessat nec minus quam tota manus semper in officio
> est: unde apud Graecos ἀντίχειρ (inquit) vocatur,
> quasi manus altera. 15. pollici vero vicinus nudus et

---

[114] Sim. Lact. *On the Craftsmanship of God* 10.24 (cited at
LALE 482).

[115] The Greek term reflects the fact that humans have an op-
posable thumb: i.e., it is opposite (*anti*) the hand (*kheir*). Ateius,
however, seems to have understood *anti* in another sense it can
have, "in place of / equivalent to."

gods, he went on to say also why a ring is worn on this finger and on this hand. 12. "The ancients," he said (fr. 15 *IAH* 2.1:276 = fr. 10 *IAR*[6]),

wore a ring not as an ornament but to seal documents. For that reason, having more than one ring was not allowed and only a freeman could have one, since they alone were worthy of the credit that the seal implied; accordingly, slaves in the household did not have the right to wear a ring. A figure was engraved on the material of the ring—whether it was iron or gold—and the ring was worn according to each person's whim, on either hand and on any finger. 13. Afterward (Ateius continues), in an age of luxury, it began to be the practice to engrave the devices on precious gems, and peoples' imitation of one another, and their rivalries, reached the point that they boasted of the inflated prices they paid for stones to engrave. That is the point at which the right hand, which is the busier hand, ceased to be used for wearing a ring, and the function was transferred to the left, which is idler, lest the right hand's frequent movement and duties smash the precious stones. 14. Furthermore (he adds) the finger next to the pinky on the left hand was chosen as being more suitable than the others for being entrusted with a valuable ring. The thumb [*pollex*], which was so named because of its strength [*pollet*],[114] is not idle even on the left hand and is always as engaged in activity as the hand as a whole: that's why (he says) the Greeks call it the *antikheir*, that is, "second hand."[115] 15. But the finger next to the thumb seemed ex-

sine tuitione alterius adpositi videbatur. nam pollex
ita inferior est ut vix radicem eius excedat. medium
et minimum vitaverunt (inquit) ut ineptos, alterum
magnitudine, brevitate alterum; et electus est qui
ab utroque clauditur et minus officii gerit et ideo
servando anulo magis adcommodatus est.

16. haec sunt quae lectio pontificalis habet. unus quisque
ut volet vel Etruscam vel Aegyptiacam opinionem sequatur.'

17. Inter haec Horus ad consulendum reversus, 'scis,'
inquit, 'Dysari, praeter hunc vestitum qui me tegit nihil
me in omni censu aliud habere. unde nec servus mihi est,
nec ut sit opto, sed omnem usum qui vivo ministrandus est,
ego mihimet subministro. 18. nuper ergo cum in Ostiensi
oppido morarer, sordidatum pallium meum in mari diutule lavi et super litus sole siccavi, nihiloque minus eae-
dem in ipso post ablutionem maculae sordium visebantur.
cumque me res ista stupefaceret, adsistens forte nauta,
"quin potius," ait, "in fluvio ablue pallium tuum si vis ema-
culatum." parui ut verum probarem, et aqua dulci ablutum
atque siccatum vidi splendori suo redditum, et ex illo causam requiro cur magis dulcis quam salsa aqua idonea sit
sordibus abluendis?'

19. 'Iamdudum,' Dysarius inquit, 'haec quaestio ab

---

116 Represented by Ateius' treatise on priestly law, much of
which the Romans derived from the Etruscans.

117 I.e., as a Cynic Horus renounced all ties to worldly goods in
the manner of the sect's founder, Diogenes of Sinope: cf. 7.3.21.

118 §§18–27 are based on Plut. *Mor.* 626F–627F.

posed, left undefended by its neighbor, the thumb, which is so much shorter that it scarcely reaches beyond the other finger's base. They avoided the middle finger and the pinky (he concludes) as unsuitable, the one because it is so large, the other because it is so small. So they chose the finger that those two enclose, since it performs fewer activities and is therefore more suited to protecting a ring.

16. So much for the text on pontifical law. Let each person pursue either the Etruscan opinion[116] or the Egyptian, as he pleases.'

17. Horus, meanwhile, returned to his role as questioner and said, 'You know, Dysarius, that I have nothing in my entire estate beyond the clothing that covers me:[117] accordingly, since I neither have a slave nor wish to have on, I perform for myself all the services that living requires. 18. Recently, when I was staying in Ostia, I washed my soiled cloak for a bit in the sea and dried it on the shore in the sunshine—and yet the same stains were visible on it after it was cleaned.[118] When the situation left me dumbfounded, a sailor who chanced to be standing near said, "Why don't you wash your cloak in the river, if you want to get the stains out." I did as he said, to test the truth of it, and after it was washed in fresh water and dried, I saw that it had been restored to its proper, gleaming condition. So: my question is, why is fresh water better suited to washing dirt away than salt water?'

19. 'This question,' Dysarius said, 'has long since been

Aristotele et proposita est et soluta. ait enim aquam marinam multo spissiorem esse quam est dulcis. immo illam
esse faeculentam, dulcem vero puram atque subtilem.
hinc facilius ait vel imperitos nandi mare sustinet, cum
fluvialis aqua quasi infirma et nullo adiumento fulta mox
cedat et in imum pondera accepta transmittat. 20. ergo
aquam dulcem dixit quasi natura levem celerius immer-
gere in ea quae abluenda sunt, et dum siccatur secum sordium maculas abstrahere; marinam vero quasi crassiorem
nec facile penetrare purgando propter densitatem sui et
dum vix siccatur non multum sordium secum trahere.'

21. Cumque Horus his adsentiri videretur, Eustathius
ait, 'ne decipias, quaeso, credulum qui se quaestionemque
suam commisit fidei tuae. Aristoteles enim, ut non nulla
alia, magis acute quam vere ista disseruit. 22. adeo autem
aquae densitas non nocet abluendis ut saepe qui aliquas
species purgatas volunt, ne sola aqua vel dulci tardius hoc
efficiant, admisceant illi cinerem, vel si defuerit, terrenum
pulverem, ut crassior facta celerius possit abluere. nihil
ergo impedit marinae aquae densitas. 23. sed nec ideo quia
salsa est minus abluit. salsitas enim findere et velut aperire
solet meatus et ideo magis elicere debuit abluenda. sed
haec una causa est cur aqua marina non sit ablutioni apta,
quia pinguis est, sicut et ipse Aristoteles saepe testatus est
et sales docent quibus inesse quiddam pingue nullus igno-
rat. 24. est et hoc indicium pinguis aquae marinae quod,
cum inspergitur flammae, non tam extinguit quam pariter accenditur, aquae pinguedine alimoniam igni sub-

---

119 Arist. *Prob. phys.* fr. 217 Rose, cf. [Arist.] *Prob.* 23.7 932a–
b, 23.13 933a.

120 Cf. [Arist.] *Prob.* 23.9 932b, 23.15 933a, 23.32 935a.

posed and answered by Aristotle,[119] who says that sea water is much thicker than fresh—or rather, that it's filled with impurities, whereas fresh water is pure and fine. That's why (he says) the sea supports even inexperienced swimmers, but river water, being weak, in a sense, and lacking any support, soon gives way and sends to the bottom any weight it receives. 20. He said that fresh water, being naturally light, therefore enters the things that need washing and draws out the dirty stains as it dries; but sea water, being thicker, is prevented by its own density from easily penetrating and cleaning and, since it dries only with difficulty, does not draw out much dirt.'

21. When this seemed to meet with Horus' assent, Eustathius said, 'Please, don't deceive a credulous man who has entrusted himself and his question to your good faith. Aristotle's account in this matter—as in some others—was more clever than true. 22. The density of water is so far from harming laundry that those who want to clean some articles often mix in ash or, if that's not available, dirt, to do the job more quickly than they could with water alone, even fresh water: the idea is to make the water thicker so it can clean more quickly. Seawater's density, then, is no obstacle to cleaning. 23. Nor is it less effective for being salty. Saltiness usually creates fissures and, as it were, opens passages and so ought more effectively draw out what needs to be washed away. But here's the sole reason that sea water is not good for cleaning: it's greasy, as Aristotle himself said on a number of occasions[120] and as is shown by salt itself, in which everyone knows there's something greasy. 24. There is this further indication that sea water is greasy: when it's sprayed on a flame, it doesn't so much quench it as catch fire along with it, as the water's

ministrante. 25. postremo Homerum sequamur qui solus
fuit naturae conscius. facit enim Nausicaam Alcinoi filiam
abluentem vestes cum super mare esset, non in mari sed
in fluvio. idem locus Homeri docet nos marinae aquae
quiddam inesse pingue permixtum. 26. Vlixes enim cum
iamdudum mare evasisset et staret siccato corpore, ait ad
Nausicaae famulas,

> ἀμφίπολοι, στῆθ' οὕτω ἀπόπροθεν, ὄφρ' ἐγὼ
>   αὐτός
> ἅλμην ὤμοιιν ἀπολούσομαι.

post haec cum descendisset in fluvium,

> ἐκ κεφαλῆς ἔσμηχεν ἁλὸς χνόον.

27. divinus enim vates, qui in omni re naturam secutus est,
expressit quod fieri solet, ut qui ascendunt de mari, si in
sole steterint, aqua quidem celeriter sole siccetur, maneat
autem in corporis superficie veluti flos quidam qui et in de-
tergendo sentitur, et hoc est aquae marinae pinguedo quae
sola impedit ablutionem.

14   'Et quia a ceteris expeditus mihi te paulisper indulges,
modo autem nobis de aqua sermo fuit, quaero cur in aqua
simulacra maiora veris videntur? quod genus apud popi-
natores pleraque scitamentorum cernimus proposita am-
pliore specie quam corpore, quippe videmus in doliolis vi-
treis aquae plenis et ova globis maioribus et iecuscula fibris

greasy quality provides fuel to the fire. 25. Finally, let's follow Homer, who was uniquely knowledgeable about nature. He has Alcinoüs' daughter, Nausicaä, at the seaside washing clothes not in the sea but in a stream (*Od.* 6.85–95), and in the same passage shows us that there's something greasy intermingled with sea water: 26. when Ulysses has long since emerged from the sea and is standing with his body already dry, he says to Nausicaä's slaves (*Od.* 6.218–19),

> Stand there at a distance, attendants, until I
> wash the brine from my shoulders.

After, when he's gone down into the river (*Od.* 6.226),

> he cleaned the salt-foam from his head.

27. The god-like bard, who followed nature in every respect, represented the common experience of coming out of the sea, standing in the sun so that the sun quickly dries the water, and yet having stick to the body's surface a kind of film, if I can put it like that, which we also feel when we wash things. This is seawater's greasy quality, which is the only thing that gets in the way of cleaning.

'Since you've acquitted yourself of all our companions 14 and are indulging me for a bit, with water our recent topic, I'd like to ask why images in water appear larger than the objects actually are.[121] This is the sort of thing we find food peddlers doing, when their morsels are usually presented looking larger than they really are—in water-filled glass jars we see exceptionally large, round eggs and little livers

[121] With §§1–2 cf. [Alex. Aphrod.] *Prob.* 1.36.

tumidioribus et bulbos[45] spiris ingentibus. et omnino ipsum videre qua nobis ratione constat, quia solent de hoc non nulli nec vera nec veri similia sentire?'

2. Et Dysarius, 'aqua,' inquit, 'densior est aëris tenuitate et ideo eam cunctantior visus penetrat, cuius offensa repercussa videndi acies scinditur et in se recurrit. scissa dum redit, iam non directo ictu sed undique versum incurrit liniamenta simulacri, et sic fit ut videatur imago archetypo suo grandior. nam et solis orbis matutinus solito nobis maior apparet quia interiacet inter nos et ipsum aër adhuc de nocte roscidus, et grandescit imago eius tamquam in aquae speculo visatur. 3. ipsam vero videndi naturam non insubide introspexit Epicurus, cuius in hoc non est ut aestimo improbanda sententia, adstipulante praecipue Democrito, quia sicut in ceteris ita et in hoc paria senserunt. 4. ergo censet Epicurus ab omnibus corporibus iugi fluore quaepiam simulacra manare, nec umquam tantulam moram intervenire quin ultro ferantur inani figura cohaerentes corporum exuviae, quarum receptacula in nostris oculis sunt et ideo ad deputatam sibi a natura sedem proprii sensus recurrunt. haec sunt quae vir ille commemorat, quibus si occurris obvius, expecto quid referas.'

5. Ad haec renidens Eustathius, 'in propatulo est,' inquit, 'quod decepit Epicurum. a vero enim lapsus est aliorum quattuor sensuum secutus exemplum, quia in audiendo et gustando et odorando atque tangendo nihil e nobis

---

45 bulbos *Jan*: bulvas ω (vulvas *paene malim*)

---

122 Or perhaps, reading *vulvas*, "sows wombs [a delicacy] with large folds."   123 §§3–4: cf. Lucr. 4.216–378, Gell. 5.16.3, Apul. *Apology* 15, Diog. Laert. 10.46–52.

with inflated lobes and onions with huge rings.[122] For that matter, what is the principle behind vision itself—a question on which some people hold views that are neither true nor plausible?'

2. Dysarius said, 'Water is denser, air thinner, and so our vision penetrates the former more slowly: striking up against it and bouncing back, our line of vision becomes divided and collides with itself. When it turns back after being divided, it meets the image's contours not head on but from every direction, and so it happens that the image we see seems larger than its original. The sun's orb in the morning also appears larger than usual because the atmosphere between the sun and us is still dewy from the night, and the sun's image increases in size as though it were being seen in a pool of water. 3. As for the nature of vision itself, Epicurus had some acute insights,[123] and I don't think his opinion on this matter should be rejected, especially given the support of Democritus, since in this as in all other matters they held similar views. 4. Epicurus, then, holds that images of a sort emanate from all objects in a continuous stream, nor does a moment go by in which objects do not throw off cohesive but insubstantial trace-images of themselves: repositories for these images are located in our eyes, and that is why these sensations appropriately hasten toward the seat assigned to them by nature. These are the great man's views: if you oppose them, I look forward to learning what you have to say.'

5. Eustathius replied with a smile, 'It's clear what misled Epicurus: he diverged from the truth by relying on the analogy of the other four senses, since in hearing, tasting, smelling, and touching we emit nothing from ourselves but

emittimus, sed extrinsecus accipimus quod sensum sui
moveat. 6. quippe et vox ad aures ultro venit, et aurae in
nares influunt, et palato ingeritur quod gignat saporem, et
corpori nostro adplicantur tactu sentienda. hinc putavit et
ex oculis nihil foras proficisci sed imagines rerum in oculos
ultro meare. 7. cuius opinioni repugnat quod in speculis
imago adversa contemplatorem suum respicit, cum debeat, si quidem a nobis orta recto meatu proficiscitur, pos-
teram sui partem cum discedit ostendere, ut laeva laevam
dextera dexteram respiciat. nam et histrio personam sibi
detractam ex ea parte videt qua induit, scilicet non faciem
sed posteriorem cavernam. 8. deinde interrogare hunc virum vellem an tunc imagines e rebus avolant cum est qui
velit videre, an et cum nullus aspicit, emicant undique simulacra. 9. nam si quod primum dixi teneat, quaero cuius
imperio simulacra praesto sint intuenti et quotiens quis vo-
luerit ora convertere, totiens se et illa convertant. 10. si secundo inhaereat, ut dicat perpetuo fluore rerum omnium
manare[46] simulacra, quaero quam diu cohaerentia perma-
nent nullo coagulo iuncta ad permanendum. aut si manere
dederimus, quem ad modum aliquem retinebunt colorem,
cuius natura cum sit incorporea, tamen numquam potest
esse sine corpore? 11. dein quis potest in animum inducere simul atque oculos verteris incurrere imagines caeli,
maris, litoris, prati, navium, pecudum et innumerabilium
praeterea rerum, quas uno oculorum iactu videmus, cum

46 manare A²C: -ere ω

124 Cf. Arist. *On Perception* 4 442a30–b1, criticizing Democritus et al. for reducing all perception to touch.

receive from the outside something that moves us to perceive it.[124] 6. Certainly, an utterance reaches our ears on its own, and scents waft into our nostrils, and the source of taste impinges on the palate, and things that are to be perceived by touch come into contact with our body. From this he reckoned that nothing emerges from our eyes but that images of things pass on their own into the eyes. 7. Against this view is the fact that in mirrors the image across from the viewer looks right back at him, though if indeed it emerges from us and sets out in a straight line, it ought to show us its back as it departs, with the left side corresponding to the left, the right to right: compare the actor who looks at the mask he's taken off from the side on which he put it on, which is to say, not the face but the hollowed-out back. 8. Next I'd like to ask this fellow whether images go flying off from objects only when there's someone who wants to see them or whether there are images darting off on every side even when no one is watching. 9. If he should hold the former, my question is, who gives the order for the images to present themselves to the onlooker and meet his gaze whenever he chooses to look in that direction. 10. If he should cling to the latter position, and so claim that images of all objects are flowing in a steady stream, my question then is: how long do they maintain their shapes intact when there's no substance to bind them so they stay together? Or if we should grant that they stay together, how will they retain any color, which itself though naturally incorporeal can never exist independent of a physical body? 11. Furthermore, who can convince himself that as soon as he turns his eyes, images—of heaven, sea, shore, meadow, ships, cattle, and countless things besides that we take in with a single glance—thrust

sit pupula quae visu pollet oppido parva? et quonam modo
totus exercitus visitur? an de singulis militibus profecta simulacra se congerunt atque ita collata tot milia penetrant
oculos intuentis?

12. 'Sed quid laboramus opinionem sic inanem verbis
verberare, cum ipsa rei vanitas se refellat? constat autem
visum nobis hac provenire ratione. 13. genuinum lumen
e pupula, quacumque eam verteris, directa linea emicat.
id oculorum domesticum profluvium, si reppererit in cir-
cumfuso nobis aëre lucem, per eam directim pergit quam
diu corpus offendat, et si faciem verteris ut circumspicias,
utrobique acies videndi directa procedit. ipse autem iac-
tus, quem diximus de nostris oculis emicare, incipiens a tenui radice in summa fit latior sicut radii a pictore fingun-
tur: ideo per minutissimum foramen contemplans oculus
videt caeli profunditatem. 14. ergo tria ista necessaria nobis sunt ad effectum videndi: lumen, quod de nobis emittimus, et ut aër qui interiacet lucidus sit, et corpus quo
offenso desinat intentio; quae si diutius pergat, rectam
intentionem lassata non obtinet sed scissa in dextram lae-
vamque diffunditur. 15. hinc est quod ubicumque terrarum steteris, videris tibi quandam caeli conclusionem
videre, et hoc est quod horizontem veteres vocaverunt.
quorum indago fideliter deprehendit directam ab oculis
aciem per planum contra aspicientibus non pergere ultra
centum octoginta stadia et inde iam recurvari. per planum

---

[125] This "ocular emanation" theory is most closely associated
with Plato: cf. *Timaeus* 45B–D with Lindberg 1976, 3–6.

[126] 180 stades = ca. 111,245 Roman feet = ca. 31 km; in fact the
horizon at sea level is just over 5 km distant when viewed by an eye
five and one half feet above the ground.

themselves at him, when the pupil that is a crucial element in vision is quite small? How in the world can an entire army be seen? Do the images that emerge from the individual soldiers mass themselves and, thus marshaled in their thousands, penetrate the onlooker's eyes?

12. 'But why belabor such an empty view, when its very emptiness is self-refuting? There is no doubt, however, that we experience vision for the following reason. 13. An innate light flashes from the pupil in a straight line wherever you turn:[125] if that natural emanation of the eyes should find the surrounding air to be clear, it continues straight through it until it strikes up against an object, and if you turn your face to look around, your line of vision moves straight ahead in both directions. But the emission itself, which I've said darts out from our eyes, begins from a slender base and ends by becoming broader, like rays represented by a painter: that's why the eye sees to the depths of heaven while looking through the teeniest hole. 14. There are, then, three things we need to see: the light that we give off, clear air intervening, and an object for our gaze to strike against and stop; should that gaze continue on too long, it becomes tired and doesn't maintain its direction straight on but become split and is diffused to the left and the right. 15. This is why wherever on earth you stand, the sky appears to have an end-point, and this is what the ancients called the horizon: their research reliably discovered that a glance directed by eyes looking ahead through a flat area cannot continue more than 180 stades[126] and from that point curves back. I added the qualification "through a flat area" because we see elevated

ideo adieci quia altitudines longissime aspicimus, quippe qui et caelum videmus.

16. ʽErgo in omni horizontis orbe ipse qui intuetur centron est. et quia diximus quantum a centro acies usque ad partem orbis extenditur, sine dubio in horizonte διάμετρος orbis trecentorum sexaginta stadiorum est, et si ulterius qui intuetur accesserit seu retrorsum recesserit, similem se circa orbem videbit. 17. sicut igitur diximus, cum lumen quod pergit e nobis per aëris lucem in corpus inciderit, impletur officium videndi; sed ut possit res visa cognosci, renuntiat visam speciem rationi sensus oculorum, et illa advocata memoria recognoscit. 18. ergo videre oculorum est, iudicare rationis. quia trinum est officium quod visum complet ad dinoscendam figuram, sensus, ratio, memoria, sensus rem visam rationi refundit, illa quid visum sit recordatur. 19. adeo autem in tuendo necessarium est rationis officium ut saepe in uno videndi sensu etiam alium sensum memoria suggerente ratio deprehendat. nam si ignis appareat, scit eum et ante tactum ratio calere; si nix sit illa quae visa est, intellegit in ipsa ratio etiam tactus rigorem. 20. hac cessante visus inefficax est, adeo ut quod remus in aqua fractus videtur, vel quod turris eminus visa, cum sit angulosa, rotunda existimatur, faciat rationis neglegentia, quae si se intenderit, agnoscit in turre angulos et in remo integritatem.

---

127 Cf. *Comm.* 1.15.17–19.

128 Cf. Pl. *Tim.* 45C–D.

129 Cf. [Alex. Aphrod.] *Prob.* 1.37. Tower: Lucr. 4.353–63, Petron. Fr. 29, Tert. *On the Soul* 17.6, Sext. Emp. *Outlines of Pyrrhonism* 1.32, Diog. Laert. 9.107, Nemesius *On Human Nature* p. 62.11–12. Oar: Lucr. 4.438–42, Cic. *Academica* 2.19, Sen. *Natural*

places from a very great distance, in as much as we're also seeing the sky.[127]

16. 'In the whole circuit of the horizon, then, the viewer is the center, and since I've said how far the gaze extends from the center to a point on the circuit, the diameter of the horizon's circuit must be 360 stades, and whether the viewer advances or retreats, he will have a similar circuit surrounding him. 17. So as I said, when the light that proceeds from us through the clear air strikes an object, the tasks necessary for sight are satisfied; but so that the thing seen can be recognized, the eyes' perception reports back to our reason the appearance of the thing seen, a memory is summoned up, reason performs the recognition.[128] 18. Sight, then, is the function of the eyes, judgment the function of reason: distinguishing a shape and thereby completing the act of seeing requires the function of three faculties—perception, reason, memory—with perception reporting the thing seen to reason, and reason recalling what it has seen. 19. But the function of reason is so necessary in seeing that reason often catches out, in a single perception, another sensation, too, at the prompting of memory: if fire is visible, reason knows that it's hot even before touching it; if it sees snow, reason knows per se that it's freezing cold to the touch. 20. If reason fails, vision cannot do its job, to the extent that when an oar in the water appears broken or a tower seen from a distance appears round even though it's angular, it's owing to the failure of reason, though if it concentrates it recognizes the angles in the tower and the oar's intact state.[129]

Questions 1.3.9, Tert. ibid., Serv. on *E.* 2.27, John Philop. *Comm. on Arist. "On the Soul" CAG* 15:525.27–29.

21. 'Et omnia illa discernit quae Academiacis damnandorum sensuum occasionem dederunt; cum sensus[47] inter certissimas res habendi sint comitante ratione, cui non numquam ad discernendam speciem non sufficit sensus unus. 22. nam si eminus pomi quod malum dicitur figura visatur, non omni modo id malum est; potuit enim ex aliqua materia fingi mali similitudo. advocandus est igitur sensus alter ut odor iudicet. sed potuit inter congeriem malorum positum auram odoris ipsius concepisse. hic tactus consulendus est qui potest de pondere iudicare. sed metus est ne et ipse fallatur, si fallax opifex materiam quae pomi pondus imitaretur elegit. confugiendum est igitur ad saporem, qui si formae consentiat, malum esse nulla dubitatio est. 23. sic probatur efficaciam sensuum de ratione pendere. ideo deus opifex omnes sensus in capite id est circa sedem rationis locavit.'

15   His dictis favor ab omnibus exortus est admirantibus dictorum soliditatem, adeo ut attestari vel ipsum Evangelum non pigeret. Dysarius deinde subiecit, 'isti plausus sunt qui provocant philosophiam ad vindicandos sibi de aliena arte tractatus, unde saepe manifestos incurrit errores. ut Plato vester dum nec anatomica quae medicinae propria est abstinet, risum de se posteris tradidit. 2. dixit enim divisas esse vias devorandis cibatui et potui, et cibum quidem per stomachum trahi, potum vero per ἀρτήριαν

---

47 sensus C: sensus unus ω

---

130 Cf. Cic. *Academica* 2.61, *On the Nature of the Gods* 2.147.
131 Cf. 5.2.1n.
132 Cf. *Comm.* 1.6.81, Cic. *On the Nature of the Gods* 2.140.
133 §§2–7 are based on Gell.17.11.1–5.

21. 'Reason also makes sense of all the things that gave the Academics an opportunity to condemn the senses,[130] though the senses ought to be considered among the more reliable things when they're accompanied by reason, which sometimes finds a single sense insufficient for identifying a specific object. 22. If one should spot from a distance the shape of a fruit that's called an apple, it is not necessarily an apple but could have been fashioned from some material to look like an apple: another sense—smell—must be called on to judge. But if the thing was placed amid a heap of apples it could have acquired a whiff of the very odor: here touch must be consulted, to judge by the weight. But there's concern that touch itself might also be fooled, if a deceitful craftsman chose a substance that could imitate the weight of a fruit. We must then take refuge in taste, and should it agree with the shape, then it is an apple beyond doubt. 23. This demonstrates that the senses depend on reason to do their job, and for that reason god the craftsman[131] placed all the senses in the head, which is to say, around the seat of reason.'[132]

This account was well received by all, who marveled at how well-founded everything he said was, to the extent that even Evangelus himself was not loath to add his testimony. Dysarius then interposed, 'It's applause of that sort that leads philosophy on to claim to deal with matters alien to its expertise, with the result that it often plunges into obvious errors. For example, while your Plato didn't avoid dealing with anatomy—the proper sphere of medicine— he handed on to posterity an opportunity to mock him. 2. For he said that there were separate paths for swallowing food and drink,[133] with the food, to be sure, being drawn down through the stomach, but drink sliding down

15

quae τραχεῖα dicitur fibris pulmonis inlabi. quod tantum virum vel aestimasse vel in libros rettulisse mirandum est vel potius dolendum. 3. unde Erasistratus, medicorum veterum nobilissimus, in eum iure invectus est dicens rettulisse illum longe diversa quam ratio deprehendit. 4. duas enim esse fistulas instar canalium, easque ab oris faucibus proficisci deorsum, et per earum alteram induci delabique in stomachum esculenta omnia et poculenta, ex eoque ferri in ventriculum, qui[48] Graece appellatur ἡ κάτω κοιλία, atque illic subigi digerique ac deinde aridiora ex his retrimenta[49] in alvum convenire, quod Graece κόλον dicitur, umidiora autem per renes in vesicam trahi; 5. et per alteram de duabus superioribus fistulam, quae Graece appellatur τραχεῖα ἀρτηρία, spiritum a summo ore in pulmonem atque inde rursum in os et in nares commeare, perque eandem vocis fieri meatum; 6. ac ne potus cibusve aridior, quem oporteret in stomachum ire, procideret ex ore labereturque in eam fistulam per quam spiritus reciprocatur, ex eaque offensione intercluderetur animae via, impositam esse arte quadam et ope naturae ἐπιγλωττίδα quasi claustrum mutuum utriusque fistulae, quae sibi sunt cohaerentes, 7. eamque ἐπιγλωττίδα inter edendum bibendumque operire ac protegere τὴν τραχεῖαν ἀρτηρίαν, ne quid ex esca potuve incideret in illud quasi aestuantis animae iter; ac propterea nihil umoris influere in pulmonem ore ipso arteriae communito.

8. ʽHaec Erasistratus, cui ut aestimo vera ratio consen-

48 qui *ed. Basil. 1535*: quod ω
49 retrimenta A²C (*cf. 7.15.19, 20*): recrementa ω

through the *artêria* ["windpipe"] that's called *trakheia* ["rough"] to the lobes of the lung.[134] That such a great man formed such a judgment or committed it to writing is astounding—or rather, lamentable. 3. So Erasistratus, most renowned of ancient physicians, rightly attacked him, saying that his account was very different from that discovered by reason. 4. For there are two channel-like tubes that go downward from the opening of the throat. All food and drink is ingested through one of them, slips down into the stomach, and from there is carried into the abdomen, which the Greek call *hê kata koilia* ["the lower cavity"], where it is worked and digested until the drier waste that results gathers in the bowel, which the Greeks call the *kolon*, while the damper waste is drawn through the kidneys to the bladder. 5. Through the second of the upper tubes, which the Greeks call the *trakheia artêria*, the breath passes from the mouth on top into the lung and then back into the mouth and nostrils, and the voice passes through the same tube. 6. To keep drink and drier food, which ought to go to the stomach, from tumbling from the mouth and falling into the same tube through which the breath is exchanged—thereby blocking the soul's path— nature's skill and craftsmanship has imposed the *epiglôttis* as a kind of shared barrier of both tubes, which are conjoined: 7. while one is eating and drinking the *epiglôttis* covers and protects the *trakheia artêria*, to keep any food or drink from falling into the path of the soul as it (so to speak) ebbs and flows; and with the opening of the windpipe thus fortified, no liquid flows into the lung.

8. 'Thus Erasistratus, who has true reason's agreement,

---

[134] Cf. Pl. *Tim.* 70C–D, 91A.

tit. cum enim cibus non squalidus siccitate, sed umoris temperie mollis, ventri inferendus sit, necesse est eandem viam ambobus patere, ut cibus potu temperatus per stomachum in ventre condatur, nec aliter natura componeret nisi quod salutare esset animali. 9. deinde cum pulmo et solidus et levigatus sit, si quid spissum in ipsum deciderit, quem ad modum penetrat aut transmitti potest ad locum digestionis, cum constet si quando casu aliquid paulo densius in pulmonem violentia spiritus trahente deciderit, mox nasci tussim nimis asperam et alias quassationes usque ad vexationem salutis? 10. si autem naturalis via potum in pulmonem traheret, cum polenta⁵⁰ bibuntur vel cum hauritur potus admixtis granis ex re aliqua densiore, quid his sumptis pulmo pateretur? 11. unde ἐπιγλωττίς natura provisa est, quae cum cibus sumitur, operimento sit arteriae, ne quid per ipsam in pulmonem spiritu passim trahente labatur, sicut et cum sermo emittendus est, inclinatur ad operiendam stomachi viam ut ἀρτηρίαν voci patere permittat. 12. est et hoc de experientia notum, quod qui sensim trahunt potum ventres habent umectiores, umore qui paulatim sumptus est diutius permanente: si quis vero avidius hauserit, umor eodem impetu quo trahitur praeterit in vesicam, et sicciori cibo provenit tarda digestio. haec autem differentia non nasceretur, si a principio cibi et potus divisi essent meatus. 13. quod autem Alcaeus poeta dixit et vulgo canitur,

⁵⁰ polenta PJ² *cod. Bern 404*: pulenta ω (corpulenta C, poculenta A, pulmenta Jᵐ)

---

135 §§8–13, 16–24 are based on Plut. *Mor.* 697F–700B.

I think.[135] Since food that's not dry and rough but softened by moisture's tempering effect must be conveyed to the stomach, the same path must be open to both, so that food that's tempered by drink might be brought through the stomach and stored away in the belly. Nature would make no arrangement that was not healthy for the creature. 9. Furthermore, if some dense matter should descend into the lung, which is solid and light, how does it reach the place of digestion, or how can it be passed along to it, since it's well known that whenever by chance something a bit denser than usual descends to the lung with a violent intake of breath, harsh coughing and other wracking movements soon occur, to the point of causing real distress? 10. If, however, there were a natural pathway drawing drink into the lung, what would the lung suffer when gruel is drunk down or a draft drained with an admixture of kernels of some denser material? 11. That's why nature took the precaution of the *epiglôttis*, which covers the windpipe when food is eaten, to keep anything from falling through it and into the lung when a breath happens to draw it in, just as when it changes direction to cover the stomach's pathway when one has to speak, in order to open the *artêria* to the voice. 12. We also know from experience that those who drink slowly have moister bellies, as the moisture that was taken in gradually remains longer; but whenever someone drinks too greedily, the moisture passes to the bladder as aggressively as it was ingested, and drier food is digested slowly. This difference wouldn't occur if the passageways of food and drink were distinct from the start. 13. As for the often-sung lyric that the poet Alcaeus produced (fr. 347.1 L.-P.),

289

οἴνῳ πνεύμονα τέγγε,[51] τὸ γὰρ ἄστρον
περιτέλλεται,

ideo dictum est quia pulmo re vera gaudet umore sed trahit quantum sibi aestimat necessarium. vides satius fuisse philosophorum omnium principi alienis abstinere quam minus nota proferre.'

14. Ad haec Eustathius paulo commotior, 'non minus te,' inquit, 'Dysari, philosophis quam medicis inserebam, sed modo videris mihi rem consensu generis humani decantatam et creditam oblivioni dare, philosophiam artem esse artium et disciplinam disciplinarum: et nunc in ipsam invehitur parricidali ausu medicina, cum philosophia illic se habeatur augustior ubi de rationali parte, id est de incorporeis, disputat; et illic inclinetur ubi de physica, quod est de divinis corporibus vel caeli vel siderum, tractat. 15. medicina autem physicae partis extrema faex est, cui ratio est cum testeis terrenisque corporibus. sed quid rationem nominavi, cum magis apud ipsam regnet coniectura quam ratio?—quae ergo conicit de carne lutulenta, audet inequitare philosophiae de incorporeis et vere divinis certa ratione tractanti. sed ne videatur communis ista defensio tractatum vitare pulmonis, accipe causas quas Platonica maiestas secuta est.

16. ἐπιγλωττίς, quam memoras, inventum naturae est ad tegendas detegendasque certa alternatione vias cibatus

51 οἴνῳ πνεύμονα τέγγε (codd. Athen. 1 22E, Eustath. ad Od. 1.9, Suda T.212)] τέγγε πλεύμονας οἴνῳ Plut. Mor. 697F, Gell. 17.11.1, Athen. 10 430B, Σ Hes. Op. 582–7

> moisten your lung with wine, as the Dog-Star comes
>   over the horizon,

that's so said because the lung delights in moisture but
draws in only as much as it thinks necessary. You see that it
would have been better for the prince of all philosophers
to avoid matters alien to him than to pronounce on things
unfamiliar to him.'

14. At this, Eustathius said, with a bit more heat than
usual, 'I counted you no less a philosopher than a physician, Dysarius, but now you seem to consign to oblivion a
fact repeated and believed as a matter of universal consen-
sus, that philosophy is the very essence of all arts and disciplines. Now, with the brazenness of a parricide, medicine
launches an attack upon it, since philosophy is considered the more reverend when it treats the rational side of
things, which is to say, incorporeal matters, and lowers itself when it treats of physics, which is to say the divine bodies of the heavens and the stars. 15. But medicine is the
lowest dregs of the physical side of things, a system concerned with bodies of clay and earth. But why did I use the
word "system," when medicine is more the realm of guess-
work than system? So an art that works by conjecture on
filthy flesh has the nerve to mount a charge against philosophy, which deals with incorporeal and truly divine matters
according to a reliable system. But lest this general de-
fense seem to avoid the specific topic of the lung, hear the
rationale that Plato's majestic genius followed.

16. 'The *epiglôttis*, which you mention, is nature's de-
vice for covering and opening, in regular alternation, the
paths of food and drink, to convey the former to the stom-

et potus ut illum stomacho transmittat, hunc pulmo suscipiat. propterea tot meatibus distinctus est et interpatet rimis, non ut spiritus egressiones habeat, cui exhalatio occulta sufficeret, sed ut per eos si quid cibatus in pulmonem deciderit, sucus eius mox migret in sedem digestionis. 17. deinde ἀρτηρία si quo casu scissa fuerit, potus non devoratur, sed quasi fisso meatu suo reiectatur foras incolumi stomacho. quod non contingeret nisi ἀρτηρία via esset umoris. 18. sed et hoc in propatulo est, quia quibus aeger est pulmo accenduntur in maximam sitim, quod non eveniret nisi esset pulmo receptaculum potus. hoc quoque intuere, quod animalia quibus pulmo non est potum nesciunt. natura enim nihil superfluum sed membra singula ad aliquod vivendi ministerium fecit, quod cum deest usus eius, non desideratur.

19. 'Vel hoc cogita, quia si stomachus cibum potumque susciperet, superfluus foret vesicae usus. poterat enim utriusque rei stomachus retrimenta intestino tradere, cui nunc solius cibi tradit; nec opus esset diversis meatibus quibus singula traderentur, sed unus utrique sufficeret ab eadem statione transmisso. modo autem seorsum vesica et intestinum seorsum saluti servit, quia illi stomachus tradit, pulmo vesicae. 20. nec hoc praetereundum est, quod in urina, quae est retrimentum potus, nullum cibi vestigium reperitur, sed nec aliqua qualitate illorum retrimentorum vel coloris vel odoris inficitur; quod si in ventre simul fuis-

---

136 Cf. Arist. *Parts of Animals* 3.3 664b5–19.

137 Animals without lungs include, besides fish (Arist. *Parts of Animals* 3.5 668a5–8, *On Youth and Old Age* 16 478a31–32), those also in the category of "animals without blood," which lack viscera entirely, cf. 7.13.4n.

ach while the lung receives the latter.[136] The lung is divided by so many passageways and gapes with so many fissures, not to provide exits for the breath (an unseen process of exhalation would be enough for that), but so that the juice could quickly pass over to the seat of digestion if some food fell into the lung. 17. Further, if the *artêria* chances to be severed, drink cannot be swallowed, but with its proper path as it were split, it's heaved back up and out, leaving the stomach unaffected: this wouldn't happen if the *artêria* were not the path of moisture. 18. But this point is obvious, too: people with an ailing lung burn with extreme thirst, and that wouldn't happen if the lung were not drink's proper repository. Consider this point too: creatures without lungs do not drink.[137] Nature created nothing superfluous, but made the several limbs so that they would somehow support life: when there is no use for it, it is not missed.

19. 'Or reflect on this: if the stomach received food and drink, the bladder would have no use, since the stomach could pass on the waste of both to the intestine, which now receives only the waste of food, and there would be no need for distinct passageways to convey them separately, but a single passageway would be enough for both as they were passed on from the same staging-point. As it is, the bladder on one side and intestine on the other serve the cause of health, since the stomach hands off to the latter, the lung to the bladder. 20. Nor should we omit the fact that in urine, the waste product of drink, no trace of food is found, and it is not imbued with any property of food's waste, either in color or odor: but if they had been together

293

sent, aliqua illarum sordium qualitas[52] inficeretur. 21. nam
postremo lapides qui de potu in vesica nascuntur cur numquam in ventre coalescunt, cum non nisi ex potu fiant et
nasci in ventre quoque debuerint si venter esset receptaculum potus? 22. in pulmonem defluere potum nec poetae
nobiles ignorant. ait enim Eupolis in fabula quae inscribitur *Colaces*,

πίνειν γὰρ[53] Πρωταγόρας ἐκέλευεν,[54] ἵνα
πρὸ τοῦ κυνὸς τὸν πνεύμονα[55] ἔκλυρον[56] ἔχῃ.[57]

23. et Eratosthenes testatur idem:

καὶ βαθὺν ἀκρήτῳ πλεύμονα τεγγόμενος.

Euripides vero huius rei manifestissimus adstipulator est:

οἶνος περάσας πλευμόνων διαρροάς.

24. cum igitur et ratio corporeae fabricae et testium nobilis
auctoritas adstipuletur Platoni, nonne quisquis contra sentit insanit?'

16   Inter haec Evangelus gloriae Graecorum invidens et
inludens, 'facessant,' ait, 'haec quae inter vos in ostentatio-
nem loquacitatis agitantur; quin potius si quid callet vestra
sapientia, scire ex vobis volo ovumne prius extiterit an gal-

[52] qualitate C, *haud absurde* [53] γὰρ] γὰρ ὁ *Plut. Mor.*
699A, γὰρ αὐτὸν *Grotius* [54] ἐκέλευεν] ἐκέλευσ' *Plut.*
ibid., ἐκέλευ' *Meineke* [55] πνεύμονα (*plene scriptum a*
nostro)] πνεύμον' *edd. Eupol.* [56] ἔκλυρον (*Plut. ibid., cf.*
Hesych. E, 1506)] ἔκλυτον *Athen.* 1 22F, ἔκκλυστον *Reiske,* ἔκ-
πλυτον *Fritzsche* (*v. Kaster 2010, 77*)
[57] ἔχῃ P: φορῇ *Plut., Athen., Willis*

in the belly, some property of that filth would be imparted. 21. Finally, why do the stones that occur in the bladder from drinking never form in the belly, since they occur only as a result of drinking and should occur in the belly, too, if the belly were the receptacle of drink? 22. Nor are renowned poets unaware that drink flows down into the lung. Eupolis, in the play called *Flatterers*, says (fr. 158 *PCG* 5:383),

> Indeed, Protagoras called for drink, that he might
> have a moist lung before the Dog-Star's rising,

23. and Eratosthenes gives the same testimony (fr. 25 *CA* p. 65):

> . . . and moistening the lung deep with unmixed wine.

But Euripides is the most explicit support on this point (fr. 983 *TGrF* 5,2:973):

> the wine passed through the lungs' channels.

24. Since, then, both a rational understanding of the body's make-up and the noble authority of witnesses supports Plato, isn't anyone who holds an opposing opinion just insane?'

Evangelus, meanwhile, begrudging the Greeks their glory[138] and in a trifling mood, said, 'Away with these subjects, which you ventilate only to parade your chatter: instead, if your wisdom has the skill, I want to learn from you whether the egg or the chicken existed first.'

[138] Cf. 7.2.8.

lina.' 2. 'inridere te putas,' Dysarius ait, 'et tamen quaestio quam movisti et inquisitu et scitu digna est. iocum[58] enim tibi de rei vilitate comparans, consuluisti utrum prius gallina ex ovo an ovum ex gallina coeperit; sed hoc ita seriis inserendum est ut de eo debeat vel anxie disputari. et proferam quae in utramque partem mihi dicenda subvenient, relicturus tibi utrum eorum verius malis videri.

3. 'Si concedimus omnia quae sunt aliquando coepisse, ovum prius a natura factum iure aestimabitur. semper enim quod incipit imperfectum adhuc et informe est, et ad perfectionem sui per procedentis artis et temporis additamenta formatur. ergo natura fabricans avem ab informi rudimento coepit et ovum, in quo necdum est species animalis, effecit. ex hoc perfectae avis species extitit, procedente paulatim maturitatis effectu. 4. deinde quicquid a natura variis ornatibus comptum est, sine dubio coepit a simplici et ita contextionis accessione variatum est. ergo ovum visu simplex et undique versum pari specie creatum est, et ex illo varietas ornatuum quibus constat avis species absoluta est. 5. nam sicut elementa prius extiterunt et ita reliqua corpora de commixtione eorum creata sunt, ita rationes seminales quae in ovo sunt, si venialis erit ista translatio, velut quaedam gallinae elementa credenda sunt. 6. nec importune elementis, de quibus sunt omnia, ovum comparaverim. in omni enim genere animantium quae ex coitione nascuntur invenies ovum aliquorum esse principium

---

[58] iocum *Jan* (locum C, *haud absurde*): cum ω

---

139 §§2–14 are based on Plut. *Mor.* 635E–638A.

2. 'You think you're making fun,' Dysarius said, 'and yet the question you've raised is worth investigating and learning the answer.[139] Basing your joke on the trivial character of the subject, you asked whether the hen first came from the egg or the egg from the hen: but this should be counted such a serious question that there ought to be quite a meticulous discussion of it. I'll put before you what it occurs to me to say on both sides of the question, leaving to you which of the two you prefer to think more correct.

3. 'If we grant that all things that exist came into being at some point, the egg will rightly be judged to have been made first by nature. For the first stage of anything is still incomplete and unformed and is shaped and perfected as time passes and skill grows. So nature, in fashioning the bird, began with a shapeless first stage and produced the egg, which does not yet have a creaturely appearance. From the egg there emerged the bird complete in form, as it gradually came to be fully developed. 4. Further, whatever nature has arrayed with varied adornments surely was simple to begin with and gained in variety as elaboration was added. Thus the egg at its creation was simple in appearance and looked the same whichever way it was turned, and from that beginning there came to be completed the range of adornments that gives the bird the appearance it has. 5. For just as the elements existed first and all other objects were created from their combination, so the germinative principles in the egg must be regarded as—if you'll indulge the metaphor—the elements of the chicken. 6. Nor would I compare the egg with the elements of which all things are composed without having a point: in every kind of living creature that is produced by intercourse, you will find that an egg is the first stage—like

297

instar elementi. aut enim gradiuntur animantia aut serpunt aut nando volandove vivunt. 7. in gradientibus lacertae et similia ex ovis creantur; quae serpunt, ovis nascuntur exordio; volantia universa de ovis prodeunt, excepto uno quod incertae naturae est, nam vespertilio volat quidem pellitis alis, sed inter volantia non habendus est, quia quattuor pedibus graditur formatosque pullos parit et nutrit lacte quos generat. nantia paene omnia de ovis oriuntur generis sui, crocodilus[59] vero etiam de testeis qualia sunt volantium. 8. et ne videar plus nimio extulisse ovum elementi vocabulo, consule initiatos sacris Liberi patris, in quibus hac veneratione ovum colitur ut ex forma tereti ac paene sphaerali atque undique versum clausa et includente intra se vitam, mundi simulacrum vocetur, mundum autem consensu omnium constat universitatis esse principium.

9. 'Prodeat qui priorem vult esse gallinam, et in haec verba temptet quod defendit adserere:

'Ovum rei cuius est nec initium nec finis est. nam initium est semen, finis avis ipsa formata, ovum vero digestio est seminis. cum ergo semen animalis sit et ovum seminis, ovum ante animal esse non potuit, sicut non potest digestio cibi fieri antequam sit qui edit. 10. et tale est dicere ovum ante gallinam factum ac si quis dicat matricem ante mulierem factam: et qui interrogat, quem ad modum gallina sine ovo esse potuit similis est interroganti quonam pacto homines facti sint ante pudenda de quibus homines pro-

---

[59] crocodi(l)lus SG: -drillus ω

an element—of a certain number of them. Now, living creatures either walk or creep or they live by swimming or flying. 7. Among those that walk, lizards and the like are created from eggs; those that creep have the first stage of their being in an egg; all flying creatures are produced from eggs save for one whose nature is uncertain—for the bat certainly flies with wings of hide, but should not be counted among the flying creatures because it walks on four feet and bears fully-formed whelps and nurses them from the milk it produces. Almost all swimming creatures are born from eggs of their own kind, though the crocodile is born from hard-shelled eggs like those of flying creatures. 8. And lest I seem to have exalted the egg excessively by calling it an element, consider those initiated in the rites of father Liber, in which an egg is so worshipped that—being rounded and almost spherical, perfectly enclosed on all sides, and keeping life shut up within it—it is called a likeness of the universe, which by general agreement is held to be the first beginning of all that is.

9. 'Now let the champion of the chicken's priority come forward and try to maintain his position, along these lines:

'An egg is neither the beginning nor the end of that to which it belongs: the beginning is the seed, the end is the fully formed bird, while the egg is the processing of the seed. Since, then, the seed derives from the creature and the egg from the seed, the egg could not pre-exist the creature, just as the processing of food could not occur before there is someone to eat it. 10. To say that the egg was produced before the chicken is like saying a womb came to be before a woman: asking how a chicken could exist without an egg is like asking how humans were produced before the genitals instrumental in their procreation. So just as no

creantur. unde sicut nemo recte dicet hominem seminis
esse sed semen hominis, ita nec ovi gallinam sed ovum esse
gallinae. 11. deinde si concedamus ut ab adversa parte
dictum est, haec quae sunt ex tempore aliquo sumpsisse
principium, natura primum singula animalia perfecta for-
mavit, deinde perpetuam legem dedit ut continuaretur
procreatione successio. 12. perfecta autem in exordio fieri
potuisse testimonio sunt nunc quoque non pauca animantia quae de terra et imbre perfecta nascuntur, ut in Aegypto mures, ut aliis in locis ranae serpentesque et similia.
ova autem numquam de terra sunt procreata, quia in illis
nulla perfectio est, natura vero perfecta format et de per-
fectis ista procedunt, ut de integritate partes. 13. nam ut
concedam ova avium esse seminaria, videamus quid de semine ipso philosophorum definitio testatur, quae ita san-
cit: semen est generatio ad eius ex quo est similitudinem
pergens. non potest autem ad similitudinem pergi rei quae
necdum est, sicut nec semen ex eo quod adhuc non subsis-
tit emanat. 14. ergo in primo rerum ortu intellegamus,
cum ceteris animantibus quae solo semine nascuntur,
de quibus non ambigitur quin prius fuerint quam semen
suum, aves quoque opifice natura extitisse perfectas, et
quia vis generandi inserta sit singulis, ab his iam procedere
nascendi modos quos pro diversitate animantium natura
variavit.

---

[140] For the belief cf. Diod. Sic. 1.10.2, Ov. *Met*. 1.422–29,
Pliny *Natural History* 9.179, Aelian *On the Nature of Animals*
2.56, and more generally [Arist.] *Prob*. 10.13 892a.

[141] Cf. [Arist.] *Prob*. 4.13 878a24–26, Chrysippus fr. 741 *SVF*
2:211, [Plut.] *Mor*. 905A.

one will rightly say that a human being is derived from seed, rather than seed is derived from a human being, so one cannot say that the chicken is derived from the egg, but rather the egg is derived from the chicken. 11. Further, if we should grant the other side's statement that the things that now exist took their beginning from some point in time, it follows that nature first completely formed the individual living creatures, then established the eternal law that one generation would follow the next in an unbroken line by means of procreation. 12. Now, as evidence that things could have been completely formed at the outset we even now have a considerable number of living things that arise completely formed from the earth and rain, like mice in Egypt and like frogs, snakes, and similar creatures elsewhere.[140] Eggs, however, have never been produced from the earth, since there is nothing completely formed about them, whereas nature shapes completely formed things, and eggs are derived from the things completely formed, like parts from a whole. 13. For on the supposition that eggs are the seedbeds from which birds derive, let's see what evidence is provided about seed itself by the philosophers' definition, which holds that seed is a germ tending toward a likeness of its source.[141] But there can be no aim to produce a likeness of that which does not yet exist, just as seed does not flow from that which does not yet exist. 14. Let us take it, then, that at the first beginning of things, along with all other living creatures born from seed alone—and there is no doubt in their case that they existed before their seed—birds too came forth completely formed by nature the craftsman; and that because the power of generation was implanted in each and every one, they developed ways of giving birth that nature caused to vary according to the differences among living things.

'Habes, Evangele, utrobique quod teneas, et dissimulata paulisper inrisione tecum delibera quid sequaris.'

15. Et Evangelus: 'quia et ex iocis seria facit violentia loquendi, hoc mihi absolvatis volo, cuius diu me exercuit vera deliberatio. nuper enim mihi de Tiburti agro meo exhibiti sunt apri quos obtulit silva venantibus et quia diutule continuata venatio est, perlati sunt alii interdiu, noctu alii. 16. quos perduxit dies, integra carnis incolumitate durarunt, qui vero per noctem lunari plenitudine lucente portati sunt putruerunt. quod ubi scitum est, qui sequenti nocte deferebant, infixo cuicumque parti corporis acuto aëneo, apros carne integra pertulerunt. quaero igitur cur noxam, quam pecudibus occisis solis radii non dederunt, lunare lumen effecerit.'

17. 'Facilis est,' Dysarius inquit, 'et simplex ista responsio. nullius enim rei fit aliquando putredo nisi calor umorque convenerint. pecudum autem putredo nihil aliud est nisi cum defluxio quaedam latens soliditatem carnis in umorem resolvit. 18. calor autem si temperatus sit et modicus, nutrit umores, si nimius exsiccat et habitudinem carnis extenuat. ergo de corporibus enectis sol ut maioris caloris haurit umorem, lunare lumen, in quo est non manifestus calor sed occultus tepor, magis diffundit umecta et inde provenit iniecto tepore et aucto umore putredo.'

19. His dictis Evangelus Eustathium intuens, 'si rationi

---

142 With §17 cf. [Alex. Aphrod.] *Prob.* 1.66; §§18–34 are based on Plut. *Mor.* 658A–659E. On the effects of moonlight cf. also Cic *On the Nature of the Gods* 2.50 (with A. S. Pease's note), Pliny *Natural History* 2.223, Plut. *Mor.* 367D.

'There you have a position to take on either side, Evangelus, and if you you'll suppress your mockery a bit, you may ponder your choice.'

15. Evangelus said, 'Since your aggressive chatter turns even jokes into sober discussions, I'd like the two of you to solve this puzzle for me, which I've really pondered for a while. I was recently shown boars that the forest had offered up to hunters on my estate at Tibur: since the hunt went on for a while, some were brought in during the daytime, others at night. 16. The meat of the former continued to be intact and untainted, whereas those brought in at night under a full moon turned putrid. When this was discovered, the porters on the following night inserted a piece of sharpened bronze in one or another part of the body and brought the boars in with their flesh intact. Hence my question: why did the moonlight harm the game that was killed while the sun's rays did not?'

17. 'The answer is simple and straightforward,' Dysarius said.[142] 'Nothing ever putrefies save when heat and moisture combine, and game putrefies only when a kind of hidden discharge of fluid undermines the meat's solidity and turns it into liquid. 18. Now, if heat is balanced and moderate, it favors the formation of moisture, while if it's excessive, it dries it up and reduces the meat's bulk. Thus the sun, being the greater source of heat, drains moisture from the carcasses, whereas the moonlight, which lacks outright heat but does have an imperceptible warmth, does more to spread the moisture, and the result—with the added warmth and increased moisture—is putrefaction.'

19. When Dysarius was finished, Evangelus looked at Eustathius and said, 'If you agree with this account, you

303

dictae adsentiris,' ait, 'annuas oportet, aut si est quod moveat, proferre non pigeat, quia vis vestri sermonis obtinuit ne invita aure vos audiam.'

20. 'Omnia,' inquit Eustathius, 'a Dysario et luculente et ex vero dicta sunt. sed illud pressius intuendum est, utrum mensura caloris sit causa putredinis, ut ex maiore calore non fieri et ex minore ac temperato provenire dicatur. solis enim calor qui nimium fervet quando annus in aestate est et hieme tepescit, putrefacit carnes aestate, non hieme. 21. ergo nec luna propter submissiorem calorem diffundit umores, sed nescio quae proprietas, quam Graeci ἰδίωμα vocant, et quaedam natura inest lumini quod de ea defluit, quae umectet corpora et velut occulto rore madefaciat cui admixtus calor ipse lunaris putrefacit carnem cui diutule fuerit infusus. 22. neque enim omnis calor unius est qualitatis, ut hoc solo a se differat, si maior minorve sit, sed esse in igne diversissimas qualitates nullam secum habentes societatem, rebus manifestis probatur. 23. aurifices ad formandum aurum nullo nisi de paleis utuntur igne, quia ceteri ad producendam hanc materiam inhabiles habentur; medici in remediis concoquendis magis de sarmentis quam ex alio ligno ignem requirunt. 24. qui vitro solvendo formandoque[60] curant de arbore cui myricae nomen est igni suo escam ministrant; calor de lignis oleae cum sit corporibus salutaris, perniciosus est balneis et ad dissolvendas iuncturas marmorum efficaciter noxius. non est ergo mirum si ratione proprietatis quae singulis inest calor solis arefacit, lunaris umectat.

---

[60] formandoque J²W¹: firm- ω

---

[143] Plutarch *Mor.* 658C says "peculiarity" (ἰδιότητα).

should indicate your assent, or if something leaves you unsettled, don't be slow to raise it, since the forceful speech of you Greeks has made me a willing listener.'

20. 'Dysarius' whole account,' Eustathius said, 'was brilliantly said and correct. But we should consider more closely whether the degree of heat is the cause of putrefaction, so that it can be said that greater heat does not cause it, but it issues from a lesser, moderate heat. For the sun's heat, which is too hot in the summer and mild in the winter, causes meat to putrefy in the summer, not the winter. 21. The moon, then, doesn't spread moisture because its heat is milder, but moonlight has a certain peculiar property—the Greek term is *idiôma*[143]—and there is a certain essence in the light which issues from it that makes bodies moist and steeps them in a kind of imperceptible dew that, mingled with the moon's warmth, putrefies meat that's been infused with it for any length of time. 22. Not all heat is of a single sort, so that the sole difference is whether it's greater or less, but as very clear evidence shows, there are different kinds of fire that have nothing in common. 23. Goldsmiths use only fire fueled by wheat chaff to shape their gold, since all other sorts are considered unsuitable for working that material; but physicians prefer fire from cut twigs to any other kind for concocting their cures. 24. Those who melt and shape glass feed their fire with wood from the tree called the tamarisk; heat from olive logs promotes the body's health but is destructive for baths and does great harm in loosening the joins of marble. It's not surprising, then, that the sun's heat dries while the moon's moistens, by reason of the peculiar quality of each.

25. hinc et nutrices pueros fellantes[61] operimentis obtegunt, cum sub luna praetereunt, ne plenos per aetatem naturalis umoris amplius lunare lumen umectet et, sicut ligna adhuc virore umida accepto calore curvantur, ita et illorum membra contorqueat umoris adiectio. 26. hoc quoque notum est, quia si quis diu sub luna somno se dederit, aegre excitatur et proximus fit insano, pondere pressus umoris qui in omne eius corpus diffusus atque dispersus est proprietate lunari quae ut corpus infundat omnes eius aperit et laxat meatus. 27. hinc est quod Diana, quae luna est, Ἄρτεμις dicitur, quasi ἀερότεμις, hoc est aërem secans. Lucina a parturientibus invocatur, quia proprium eius munus est distendere rimas corporis et meatibus viam dare, quod est ad celerandos partus salutare. 28. et hoc est quod eleganter poeta Timotheus expressit:

διὰ λαμπρὸν[62] πόλον ἄστρων
διά τ᾽ ὠκυτόκοιο σελάνας.

29. ʻNec minus circa inanimata lunae proprietas ostenditur. nam ligna quae luna vel iam plena vel adhuc crescente deiecta sunt, inepta sunt fabricis quasi emollita per umoris conceptionem, et agricolis curae[63] est frumenta de

61 fellantes *Meurs*: fallentes ω (pallentes PA, lactentes C, alentes JᵐWᵐ)   62 λαμπρὸν] κυάνεον *Plut. Mor. 282C, 659A*
63 curae *ed. Ven. 1472*: cura ω

144 Cf. Galen 9:903.
145 Cf. 1.15.20.
146 The Roman goddess of childbirth, variously identified with Juno or Diana: the surrounding refs. suggest the latter is intended here.

25. This is why nurses, too, in giving suck to children, cover them with blankets when they pass by beneath the moon: so the moonlight won't make even more moist those who are naturally full of moisture because of their age, and so the added moisture won't twist their limbs, just as logs that are still green and moist become warped when subjected to heat.

26. 'Here's another well-known fact:[144] if someone sleeps a long time under the moon, it's very difficult to wake him and he nearly goes mad, once he's been overwhelmed by the weight of the moisture that has suffused his entire body and been spattered with the moon's peculiar property, which loosens and opens all the body's passageways so that it might seep into the body itself. 27. This is why Diana, who is the moon, is called in Greek *Artemis*, as though *aërotemis*, that is, cutting through the air.[145] Women in labor call upon Lucina,[146] whose peculiar function it is to enlarge the body's crevices and provide a pathway for movement, a salutary thing when it comes to accelerating childbirth. 28. Consider too the poet Timotheus' fine expression (fr. 27 *PMG*):

> Through the stars' brilliant vault of heaven
> and through the moon's, that speeds childbirth.

29. 'The peculiar quality of the moon is made no less plain where inanimate objects are concerned. Logs cut when the moon is already full or still waxing are unsuited for building, because they've taken on moisture and become soft,[147] and farmers take care to gather grain from

---

[147] Cf. Varro *On Agriculture* 1.37.1, Col. 11.2.11, Pliny *Natural History* 16.190, Plut. fr. 109 Sandbach, DServ. on *G.* 1.256.

areis non nisi luna deficiente colligere ut sicca perma-
neant. 30. contra quae umecta desideras luna crescente
conficies. tunc et arbores aptius seres maxime cum illa est
super terram, quia ad incrementa stirpium necessarium
est umoris alimentum. 31. aër ipse proprietatem lunaris
umoris et patitur et prodit. nam cum luna plena est vel
cum nascitur—et tunc enim a parte qua sursum suspicit
plena est—aër aut in pluviam solvitur, aut si sudus sit, multum de se roris emittit, unde et[64] Alcman lyricus dixit ro-
rem aëris et lunae filium. 32. ita undique versum probatur ad umectandas dissolvendasque carnes inesse lunari
lumini proprietatem, quam magis usus quam ratio deprehendit.

33. 'Quod autem dixisti, Evangele, de acuto aëneo, ni
fallor coniectura mea a vero non deviat. est enim in aere vis
acrior, quam medici stypticam vocant, unde squamas eius
adiciunt remediis quae contra perniciem putredinis advo-
cantur. deinde qui in metallo aeris morantur, semper oculorum sanitate pollent, et quibus ante palpebrae nudatae
fuerant, illic convestiuntur. aura enim quae ex aere procedit, in oculos incidens haurit et exsiccat quod male influit.
34. unde et Homerus modo εὐήνορα modo νώροπα χαλ-

---

[64] et *ed. Paris. 1585, om.*ω

---

[148] Cf. Varro ibid., Pliny *Natural History* 18.322.
[149] Cf. Col. 5.11.2, Pliny ibid.   [150] M. appears to mean
that at the full moon the orb's "lower" part, which looks "downward" (sc. toward the earth), is entirely illuminated from a terres-
trial perspective, whereas at the new moon (or, more properly,
conjunction) the part that looks "upward" and away from earth is
entirely visible from the opposite perspective, on the "far side."

the threshing floor only under a waning moon, so that it will stay dry.[148] 30. On the other hand, under a waxing moon you'll complete tasks that call for moisture: that's a better time to plant trees, especially when the moon has risen, since it provides the nourishing moisture that tree-stocks need to grow.[149] 31. The very air both experiences and reveals the peculiar quality of the moon's moisture: when the moon is full, or when it's new—for then, too, it's full in the part that looks upward[150]—the air either lets loose a downpour or, if the sky's clear, produces a lot of dew: that's why the lyric poet Alcman said that dew is the child of air and moon (cf. fr. 57 *PMG*). 32. So from every point of view it's plain that there's a peculiar quality in moonlight that moistens and dissolves meat, a quality that experience apprehends rather than reason.

33. 'As for your remark about sharpened bronze, Evangelus, if I'm not mistaken I have a conjecture that's not wide of the truth. Bronze has quite a sharp force, which physicians call "styptic," and that's why they add flakes of bronze to medicine called on to fight the danger of gangrene. Furthermore, those who deal extensively with bronze always have very good eyesight, and people who lacked eyelashes previously grow a thick set:[151] bronze gives off an emanation that falls upon the eyes, draining and drying any unhealthy influxes.[152] 34. It's in line with these reasons that Homer calls bronze now "a boon to

The idea (which has no counterpart in the corresponding passage of Plutarch) is somewhat oddly put.   [151] Cf. [Arist.] *Marvels Heard* 58 834b.   [152] Cf. Galen 12:242, on "blossom of bronze," a copper sulphate salve used to cure ulcerations of the eyelid (sim. Hippocratic Corpus *On Vision* 6).

κόν has causas secutus appellat. Aristoteles vero auctor est vulnera quae ex aëreo mucrone fiunt minus esse noxia quam ex ferro faciliusque curari: "quia inest," inquit, "aeri vis quaedam remedialis et siccifica, quam demittit in vulnere." pari ergo ratione infixum corpori pecudis lunari repugnat umori . . ."[65]

[65] *post* umori *nihil* P (*fol. reciso*), MACROBII THEODOSII V.C. ET INLUSTRIS CONVIVIORUM PRIMI DIEI SATURNALIORUM EXPLICIT G, MACROBII THEODOSII V.C. & INL. CONVIVIORUM TERTII DIEI β_2 (*cui* expliĉ *add.* F, explicit felicit(er) W, finit H)

men" (*Od.* 13.19), now "flashing" (*Il.* 2.578 *et al.*).[153] We have it on Aristotle's authority that wounds made by a bronze blade are less harmful and easier to cure than those made by iron (*Prob.* 1 863a25–30), "because," he says, "bronze has some curative drying power that it deposits in the wound." For the same reason bronze inserted in an animal's body counteracts the moon's moisture . . .'"

[153] M. means to link the second epithet, *nôropa*, to the root *op-*, pertaining to the eye (cf. Σ *Od.* 24.467).

INDEX OF NAMES

This index includes the names of persons (historical and mythological), divinities, days, months, festivals, peoples, and places. Personal names are generally listed according to the form that Macrobius uses; parts of a Roman name that Macrobius does not use are given in parentheses: so, e.g., "Cato, (Marcus Porcius)" rather than "Porcius Cato, Marcus." I have excluded names that appear only in texts that Macrobius quotes.

INDEX

Adad (god of "Assyrians")
  identified with Sun:
  1.23.17–19
    image of: 1.23.19
Adargatis (consort of Adad)
  identified with Adad:
  1.23.18–19
    image of: 1.23.19–20
Adonis
  cult paid by "Assyrians"
  and Phoenicians: 1.21.1–2
  identified with Sun:
  1.21.1–6
    image of: 1.21.9
    killed by boar: 1.21.4
Adriatic Sea: 7.12.35
Aegean Sea: 7.12.35
Aemilia (Vestal Virgin, 114
  BCE), condemnation of:
  1.10.5
Aemilius (Mamercus, Lucius)
  (military tribune with consular powers, 389 BCE):
  1.16.22
Aemilius Lepidus. *See* Lepidus
Aemilius Regillus, (Lucius)
  (praetor 190 BCE), vows temple to Lares: 1.10.10
Aeneas (protagonist of *Aeneid*):
  1.12.8, 4.3.7, 15, 4.4.6, 9,
  4.5.4, 4.6.7, 5.11.7, 5.13.35–
  36, 5.15.11, 5.17.4, 5.2.6, 8,
  11,13, 15, 5.4.4, 5.6.1, 6.8.14,
  23, 7.2.16; ritually correct actions of: 3.1–12 passim
Aeschylus (tragic poet, ca. 525/
  24–456/55 BCE), cited as authority: 5.19.17, 24, 5.20.16,
  5.22.12–13

Aesculapius
  identified with Sun: 1.20.1–
  2, 4–5
    images of, with serpent:
    1.20.1–2
    prophetic power of:
    1.20.4–5
Aesopus (tragic actor, 1st cent.
  BCE)
    becomes wealthy: 3.14.14
    befriended by Cicero:
    3.14.11
Aetna, Mount, eruption of, described by Virgil and Pindar:
  5.17.7–14
Aetolians
    customs of: 5.18.16, 19–
  20
    war of, with Romans:
  1.13.21
Afranius, (Lucius) (author of
  comedies in Roman dress, fl.
  150–125 BCE)
    cited as authority: 3.20.4,
  6.1.4, 6.8.13
    usage of, as precedent for
  Virgil: 6.4.12, 6.5.6
Agamemnon (leader of Greek
  host against Troy): 4.3.12,
  4.4.22, 5.2.15; as host: 1.7.10
Agathon (tragic poet, late 5th–
  early 4th cent. BCE)
    host of Plato's Symposium:
  2.1.2, 6, 7.1.13
    lover of Plato: 2.2.15
Agesilaos (error for "Acusilaus"
  of Argos, mythographer of
  6th cent. BCE), cited as authority: 5.18.10

314

INDEX

cited as authority: 5.18.9–12,
5.22.10

Diogenes (of Babylon: Stoic
philosopher, 2nd cent. BCE),
embassy of, to Rome: 1.5.15–
16

Diogenes (of Sinope: most
noted Cynic philosopher of
antiquity, 4th cent. BCE)
enslavement of: 1.11.7
praises Antisthenes: 7.3.21
sold into slavery: 1.11.42–43

Diomedes (Greek in *Iliad*):
5.2.15, 5.13.34

Dionysos, name of Liber:
1.18.12–15

Dionysus. *See* Liber

Dis, days when *mundus* is open
sacred to: 1.16.17. *See also*
Hades

Dodona, oracle at: 1.7.28

Dolon (Trojan in *Iliad*): 5.16.9

Domitian (Titus Flavius
Domitianus: Roman emperor,
r. 81–96 CE): 7.3.15; attempts
to rename September and
October: 1.12.36–37

Domitius (Ahenobarbus),
Gnaius (cos. 96, cens. 92
BCE), criticizes luxury of
Crassus: 3.15.4–5

Domitius (Calvinus), Gnaius
(cos. 53 BCE), cited as authority: 1.9.14

Drances (Italian in *Aeneid*):
5.2.15

Dysarius (physician, interlocutor in *Sat.*: see Introd. §2)

answers Avienus' ques-
tions: 7.12 passim
answers questions
about digestion: 7.8.2–3,
5–6
about fasting: 7.13.2–5
about graying and baldness:
7.10.1–11
about heat: 7.8.8–15
about moonlight's effects:
7.16.17–18
about optics: 7.14.2–4
arrival of: 1.7.1
criticizes Plato's anatomical
views: 7.15.1–13
debates Eustathius on perception and digestion: 7.14–
15
eludes Evangelus' trap:
7.9.10–25
explains
cause of blushing and pallor:
7.11.4–6, 8–9
cause of dizziness: 7.9.3–7
eunuchs' high-pitched voices:
7.10.13–14
fresh water's cleansing power:
7.13.19–20
nervous system: 7.9.16–25
properties of must: 7.7.15–20
responds civilly to Eustathius: 7.5.33
serves as "consultant": 7.4–
13, 16
speaks
on drunkenness: 7.6.16–21
on egg vs. chicken question:
7.16.2–14

335

336

INDEX

Killaios, epithet of Apollo:
1.17.48

Kronos
    born from Heaven: 1.8.7
    identified
    with Khronos: 1.8.6–7, 10
    with Saturn: 1.7.36–37,
        1.8.6–7
    See also *Cronia*

Kylikrani (tribe near Heraclea):
5.21.18

Labeo, (Marcus Antistius) (Ro-
    man jurist of Augustan era),
    cited as authority: 3.10.4, 6

Laberius, Decimus (Roman au-
    thor of mimes, fl. mid-1st
    cent. BCE)
        defeated by Publilius
        Syrus: 2.7.7–9
        performs on stage: 2.7.2–4
        rewarded for stage perfor-
        mance: 2.3.10
        target of Cicero's wit:
        2.3.10
        usage of, as precedent for
        Virgil: 6.5.15
        wit of: 2.3.10, 2.6.6, 7.3.8

Labienus, (Quintus) (Roman
    turncoat, abetted Parthian
    campaign against Romans,
    40–39 BCE), protected by his
    freedmen: 1.11.18

Lacedaemonians: 5.15.2
    celebrate Hyacinthia:
    1.18.2
    cult paid
    armed Dionysus by: 1.19.2
    Apollo by: 1.18.2

have statue of Liber: 1.19.2
used freed slaves as sol-
    diers: 1.11.34

Laelius, (Gaius) (friend of
    younger Scipio Africanus,
    cos. 140 BCE), interlocutor in
    Ciceronian dialogues: 1.1.4

Laelius, Marcus (augur =
    Laelius Felix, jurist under
    Hadrian?), cited as authority:
    1.6.13

Laevius (innovative Roman
    poet, prob. early 1st cent.
    BCE)
        cited as authority: 1.18.16,
        3.8.3
        usage of, as precedent for
        Virgil: 6.5.10

Lais (Greek courtesan, 4th cent.
    BCE): 2.2.11

Lanuvium, people of, use *mane*
    to mean "good": 1.3.12

Larcius, Titus (Roman dictator,
    498 BCE), dedicates temple
    of Saturn: 1.8.1

Larentinalia, holiday of Jupiter:
    1.10.11–17

Lares
    holiday of: 1.10.10
    honored at *Compitalia*:
    1.7.34
        offerings to: 1.7.34–35
        shrine of: 1.10.10

Latin festival (*feriae Latinae*)
    movable: 1.16.6
    start of war during, forbid-
    den: 1.16.16–17

Latins, call June "Junonius":
    1.12.30

INDEX

BCE), cited as authority:
1.10.22, 3.8.3

Philocrates (alternative name of
Gaius Gracchus' slave),
loyalty of: 1.11.25

philosophers, teach that "the all
is one": 1.17.4

Philostratus (error for
"Theophrastus," Aristotle's
successor): 1.11.42

Philotis (alternative name of
Tutela), devises stratagem in
war: 1.11.38

Phoebus, tithe offered to: 1.7.28

Phoenicians
    cult paid Venus and Adonis
    by: 1.21.1–2
    fashion cult image of Janus:
    1.9.12

Phrygians
    cult paid Mother of Gods
    and Attis by, 1.21.7–10,
    1.23.20
    image of Mother of Gods
    fashioned by: 1.23.20

Pictor (perhaps an error: see n.
ad loc.), cited as authority:
3.2.3, 11

Pinarii (wardens of Hercules'
cult): 1.12.28, 3.6.12, 15

Pinarius (Mamercinus Rufus),
Lucius (cos. 472 BCE), passes
law on intercalation: 1.13.21

Pindar (Greek lyric poet, end of
6th–1st half of 5th cent.
BCE), imitated by Virgil:
5.17.7–14

Pisa: 5.15.4

Pisander (of Laranda: Greek
poet, wrote on marriages of
gods, early 3rd cent. CE), said
(erroneously) to be imitated
by Virgil: 5.2.4–5

Pisces (sign of zodiac), symbolizes Sun: 1.21.27

Pisistratus (tyrant of Athens, fl.
mid-6th cent., d. 527 BCE):
7.1.12

Piso (Frugi), (Gaius Calpur-
nius) (son-in-law of Cicero),
butt of joke: 2.3.16

Piso (Frugi), (Lucius Calpur-
nius) (Roman historian, cos.
133, cens. 120 BCE), cited as
authority: 1.12.18, 3.2.13

Plancus, (Lucius) Munatius (political opportunist, cos. 42,
censor 22 BCE)
    butt of joke: 2.2.6
    judges wager of Antony
    and Cleopatra: 3.17.16–17

Plato (Greek philosopher, ca.
429–347 BCE)
    anachronisms of: 1.1.5–6
    anatomical views of
    criticized: 7.15.1–13
    defended: 7.15.15–24
    cited as authority: 1.17.7,
    46, 1.23.5–8
    enslavement of: 1.11.7
    epigram of: 2.2.15
    names *Phaedo* after slave:
    1.11.41
    Symposium of: 1.1.3
    views of, on wine: 2.8.4–8

Plautus, (Titus Maccius) (Ro-

(Roman historian, cos. 129 BCE), cited as authority: 1.13.21, 1.16.32

Tullia (d. of Cicero), butt of joke: 2.3.16

Tullius, Servius. *See* Servius

Tullius Cicero. *See* Cicero

Tullus Hostilius (Rome's 3rd king, r. 672–641 BCE)
  adopts Etruscan insignia: 1.6.7
  consecrates shrine to Saturn and establishes Saturnalia: 1.8.1
  defeats Albans and Sabines: 1.8.1

Turnus (Aeneas' Italian rival in *Aeneid*): 3.3.6, 4.4.20, 4.6.10, 21, 5.1.16, 5.2.15, 5.13.35, 39, 5.15.5, 7, 12

Tusculum
  best figs produced in: 3.16.12
  people of, worship god Maius: 1.12.17

Tutela (slave), devises stratagem in war: 1.11.38

Tutilina: 1.16.8

Twelve Tables: 1.13.21

Twins (zodiac sign), symbolize the Sun: 1.21.22

"Two-fold," cult name of Janus: 1.9.15–16

Tyre, cult paid Hercules in: 1.20.7

Tyrrhenian Sea: 7.12.35

Ulysses (Gk. Odysseus: warrior in *Iliad*, protagonist of *Odys-*

sey): 5.2.6, 10, 13, 5.4.4, 5.6.1, 5.11.7

Umbrians, define "day" (as unit of time): 1.3.4–5

Umbro (Italian in *Aeneid*): 5.15.8

Umbro (otherwise unknown), cited as authority: 1.16.10

Urbinius, Gaius (quaestor of Metellus Pius, 74 BCE): 3.13.7

Urbinus (otherwise unknown), rescued by his slave: 1.11.16

Valerius Antias. *See* Antias

Valerius Catullus. *See* Catullus

Valerius Flaccus. *See* Flaccus

Valerius Maximus, (Manius) (cos. 263, censor 252 BCE), receives surname Messala: 1.6.26

Valerius Messala. *See* Messala

Valerius Probus, (Marcus) (Roman literary scholar, 2nd half of 1st cent. CE), ignorance of, criticized: 5.22.7–8

Varius (Rufus), Lucius (Roman epic and tragic poet of Augustan era): 2.4.2; imitated by Virgil: 6.1.39–40, 6.2.19–20

Varro, Marcus Terentius (greatest Roman scholar and antiquarian, 116–27 BCE)
  on cakes: 2.8.2
  cited as authority: 1.3.2–6, 1.4.14, 1.5.5, 10, 1.7.12, 28, 1.8.1, 1.9.16, 1.11.5, 1.12.13, 27, 1.13.20–21, 1.15.18, 21, 1.16.18–19, 27, 33, 1.18.4,

367

INDEX

3.2.8, 11, 3.4.2–3, 5, 7, 3.6.10,
17, 3.8.9–10, 3.12.2–3, 6,
3.13.1, 14–15, 3.15.2, 6, 8,
3.16.12–13, 3.18.5, 13
  imitates writings of
Menippus: 1.11.42
  usage of, as precedent for
Virgil: 6.4.8
Vatinius, (Publius) (tr. pl. 59,
cos. suff. 47 BCE)
  butt of jokes: 2.3.5, 2.6.1
  calls Cicero "consular buf-
foon": 2.1.12
  stoned by a crowd: 2.6.1
  target of Augustus' wit:
2.4.16
  wit of: 2.3.5
Veii, devoted to destruction:
3.9.13
Velabrum: 1.10.15
Velius Longus (Roman literary
scholar, early 2nd cent. CE),
error of: 3.6.6
Veneralia, holiday of Venus:
1.12.15
Veneto: 5.2.1
Venus
  and Mars, benefactor and
destroyer: 1.12.9
  androgynous statue of, on
Cyprus: 3.8.2
  April dedicated to: 1.21.6
  called "god": 3.8.1–3
  cult paid, on Mount Leba-
non: 1.21.5
  by "Assyrians": 1.21.1–2
  by Phoenicians: 1.21.1–2,
5–6

has no holy days in April:
1.12.12
  identified with earth's upper hemisphere: 1.21.1
  invoked as "mother":
1.12.8
  mother of Aeneas: 1.12.5, 8
  "mourning," image of:
1.21.2–3, 5
  name of, did not exist under the kings: 1.12.13
  named "Aphrodite" from
sea foam: 1.8.6, 1.12.8
  not sung of by Salii:
1.12.12
  replaces Nausicaa: 5.2.13
  source of living things:
1.8.8
  statue of, in Pantheon:
3.17.18
Venustus, (Volusius) (father of
Flavianus): 1.5.13
Veranius (Roman writer on sa-
cral law, 1st cent. BCE), cited
as authority: 3.2.3–4, 3.5.6,
3.6.14, 3.20.2
Vergilius (error for Lucius
Verginius Tricostus, military
tribune with consular powers,
389 BCE): 1.16.22
Verrius Flaccus, (Marcus) (Roman grammarian and lexicog-
rapher, ca. 55 BCE–ca. 20 CE),
cited as authority: 1.4.7,
1.6.15, 1.8.5, 1.10.7, 1.12.15,
1.15.21
Vesta, altar of,
  and Penates: 3.4.11

368

new flame kindled on:
1.12.6

Vettius (Scatto), Gaius (of
Corfinum, commander of
Marsi in Social War, 91–88
BCE), killed by slave to save
his honor: 1.11.24

Vettius (unknown), target of
Augustus' wit: 2.4.10

Viminal: 1.9.17

Vinalia, grammatical form of
name: 1.4.9

Vipsanius Agrippa. *See* Agrippa

Virbius (Italian in *Aeneid*):
5.15.8

Virgil (Publius Vergilius Maro,
70–19 BCE)
achievement a result of divine intelligence: 5.1.18
antique diction of: 6.4–5
passim
borrowings of, wrongly
criticized as thefts: 5.3.16,
6.1.2–6
borrows Greek diction:
5.17.15–19
called "Homer of Mantua":
1.16.43
carelessness of: 5.15.10–
13
catalogues of, compared
with Homer's: 5.15.1–9, 14–
18, 5.16.1–5
cited as authority: 1.3.10–
11, 1.7.23, 1.14.5, 1.16.12,
43–44, 1.17.4, 34, 1.18.23–24,
1.20.4, 1.21.23, 3.18.5, 3.18.7,
3.19.3, 5, 5.19.12

cited to elucidate Virgilian
usage: 6.7.15, 18, 6.8.3, 10–
12
command of Greek litera-
ture: 5.2–20
compared with Homer:
5.11–16 passim
comparison of, with
Cicero, declined: 5.1.3–4
departs from Homer:
5.16.8–11
disguises imitations of
Homer: 5.16.12–14
epigrams of: 5.16.7
expert
at representing and evoking
emotion: 4.1–6 passim
in oratory: 4.1–5.1
in pontifical lore: 3.1–12 passim
exploits Greek literary ar-
cana: 5.18–20 passim
flaws of: 5.17.1–6
Homer of Mantua: 1.16.43
imitates
Accius: 6.1.55–59, 6.2.17
Apollonius in *Aeneid* 4: 5.17.4
Aratus: 5.2.4
Catullus: 6.1.41–42
Cicero: 6.2.33–34
Demosthenes: 6.6.15
earlier Latin poets: 6.1–3 passim
Ennius: 6.1.8–24, 50–54, 60–
62, 6.2.16, 18, 21, 25–28,
32
Ennius imitating Homer:
6.3.2–4, 6.3.7–8

INDEX LOCORUM

INDEX

375

INDEX

INDEX

INDEX

Fr. 6 *FGrH* = *IAH* 1:45 = *IAR*[6] 1:14–15: 1.16.34

Sallust
  Catiline's War 25.2: 3.14.5
  Histories
  2.70 (ed. Maurenbrecher 1891): 3.13.7
  3.31: 1.4.6
  3.65: 7.12.34
Sappho
  Fr. 141b Lobel-Page: 5.21.6
Scholia
  Σ Aeschylus
  Σ Vetera *Persians*: 869 (ed. Dindorf 1851): 5.18.12n.
  Σ Apollonius Rhodes: 4.1377–79 (ed. Wendel 1935): 3.12.6n.
  Σ Aristophanes
  Acharnians 348b,d (ed. Wilson 1975): 1.18.3n.
  Birds 874 (ed. Dübner 1877): 1.18.11n.
  Clouds 144b (ed. Koster 1977): 1.17.45n.
  Thesmophoriazusae 489: 1.9.6n.
  Wasps 9a–b (ed. Koster 1978): 1.18.11n.
  Wealth
      39 (ed. Dübner 1877): 1.17.50n.
      359: 1.17.14n.
      636: 1.17.16n.
  Σ Dionysius Thrax
  Σ Vatican *GG* 1,3:198.1–6: 1.19.15n.

Σ Marciana *GG* 1,3:346.31: 1.17.50n.
  Σ Euripides
  Andromache 167: 5.18.12n.
  Σ Homer *Iliad*
  Σ D (ed. Heyne 1834)
      1.222: 1.23.7n.
      1.462: 7.12.28n.
      4.101: 1.17.38n.
      4.259: 7.12.28n.
      20.74: 1.15.20n.
  Σ Vetera (ed. Erbse 1969–1988)
      4.101: 1.17.38n.
      4.101b1: 1.17.36n.
      15.365: 1.17.17n.
      20.404: 5.13.11n.
      21.194: 5.18.12n.
      24.616b: 5.18.12n.
  Σ Homer *Odyssey* (ed. Dindorf 1855).
      10.152: 7.12.28n
      14.161: 1.17.39n.
      24.467: 7.16.34n.
  Σ Pindar (ed. Drachmann 1903–1927)
  Olympian 14.16: 1.17.13n.
  Pythian
      hypoth. a: 1.19.15n.
      1 inscr. b: 1.17.50n. (bis)
  Σ Sophocles *Oedipus Tyrannus* sch. Plan. 154 (ed. Longo 1971): 1.17.16n. (ter)
  Σ Theocritus (ed. Wendel 1914)
      3.48: 1.21.3n.
      4.62–63e: 1.8.9n.
Scipio Africanus
  Fr. 30 *ORF*[2]: 3.14.7

INDEX

Fr. 9: 6.4.15

Solinus (ed. Mommsen 1895)
1.5: 3.9.3n.
1.6: 1.10.8n.
1.32: 1.21.20n.
1.34: 1.12.2n.
1.35: 1.12.7n.
1.38: 1.13.1n.
1.39: 1.13.5n.
1.40: 1.13.7n.
1.42: 1.13.8n., 1.13.10n.
(ter)
1.43: 1.14.1n.
1.45: 1.14.2n.
1.46: 1.14.13n.
1.47: 1.14.14n.
1.72: 2.1.6n.

Sophocles
Ajax 550–51: 6.1.58n.
Fr. 534 TrGF 3:410:
5.19.10
Fr. 660 TrGF 4:469: 5.21.6
Fr. 701 TrGF 4:484:
1.19.16n.

Sotion
Cornucopia: 2.2.11n.

Speusippus (ed. Parente
1880)
Fr. 152: 1.17.8

Statius Tullianus
On the Names of Things
Book 1: 3.8.6

Stephanus of Byzantium (ed.
Billerbeck 2006)
1.50: 1.9.6n.
2.174: 1.18.9n.

Stobaeus (ed. Hense and
Wachsmuth 1884–1912)
3.1.4: 2.8.16n.

3.6.44: 2.8.16n.
3.15.7: 5.16.6n.
3.17.21: 2.8.16n.

Strabo
1.3.16: 1.17.22n.
1.18.7: 1.10.22n.
5.3.2: 1.10.17n.
8.3.30: 5.13.23n.
14.1.6: 1.17.21n.
14.1.22: 6.7.16n.
17.1.22: 1.21.20n.
17.1.27: 1.21.20n.
17.1.40: 1.17.40n.

Sueius
Fr. 1 FPL[3]: 3.18.12
Fr. 7 FPL[3]: 6.1.37
Fr. 8 FPL[3]: 6.5.15

Suetonius
Augustus
4.2: 7.3.7n.
16.3: 1.23.13n.
25.2: 1.11.32n.
29.5: 1.12.16n.
31.2: 1.12.35n.
34.1: 3.17.13n.
53.2: 2.4.3n.
67.1: 2.4.24n.
73.1: 2.4.14n.
85.2: 2.4.2n.
101.4: 1.4.12n.
Caligula
16.3: 1.4.12n.
57.3: 1.23.13n.
Domitian 13.3: 1.12.36n.
Julius
39.2: 2.3.10n.
45.3: 2.3.9n.
50.2: 2.2.5n.
56.7: 2.1.8n.

413

417

419

INDEX OF TOPICS

INDEX

composition
  metaphor of bees for:
  Praef. 5
  metaphor of chorus for:
  Praef. 9
  metaphor of digestion for:
  Praef. 7
  metaphor of perfumery
  for: Praef. 8
  method of: Praef. 2–11
"consecrated," meaning of:
  3.7.3–8
consul, sacrifices to Penates and
  Vesta at Lanuvium: 3.4.11
consulship
  of Aulus Albinus and
  Lucius Lucullus (151 BCE):
  Praef. 13
  of Caninius Rebilus (45
  BCE): 2.2.13, 2.3.6
  of Junius Brutus (509 BCE):
  1.7.35
  of Lucius Pinarius and
  Publis Furius (427 BCE):
  1.13.21
  of Marcus Messala and
  Gnaius Domitius (53 BCE):
  1.9.14
  of Mark Antony (44 BCE):
  1.12.34
  of Vatinius (47 BCE): 2.3.5
convivium. See symposium
craftsman
  god as: 5.2.1, 7.14.23
  nature as: 7.5.6, 7.16.14
creation, divine, compared to
  Virgil's poetry: 5.1.19–20
cremation: 7.7.5

criticism. *See* reproach
crows, longevity of: 7.5.11
cruelty, cause of: 1.11.13
cultivation, as aim of reading:
  Praef. 10
cups, Greek names of, used by
  Virgil: 5.21 passim
curule
  magistrates: 1.6.11
  seat, imported from Etruscans: 1.6.7
custom (*mos*), definition of:
  3.8.8–14
customs, of ancients, praised:
  1.5.2
cymbia, diminutive of *cymba*:
  5.21.9; Greek term used by
  Virgil: 5.21.1, 7–13

dancing, immorality of: 3.14.4–
  15
days
  appointed (*stati*): 1.16.14
  Athenian, definition of:
  1.3.4
  Babylonian, definition of:
  1.3.4
  "black"
  explained: 1.16.21–26
  include those following
  Kalends, Nones, Ides:
  1.16.21
  offerings to ancestors, forbidden on: 1.16.25
  unsuitable for voting assem-
  blies: 1.16.24
  called "Zeus" by Cretans:
  1.15.14

432

INDEX

435

INDEX

festra, meaning of: 3.12.8

figs

    best produced in
Tusculum: 3.16.12

    black, produced by trees of
bad omen: 3.20.2–3

    distinguished from fruit
(*pomum*): 3.20.4

    unripe, called *grossi* or
olynthoi: 3.20.5

    varieties of: 3.20.1–5

    white, produced by trees of
good omen: 3.20.2–3

figurative usages, devised by
Virgil: 6.6 passim

figurines, clay, used to celebrate
Sigillaria: 1.11.1, 47–49

"filled with religious scruple"
(*religiosum*), definition of:
3.3.8–12

"fishpond-fanciers" (*piscinarii*),
Cicero's contempt for:
3.15.6

flamen: 1.10.15

    attended by *camillus* (*-a*):
3.8.7

    forbidden to witness work
on festivals: 1.16.9

    homes of: 1.12.6

    of Jupiter: 1.15.16; his wife
sacrifices to Jupiter: 1.16.30

    of Vulcan: 1.12.18; wife of,
appeases gods upon hearing
thunder: 1.16.8

flaws

    of Homer, imitated by Vir-
gil: 5.14.1–4

physical, as target of jibes:
7.3.11–12

    of Virgil: 1.24.6–7

food

    different natures of:
7.4.27

    hot, handling of: 7.12.22–
23

forbearance, of Augustus:
2.4.19–31

foreigners, sons of: 1.6.12

form

    grammatical, of praeco-
cem: 6.8.13

    Greek grammatical, bor-
rowed by Virgil: 5.17.19

fortune, used to stir emotion:
4.3.6–7

freedmen

    as soldiers: 1.11.32–34

    daughters of: 1.6.13

    sons of: 1.6.12–13

frogs, spontaneous generation
of: 7.16.12

fruit (*pomum*)

    distinguished from fig:
3.20.4

    distinguished from nut:
3.19.1

    Persian: 3.19.3–4

    varieties of: 3.19.1–5

funerals, in Virgil and Homer:
5.7.9–10

games

    in Homer and Virgil:
5.2.15, 5.7.4–6, 5.13.3–5

438

INDEX

harmony, importance of:
7.1.11–13
hazel nut: 3.18.5–6
heat
  nature of: 7.13.2–5
  trait of Mars and Liber:
  1.19.3, 6
  varieties of: 7.16.21–25
herms: 1.19.14–15
hieroglyph
  of Earth: 1.19.13
  of Osiris: 1.21.12
hilarus (-ris), grammatical
  forms of: 1.4.16
historical mode, avoided by
  Homer: 5.2.9–11, 5.14.11–16
holiday
  Caprotine Nones, origin of:
  1.11.36–40
  of *Angeronia (Divalia)*:
  1.10.7
  of *Compitalia*: 1.7.34–35
  of Jupiter (*Larentinalia*):
  1.10.11–17
  of Lares: 1.10.10
  of *Opalia*: 1.10.18
  of *Parentalia*: 1.10.16–17
  of *Sigillaria*: 1.10.24,
  1.11.46–50
  of *Terminalia*: 1.13.19
holidays (*dies festi*)
  actions permitted on:
  3.3.10–12
  in January: 1.2.1
"holy" (*sanctum*), definition of:
  3.3.5–7
homoeopathy, used to stir emotion: 4.6.9

honey
  best produced in
  Tarentum: 3.16.12
  best when fresh: 7.12.9–10
  heaviest is best: 7.12.13–16
  impurities of, float: 7.12.8
horizon, distance of: 7.14.15
horoscope: 1.19.17
horse, "Trojan": 3.13.13
humor. *See* wit
humors (bodily), and digestion:
  7.4.9
hunger, issues involved in satis-
  fying: 7.12.20–21
husband, authority of, over
  wife: 1.3.9
hyperbole (figure of thought):
  4.2.4–5; used to stir emotion:
  4.6.15–16

ignorance, as cause of shame:
  7.2.5; Virgil accused of: 3.10–
  12 passim
ill-omened days. *See* days:
  "black"
illusions, optical, causes of:
  7.14.1–2, 20
im vs. *eum*, grammatical form
  of: 1.4.19
image
  of Adad: 1.23.19
  of Adargatis: 1.23.19–20
  of Adonis: 1.21.9
  of Aesculapius: 1.20.1–2
  of Angeronia: 1.10.8
  of Apollo: 1.17.66–70
  of Fortunes, at Antium:
  1.23.13

INDEX

juice, produced by digestion: 7.4.9

khilia vs. khilias, grammatical form of: 1.5.9

king, shrewdness appropriate to: 1.7.20

kissybium, relation of, to cymbia: 5.21.11–13

knight
rank of, lost by Laberius: 2.3.10, 2.7.2–5
tunic of (trabea): 1.6.2

lamentation, in Homer and Virgil: 5.2.15, 5.8.12

language. See usage

"lapper," term applied to wolf-fish: 3.16.17–18

laridum, etymology of: 7.12.2

Latin and Greek, knowledge of both: Praef. 2, 1.2.7, 1.5.16

law
of Maenius: 1.11.5
pontifical, concerning actions permitted on holidays: 3.3.10–12
proposed, promulgation of, on market days: 1.16.34–35
sumptuary: 3.17 passim
of Crassus Dives: 3.17.7–9
of Didius: 3.17.6
of Fannius: 3.13.13, 3.16.14–17, 3.17.3–8
of Orchius: 3.17.2–3
of Restio: 3.17.13
of Sulla: 3.17.13

learning
admired: 1.2.15

as source of glory: 7.2.4, 6–7
Greek, of Virgil: 5.2–22 passim

letter, of Virgil, to Augustus: 1.24.10–11

libation, poured on altar: 3.11.3–8

lictors, imported from Etruscans: 1.6.7

limbs, function of, in digestion: 7.4.23

litare, used properly of propitiation: 3.5.4

liver, function of: 7.4.11, 19–21

location, used to stir emotion: 4.3.9–15

loidoria. See insult

love, subject of sympotic discourse: 1.1.3

luck. See fortune

lungs, function of: 7.15 passim

lux, etymology of: 1.17.39

luxury
and use of rings: 7.13.13
as a moral sickness: 7.5.32
of the ancients: 3.13–17 passim

lykabas, etymology of: 1.17.39

lykos, etymology of: 1.17.41

lyre
four-stringed, attributed to Mercury: 1.19.15
seven-stringed, attributed to Apollo: 1.19.15

madness, expressed by demeanor: 4.1.4

magic, use of, by Dido: 5.19.7

442

443

TOPICS

war
  forbidden during Saturnalia: 1.10.1
  of Athenians and Amazons: 1.17.18
  of Libyans and Sicilians: 1.17.24
  of Romans and Aetolia: 1.13.21
  of Romans and Etruscans: 1.6.7, 3.2.14
  of Romans and Gauls: 1.11.37, 1.16.23
  of Romans and Sabines: 1.6.8, 1.8.1, 1.9.17–18
  of Rome and neighbors: 1.11.37–40
  Second Punic: 1.11.30–31; games of Apollo established during: 1.17.27–29
  Social: 1.11.32
  start of, forbidden on certain days: 1.16.16–20

water
  "Acheloüs" used as term for: 5.18.3–12
  fresh, purity of: 7.13.19–20
  salt, resists freezing: 7.12.31–37
  sea
  greasiness of: 7.13.23–27
  nature of: 7.13.18–27

weakness, used to stir emotion: 4.3.8

widows, permitted to wed on days of religious observance: 1.15.21

wife, subject to husband's authority: 1.3.9

windpipe (*artêria*), function of: 7.15.4, 11–12, 17–18

wine
  best, neither heaviest nor lightest: 7.12.13–16
  best produced in *ager Falernus*: 3.16.12
  called "milk" in Good Goddess' shrine: 1.12.25
  Egyptian, character of: 7.8.9–11
  Falernian: 7.12.9
  filtered, strength of: 7.12.6–7
  inhibits sexual desire: 7.6.8
  medicinal uses of: 7.6.5–7
  mixed, causes rapid intoxication: 7.4.7, 7.5.13–15
  nature of: 7.6.1–13
  offered to Ceres: 3.11.1–2, 9–10
  old is best: 7.12.9–10
  resistance of, to freezing: 7.12.28–30
  restorative power of: 2.8.6
  spoiling of: 7.12.11–12
  tests self-control: 2.8.7–9
  used
  as poultice: 7.6.3
  for irrigation: 3.13.3
  views of Plato on: 2.8.4–9

winter, represented by boar: 1.21.4

wit
  as suitable topic for discussion: 2.1.10–15
  of anonymous shoemaker: 2.2.6
  of Augustus: 2.4 passim

453